for G.R.L.

Featuring the Photography of Paul Kenward & Julian Essam
First English edition published by Colour Library Books Ltd.
© 1984 Illustrations and text: Colour Library Books Ltd.,
  Guildford, Surrey, England.
This edition published by Crescent Books
Distributed by Crown Publishers, Inc.
h g f e d c b a
Display and text filmsetting by Acesetters Ltd., Richmond,
  Surrey, England.
Colour separations by Llovet, S.A., Barcelona, Spain.
Printed and bound by JISA-RIEUSSET and EUROBINDER.
ISBN 0.517.402742
All rights reserved
CRESCENT 1984

ENGLAND'S CHURCHES

Written and Designed by

PHILIP CLUCAS MSIAD

Produced by
Ted Smart and David Gibbon

CRESCENT BOOKS
NEW YORK

INTRODUCTION

For richness and splendour the landscape and architecture of England are unsurpassed and unequalled anywhere in the world. The visual scene is still dominated by our parish and cathedral churches – their power simply as images, their magnificent variety, their enchanting detail, compel attention and demand a reverent sense of awe. On a spiritual level their continuity of religious service links us today with our medieval and Anglo-Saxon forefathers in an unbroken line of observance that may, in some instances, embrace the earliest period of the Celtic and Roman missions.

Some ten thousand medieval churches adorn our land and each has to offer its own unique quality and treasures – be it the massive splendours of our cathedral and monastic foundations – raised to create on earth a reflection of God's heaven – or the simple beauty of a small village church whose green path between the weathered inscriptions on moss-grown leaning headstones – enmeshed in briar and sweet eglantine – leads from the light and sunshine into the solemn, brooding presence of the nave, where the silent air is chill and dank – yet all is warmed and bathed by the stillness of the centuries.

High or humble, each church has the power to dazzle the eye and haunt the mind: these 'jewels' of national heritage are prayers in stone, raised on high by the sons of God – who drew their strength and resolve from implicit faith – to the eternal glory of their Father above. Thus, by its very nature, Romanesque and Gothic architecture speaks to the soul alone – in ornate and elaborate carvings, in sumptuously enriched and coloured glass, and in the very shape and construction of the building. No other age could have furnished so great a majesty (although Victorian Gothic was an interesting attempt at its revival); confidently expressing the belief that the glory due to the Lord should not be tarnished by the squalor of His house. Clearly it is impossible to encapsulate the whole field of their art, yet the 330 parish churches and cathedrals presented within this book represent that unique pinnacle to which the spirit may be uplifted.

The approach is firstly and properly a visual one, accompanied by a comprehensive text which seeks to set each of the selected churches – whether cathedral or parochial – against the backcloth of history and architecture, of religious observance and ritual requirement. Such was the hold of Christ upon the hearts of men that the fabric of England's churches is woven from the warp and woof of life – a rich tapestry that starts with the earliest Celtic fanes, and reaches its glorious climax with the full-blown flowering of Perpendicular architecture, that most uniquely English of all the Gothic styles. Within the thousand year span encompassed by these two extremes (and brought to a close by the Reformation in the 1540s) is a procession of changing emphases and styles – indeed, there is not a stage in the whole architectural evolution which does not offer overwhelming experiences. Who that has seen the Saxon minster at Brixworth, or viewed the unbuttressed towers at Barton-on-Humber and Sompting, could remain unmoved by the subtle beauty born of simplicity – of strength held in complete balance? Norman architecture is equally magnificent and sturdy – as witness Durham's nave where the immense pillars deeply channelled with zig-zag, spirals and chevrons, are as broad as the openings – or at the tiny Romanesque churches of Kilpeck, Barfreston and Iffley, which display a host of wildly lavish Norman sculpture that owe more to pagan mythology than to the Faith. Transitional and Early English architecture saw the introduction of the Gothic pointed arch, which raised vaults on high, and swept arcades forever upwards – Salisbury's unity and Canterbury's peerless Trinity are masterpieces of this style. Wells and Exeter exemplify the florid emphasis of the Decorated period: and the Perpendicular style – the last florescence of the Gothic spirit which speaks of an England rich enough to spend profusely in reverent opulence, and sought at its best to convey splendour and regularity, airy lightness and immensity. With the coming of the Renaissance and its intellectual and religious upheaval, the Church lost much of its ascendancy, yet despite the subsequent ravages of iconoclasts and 'restorers' much remains to us of this glorious heritage. England's churches are thus the highest expressions of the art and architecture of their age – the visual evidence of a triumphant striving to create a paragon of beauty for a lofty and noble purpose.

Opposite page; the Early English chancel at Cobham Church in Kent. Above, a detail of the Perpendicular carved rood-screen at Newton St Margaret's, Hereford.

ST MARY'S WARWICK

The church of St Mary at **Warwick** (1-9) is of Saxon foundation with a Norman crypt containing circular piers whose tremendous strength suggest that they must have upheld an enormous Romanesque church. The building was completed by 1123, but two hundred and forty years later the whole of St Mary's was rebuilt under the patronage of the Beauchamp Earls of Warwick. The family held the title from 1268 until 1445 – playing a great part in national affairs – and their effect upon Warwick is still to be seen, chiefly in the great strength of Warwick Castle and in the beauty

1

2

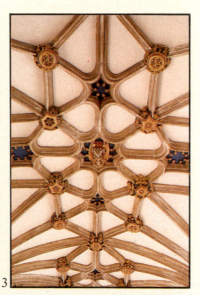

3

from head to foot.

The last and most magnificent phase of the medieval rebuilding was the erection of the chapel of Our Lady (6) – or the 'Beauchamp Chapel' as it later became known. Its founder was Richard Beauchamp, the fifth and most powerful Earl of that name, who completed the reconstruction project, begun by his father and grandfather, by the addition of this incomparable chapel to their great church. Richard's tomb (9) is at the very centre of the Perpendicular building he caused to be raised to receive it. He died in 1439 at Rouen, but had instructed, *I will*

4

5

of their church of St Mary.

It is not known why Thomas, the first Beauchamp Earl, pulled down the Norman building and started his own reconstruction on a larger and grander scale, but the Beauchamps' zestful pursuit of violence never checked their

enthusiasm for ecclesiastical building. Thomas fought in all the French wars of King Edward III's reign, and commanded forces at the Battle of Crecy, at Poitiers and at the Siege of Calais – where he contracted the plague and died in 1369. From money received by the

ransom of a French Archbishop he instigated the rebuilding programme at St Mary's, and his heir, another Thomas, continued his father's grand design. His brass (1) in the south transept is one of the finest examples of its kind, and shows the Earl encased in armour

that when it liketh God, that my Soule depart out of this World, my Body be interred within the Church Collegiate of our Lady of Warwick, where I will, that in such place as I have devised (which is known well) that there be made a Chappell of Our Lady, well faire, and goodly

ST MARY'S WARWICK

6

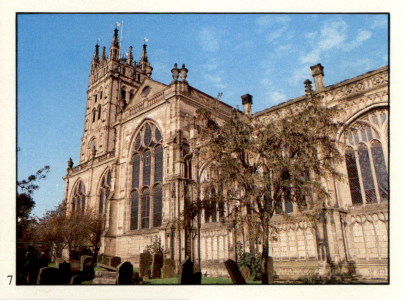

7

built, within the middle of which Chappell I will, that my Tomb be made'.

True to his behest the chapel was indeed *'well, faire and goodly built'* with only the finest of craftsmen contracted to build and embellish. The King's glazier, John Prudde, was charged to provide the windows and it was stipulated that he was only to use the best glass *'from beyond the seas'* – from Flanders. Sumptuous remains of the chapel glass (8) include the figures of Richard's favourite saints, St Thomas à Becket and the protomartyr St Alban, in which every known resource and technique was utilised to achieve the most impressive effect. Coloured jewels were inserted into the borders of robes, and the feathered angels of the tracery hold real plainsong, which is still occasionally sung by mortals in the church. A carved reredos, oak clergy stalls, white walls, gilded mouldings and a beautiful vaulted ceiling (3), with bosses in colour and gold, complete the original scheme of opulence.

Richard Beauchamp, the Commander of Calais for King Henry V, was one of the hero-figures of the 15th century, but he reaches us today somewhat tainted

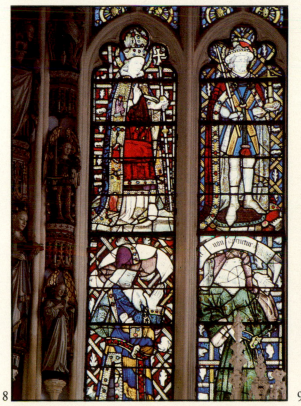

8

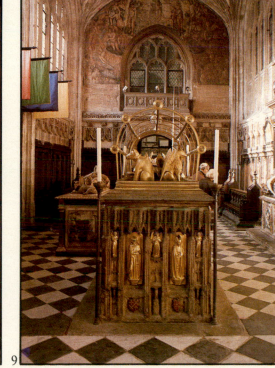

9

– as the man responsible for the imprisonment, interrogation, trial and execution of Joan of Arc. That pitiless act haunts the modern mind, but no such pangs of conscience afflicted his contemporaries, for any threat to the child-King Henry VI – whose protection was Richard's sacred trust – was, of necessity, ruthlessly suppressed. His tomb (2), constructed by John Borde in Purbeck marble, with an effigy (5) cast by William Austen of London, is one of the most beautifully sculpted in Europe – of such exquisite detail that even the veins of his temple are faithfully recorded. Its base is encircled by gilded statues, or 'weepers' (4), which occupy intricately carved niches. The monument is an excellent example of the strength and elegance of 15th century art in England – its controlled grandeur and authority is in dismissive contrast to the bombastic uncertainties of the Elizabethan tombs nearby.

STOKE D'ABERNON

The church of St Mary at **Stoke D'Abernon** (1,2,3,4 and 5) is one of the oldest in the Kingdom. It was built in the latter part of the 7th century and belongs, with a scattered group of other south-eastern churches, to the period immediately following St Augustine's mission to Kent in AD 597. Substantial portions of the original fabric survive on the south side; and Stoke D'Abernon is the earliest English example of a church which had a thegn's gallery, or Lord's seat – the doorway to which is positioned 12 ft above ground level, and was once reached by a wooden stairway. The portal is

now bricked-in, but its megalithic structure can still be clearly seen in the south wall of the nave.

After five hundred years without alteration the Normans added the north aisle c1190. The chancel, with its exceptionally fine quadripartite vault – which has a carved and gilded rose (the emblem of the Virgin, to whom the church is dedicated) at its centre – was raised in the 13th century. Within the chancel is the magnificent brass of Sir John D'Abernon, dated 1277 and acknowledged to be the oldest brass now remaining in England. Other treasured possessions include an imposing late-Elizabethan walnut pulpit of Mannerist design, and a 12th century chest which was probably one of those ordered to be made and placed in all churches in 1199 to collect alms for the Crusade. There is also a handsome and unusual Jacobean oak lectern in the form of a gilded eagle (2), and much notable stained glass – especially of pieces concerned with

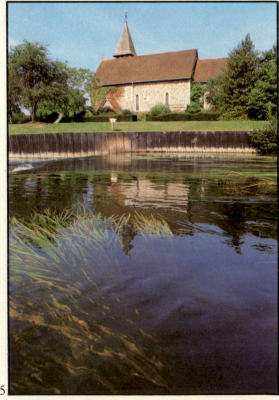

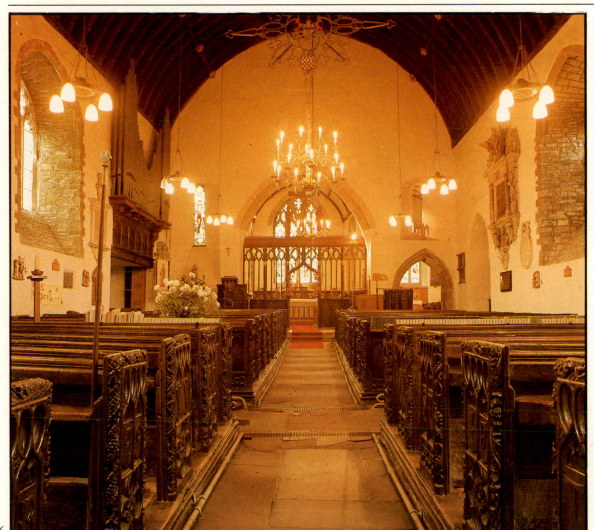

the Blessed Virgin Mary. In the north transept is an English panel of c1520, but with Flemish influence, depicting the 'Burial of the Virgin' (1) – a rare subject in Art – matched with a French panel of 1540 representing 'The Angel appearing to the Shepherds' (4). These treasures that the church shelters are augmented by the beauty of its exterior – of its ancient walls of large field-flints embowered in ivy and shady trees (3), positioned by the banks of the lovely and deep-flowing River Mole (5).

■ The church of **Braunton** (6,7,8 and 9) was founded at an even earlier date than that of the Surrey church of Stoke D'Abernon. Its first timbers were raised at least thirty years before Pope Gregory

despatched St Augustine to convert England to the Faith, by St Brannock, the son of a king of Calabria, who evangelised South Wales and spent many years engaged in missionary work for the Celtic church in North Devon. Here, at Braunton, he was instructed in a vision to build his minster at the site where he would find a white sow and her farrow: the legend is commemorated by one of the bosses of the medieval roof (7). He died in Wales in the year AD 570, and his remains were brought back to the church of his foundation and are almost certainly buried beneath the high altar.

The present church dates mostly from the 13th century, with a massive Norman tower, topped by a lead-shingled broach spire. The remarkably wide nave (6) is spanned by a fine wagon-roof, and there is a splendid collection of carved, 16th century bench-ends – one of which possesses a sculpture of the church's patron, St Brannock (8), and another displays the 'Instruments of the Passion' (9).

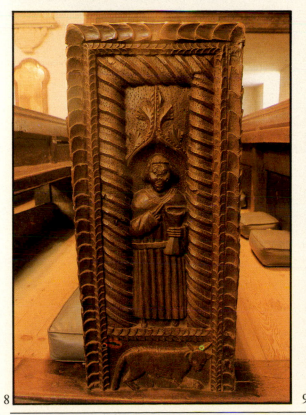

COOLING/CASTLE FROME

By the marshes of the Thames estuary stands **Cooling Church** (3 and 9), whose fame lies in the graveyard; for it is said that Charles Dickens took this for his model in the opening chapter of *Great Expectations*. Near the tower is the headstone with three winged cherubs at the top, and beside it are scattered thirteen small bodystones marking the graves of the Comport and Baker children. The three Bakers died at the ages of one, three and five months, whilst none of the ten Comport children survived beyond seventeen months. Dickens ascribed these sad tombs to the brothers and sisters of Pip, and they are now known as 'Pip's Graves': indeed, as the Kent mists roll in from the waters and the light begins to fade, an atmosphere of gloom descends upon Cooling and one can almost sense Pip's terror at the sudden appearance of the convict.

The church itself is of the 13th and 14th centuries, and is entered

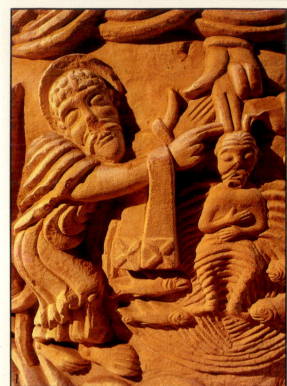

through the south porch. The walls are thick and unevenly plastered, and midway between the south and north portals stands Cooling's Norman font (9), of Purbeck type, but made of Kentish ragstone. It is upheld by circular shafts and each face of the square bowl is decorated with five trefoiled arches in low relief.

■ The 12th century font at St Michael's, **Castle Frome** (1,2,5 and 6) is the Norman church's outstanding possession. It is acclaimed as one of the masterworks of Romanesque sculpture, and is the craft of the famous Hereford school of carvers

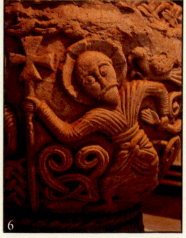

who also completed noble work at Eardisley and Kilpeck. The font stands on three crouching figures, and the centrepiece is a moving portrayal of the 'Baptism of Christ' (1). Small details are worth attention – the powerful figure of St John the Baptist wears, curiously, on his right arm, a maniple with crosses at either end. His hands join with those of God (divinely appearing from heaven) and the dove's beak, upon the head of Christ, while two pairs of fish laze in the water. The interlacing tracery bears strong Scandinavian influence; and encircling the bowl are the symbols of the Evangelists

7

8

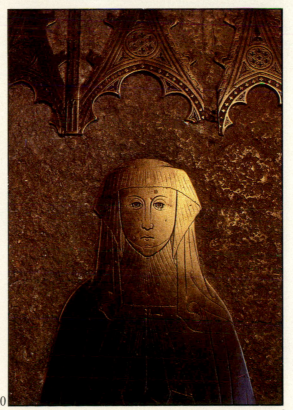

9

10

– the Eagle of St John, the Lion of St Mark (5), the Man of St Matthew (6), and the Bull of St Luke. Another fine example of craftsmanship exhibited at Castle Frome is the Unett tomb which dates from the 17th century, and displays the reclining alabaster figure of a cavalier (2) and his wife.

■ In the Middle Ages by far the most popular method of commemorating the dead was a brass – in which an effigy of the deceased was incised into a sheet of latten; cut around, and inlaid into a tombslab. It has been calculated that as many as 150,000 medieval brasses were laid down, but of that number 4,000 alone survive – the vast majority being in East Anglia. **Acton Church** (7 and 10) in Suffolk contains (according to the Victoria and Albert Museum) the finest military brass in existence, and after those of Stoke D'Abernon and Trumpington it is the third oldest brass in England. It represents Sir Robert de Bures (7) who died in 1302, and depicts him cross-legged, in complete chain mail – with the exception of his knee-pieces which are formed of *curi-bouilli.* Over his armour he wears a surcoat and his feet display single-pointed, or *pryck* spurs. On Sir Robert's left arm is a large concave shield, charged with the Arms of de Bures, and from a richly ornamented baldric hangs a large sword. Another fine brass within Acton's de Bures chapel is dated 1403, and is the effigy of Alice de Bures (10) in widow's dress with a veiled headdress, barbe, kirtle and mantel.

■ The little church of **Lullington** (8) in Sussex stands alone on the South Downs above the Cuckmere Valley, almost hidden among clumps of oak and ash, its white, weather-boarded belfry just peeping above the trees. It is now one of the smallest churches in the country, but in reality is just a portion of the chancel of a much larger Early English church – remains of which may be traced to the west of the present entrance. When and how the church was destroyed is not known but according to tradition it was slighted in Cromwellian times.

■ 4: The church of St Mary's, **Silchester** in Hampshire.

YORK MINSTER

York Minster (1-9 and 14) sets its greatest treasure, its incredible expanse of medieval stained glass, against its principal asset; its sheer, incomparable size. Nowhere could the beauty of its glass be seen to better advantage than in the enormous windows of this, the largest Gothic building north of the Alps. After the Romanesque crypt (1), the Early English transepts – completed in 1225 – are the oldest parts of the present cathedral, and their immense size set the standard for two and a quarter centuries of dedicated craftmanship, which resulted in a medieval masterpiece. Indeed, the Latin inscription near

screen displaying fifteen stone statues of kings, from the Conqueror to Henry VI. From here – the crossing (7) – one's glance is diverted upwards to the blaze of light concentrated within the lantern of the 200ft central tower (5). It was the work of the King's Master Mason, and each pier supports a thrust of four thousand tons. The tower's completion in 1480 marks the final crowning achievement of the medieval builders at York.

Their legacy is the greatest single concentration of stained and painted glass in Europe, whose quality and quantity surpasses all

the chapter-house door befits the whole of York Minster, *'as the rose is fairest of flowers, so is this the most beautiful of buildings'.*

The chapter-house, with its handsome, painted vault (4), is in the purest Decorated style, and was constructed during the years 1291 to 1307. The nave was begun in the same year, under the guidance of Archbishop John Romanus, and gradually, over a period of fifty years, the original Norman fabric was remoulded into the magnificent Gothic structure which stands today. The first impression is one of height and spaciousness; the whole nave being flooded by the light of its Great West Window, designed in 1388 by Ivo Raghton, in which may be seen (6) the distinctive stone tracery of a heart – the famous 'Heart of Yorkshire'.

In the mid-14th century the Zouche chapel (14) was raised, and later the choir was rebuilt in the Perpendicular style (9), adapted to match the nave. The two are divided by an elegant, carved

YORK MINSTER

others. When viewed from the outside, the massive bulk of the Minster's Great East Window is often compared to a sheer cliff face, yet within, the extent and wealth of its colour both amazes and delights. The window (2) measures a breathtaking 77ft by 32ft and is the world's largest sheet of medieval glazing – its size reflecting the spirit of the Perpendicular style to create 'walls of glass'. John Thornton was commissioned in 1405 to glaze the

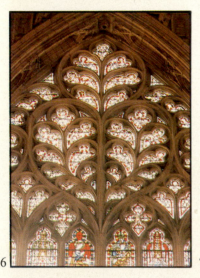

6

7

8

window and he took as his theme 'the Omnipotence of God'. The Lord sits enthroned at the very apex of the window, surrounded by the heavenly host, and holds an open book inscribed *Eqo sum Alpha et Omega* – 'I am the beginning and the end'; the inscription is faithfully interpreted in the panels beneath his feet. The first seven represent each day of the Creation; the next twenty

panels deal with stories from Exodus to the death of Absalom; and the remaining panels illustrate the Apocalypse – the end of all things. The Old Testament theme is mirrored at the opposite end of the Minster by New Testament stories.

In the northern transept is the 'Five Sisters' window (3) – a row of Early English lancets glazed with grisaille glass. This greenish-grey

9

glass is arranged in purely geometric patterns and, because it lacks human form, was thought to resemble Jewish Art. The use of a yellow stain gives much of York's glazing greater brilliance, and gives the Minster's enormous interior a marvellous honeyed appearance.

■ Although of medieval fabric, the atmosphere of **Kedington Church** (10,11,12,13 and 15) is of the 17th and 18th century. It is one of the finest of Suffolk's Puritan churches, with much exceptional woodwork – most notably the alms box made from a hollow tree trunk; the canopied pew (15) in the north arcade next to the Jacobean

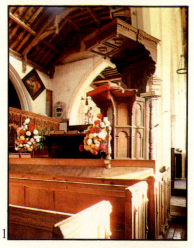

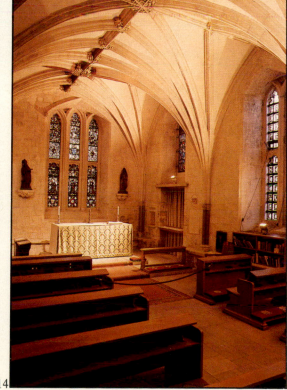

chancel screen; the three-decker pulpit and tester (11), and a west gallery of c1750. In the nave (10) are 15th century benches illuminated by skylights added to its Tudor hammer-beam roof. The vista of the stone arcade leads the eye from the nave to the chancel – with its attendant alabaster monuments and life-size effigies of members of the Barnardiston family (13).

THE DAWN OF FAITH

One of the most striking features of the history of religion is the way in which people have clung to the holy places of their far distant ancestors. Thus it is that a great many churches of Anglo-Saxon and medieval foundation occupy a site long hallowed by heathen cults. Hilltops and man-made burial chambers (1) of the Neolithic and Bronze Ages were favoured places of worship for the pagan Celts and Saxons: in turn these were rededicated to Christ with the success in England of St Augustine's mission – whose instructions from Pope Gregory were *'do not pull down the fanes of*

incumbent that she was banished to her present location near the belfry door.

Another powerful Celtic symbol adopted by the Church was the device of the severed head. The Celts were head-hunters, and set up the skulls of their enemies to guard their sacred places. Today, severed heads in stone can be seen in countless English churches – as at **Brixworth** (4) in Northamptonshire – and are distinguishable by their severed necks from the benign heads of saints on the upper walls.

Interestingly, such pagan imagery, although associated in the

1

2

the heathens but destroy their idols, purify their temples with holy water, set forth relics of the saints, and let them become temples of the true God. So that the people will have no need to change their place of concourse.'

One of the most striking examples of Christian occupation of a pagan holy place is at Knowleton in Dorset, where the medieval church was built at the centre of a Neolithic stone circle. In Yorkshire, Fimber church stands on a Bronze Age barrow. Sacred trees (especially yews) and holy wells worshipped by local people, were invariably included within the churchyard and rededicated to Christian saints. At **Braunston** (5) a carving of a Celtic earth mother stands outside the church. It represents one of Pope Gregory's *'Devils'* – a goddess who was worshipped in primitive fertility rites which took place on the site of the church two thousand years ago. The idol originally stood within the building, but her pagan nature so offended one post-Reformation

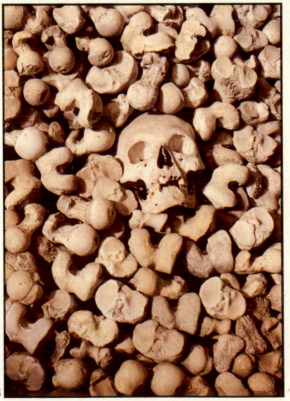

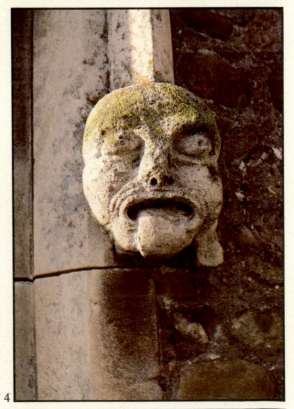

3

4

sun worship, is widely held responsible for the association between the north side of the churchyard and the Devil, and many people still have an aversion to burial in the northern part of the graveyard where the rays of the sun (8 and 9) never reach. At one time this shaded location was unhallowed ground and was used only for the graves of suicides and unbaptised infants.

■ The Kentish church at **Hythe** (2 and 3) has a crypt in which are stacked and arranged on shelves the remains of over four thousand people (3). One theory states that they are the slain of a bloody battle fought here between Britons and Saxons in AD 456, and many of the skulls display clefts, as if inflicted by a weapon. For some reason the relics attract many

'pilgrims' to this unlikely shrine, and some find the need to lay votive offerings – be it a coin or a flower – upon one or other of the assembled collection of skulls.

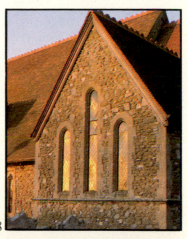

8

9

6

7

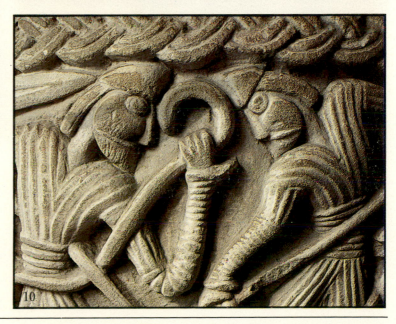

10

eyes of medieval Christians with evil, was sought to defend the church against the Devil. On the principle that like cancels out like, grotesque carvings and horrific gargoyles (6) were carved to frighten away malevolent spirits; there was also the idea that to give explicit physical form to the forces of evil was to deprive them of their power. Similarly, mystical symbolism was employed to

restrict supernatural forces – as demonstrated by **Eardisley's** vigorously carved font (7 and 10) where the prominent use of plaitwork was not merely decorative, but had the magical function of ensnaring evil (represented by warriors in combat, with pointed beards and fierce moustaches) and thereby symbolically rendering it harmless.

Another ancient religion, that of

GREAT COXWELL/BRADFORD-ON-AVON

The medieval practice of tithe payment to ecclesiastical authorities necessitated the building of great tithe-barns in which produce was stored. A few of these large stone buildings survive – as at Glastonbury and Pilton in Somerset, Abbotsbury in Dorset, and at **Great Coxwell** (5) in Berkshire. The latter has an enormous stone-tiled roof, steeply pitched, and upheld by an early example of a Queen-post vault. The barn was raised in the 13th century and is 152ft long by 44ft wide, formed in the shape of a cross. The tithe-barn at **Bradford-on-Avon** (2 and 3) is larger still, and

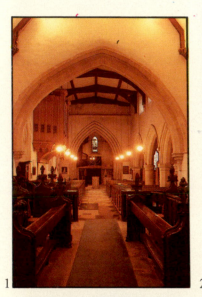

1

2

the heart of the Marshwood Vale in Dorset. Its unique treasure – the relics of St Candida – are housed in a 13th century tomb which is still the object of pilgrimage. The altar-like shrine is pierced by three oval holes so that the kneeling pilgrim could thrust his head within, and actually kiss the sacred reliquary. Little is known of St Candida's life, although a local tradition asserts that she was a Saxon woman martyred by Danes: the Viking axe and long-ship carved into the church's tower are evidence of the legend. The Saint is reputed to heal eye-ailments, and Dorset children still call the light blue,

3

4

5

was the granary of Shaftesbury Abbey.

■ As well as the payment of tithes another source of income for medieval churches was the donations of pilgrims. Many parishes possessed shrines dedicated to their own local saint

who, however humble or obscure, attracted those seeking a miraculous cure, or who merely sought penance at the shrine. At a deeper level pilgrimage tried to bridge the gap between heaven and earth – to see and touch the holy. Of the innumerable shrines and

sacred places that once peppered the map of medieval England, the only parish church with a shrine still containing bones acknowledged to be those of its patron saint is the church of St Candida and Holy Cross, at **Whitchurch Canonicorum** (6) in

starry flowers of the wild periwinkle *'St Candida's eyes'*.

■ St Michael's at **Cumnor** (1, 8 and 10) in Oxfordshire, is noted for the carved poppyheads of its choir stalls – one of which depicts the church's patron triumphing over a very Nordic-looking dragon (8).

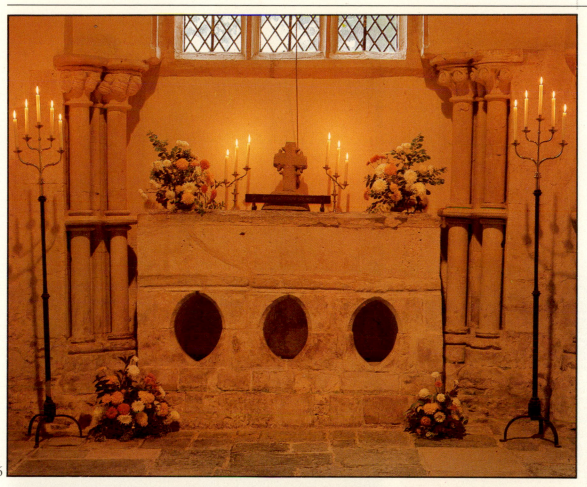

for Dudley wanted to be rid of her in order to sue for the Queen's hand in marriage. Old Cumnor Place is no more, but memories of the event are kept alive by the monuments in St Michael's. Within the medieval church is a statue of Queen Elizabeth and some of Amy Robsart's letters. At the time of her supposed murder she was the guest of Anthony Forster, a Dudley retainer who owned Cumnor Place. He kneels by his magnificent canopied tomb (10) of 1572 – his innocence or guilt remaining unknown.

■ 7: The silhouetted arch of **Newhaven's** Norman central tower

Cumnor is connected with an intriguing historical puzzle: in 1560 Amy Robsart, the wife of Robert Dudley, Queen Elizabeth's favourite, was found dead at the foot of a flight of stairs at Cumnor Place. It was widely rumoured that she had been pushed to her death,

frames the church's small 12th century chancel apse – whose simple grace and elegance find faithful echo in the massive simplicity of the crossing.

■ 4: The interior of St Materiana, at **Tintagel** in Cornwall.

CANTERBURY CATHEDRAL

Canterbury (1 – 8) has been the very heart of Christian worship in England since Whitsuntide AD 597, when St Augustine baptised Ethelbert, the Jutish King of Kent. The cathedral that grew from his mission is as rich and as grand in architecture and history as befits the mother-church of the Anglican Faith, the See of the Primate of All England, and the focal point of the cult of St Thomas à Becket – the Archbishop slain in the shadows of his own cathedral church. Four years after the martyrdom, as if to purify the dreadful sacrilege, flame swept through the old building to reduce the Norman work to a

the site chosen to house the martyr's shrine. By raising the Trinity above the level of the choir the architect, William the Englishman, achieved a feeling of triumphant ascension, evoked by successive flights of steps that led pilgrims up from the level of the nave (remodelled in the Perpendicular by Henry Yevele in 1379) and conducted them through the exceptionally long, 200ft choir, chancel and Trinity chapel, into the presence of the miracle-working tomb. As one palmer commented, *'church seems to be piled upon church, a new temple entered as soon as the first is ended'.*

charred ruin. Afforded the opportunity to develop, in a practical shape, the passion that filled the universal heart of England, the cathedral we know today was raised to Becket *'in admiration of his self-sacrifice, in veneration of his piety, and in yearning to do him honour'.* These were the moving powers which erected anew the long-drawn aisle of nave and choir; to turn the scene of his Passion into a building which is Thomas à Becket's enduring monument.

It is to the style of Canterbury Cathedral's rebuilding (1175-1220) that we owe the introduction of Gothic architecture into England. Its use of the pointed arch, to replace the Romanesque semi-circular arch, makes the style of Early English architecture one of line rather than volume – of forces held in equilibrium rather than weight supported by mass. After the choir was constructed, the transepts, the ambulatory and the corona were built, culminating in the erection of the Trinity chapel –

1

2

4

CANTERBURY CATHEDRAL

5

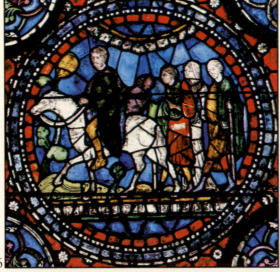

6

of c1225 ranks among the finest in the world, and must have excited almost as great a wonder as the shrine itself. One group of medallions depicts scenes – to be made famous one hundred and fifty years later by Geoffrey Chaucer in *'Canterbury Tales'* – of pilgrims travelling on horse and on foot (6 and 7) towards Canterbury, whilst another shows them at their journey's end worshipping at the holy shrine (5) – the kneeling man offers a lighted candle to the saint and another places a pouch of coins into a chest. Other panels of glass have biblical themes – the 'Adoration of the Magi' (1), the 'Tree of Jesse' (8) and portraits of Lamech, Noah and Terah (4) – all bathed in the intense ultramarine

7

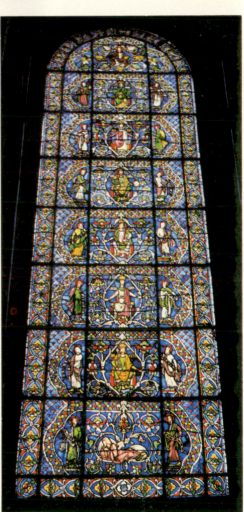

8

The goal of pilgrimage was St Thomas – *the Holy and Blissful Martyr* – whose shrine was the most glorious in medieval Europe. One visitor described it thus: *'the shrine surpasses all belief, notwithstanding its great size, covered entirely over with plates of pure gold, but the gold is hardly visible for the variety of precious stones with which* *it is studded; such as sapphires, diamonds, rubies, balasribies and emeralds. On every side that the eye turns something more beautiful than the other appears. The beauties of nature are enhanced by a human skull upon which agate, jasper and cornelians are set in relievo, some of the cameos being of such a size that I dare not mention it. But everything* *is left far behind by a ruby (the Régale de France) larger than a goose's egg. The church was darken and the sun gone down, yet I saw the ruby a good distance away as if it had been in my hand'.*

The pageant of the shrine is marvellously captured in the 'miracle windows' of the Trinity and corona – whose stained glass background, streaked with a lighter blue known as 'Canterbury blue' and flecked with mosaic-like traces of ruby red, which especially belong to the new Gothic style – as clearly as the building over which the glass has dominion.

SELBOURNE

From the steep slope of Selbourne Hanger (2) – deep shaded by mighty beech trees – one looks down upon the quiet Hampshire village clustered around the mellow stone of St Mary's church, **Selbourne** (1-6 and 8-10). This was the home of the Reverend Gilbert White, the 18th century author of *'The Natural History and Antiques of Selbourne'* and pioneer of English natural history. He was a brilliant observer and wrote with modesty and love about the flora and fauna that he encountered within his parish. White's grandfather was vicar before him, but unlike his ancestor's grave slab set with

1

5

3

4

6

honour before the high altar, the naturalist's grave is a much humbler affair – on the north-east side of the churchyard close by the vestry door. The simple headstone (1) is marked solely by his initials 'GW' and the date of his death, 1793. Gilbert White's grave and others of this era were built with a brick vault to deter body-snatchers.

A wonderfully appropriate monument to the naturalist was raised in 1920 by public subscription – a fine stained glass window (8) of St Francis preaching to the birds. It includes almost all of the species mentioned in Gilbert White's famous book; and in the background can be seen the church, the old vicarage where he was born, and the great churchyard yew. The latter (4) is a magnificent specimen nearly 28ft in girth and in all probability older than the church itself.

St Mary's may claim to be a Royal Foundation, for in the year 1049 King Edward the Confessor gave the land on which the first church was built. There is a record of that church in the Doomsday Book, together with the name of

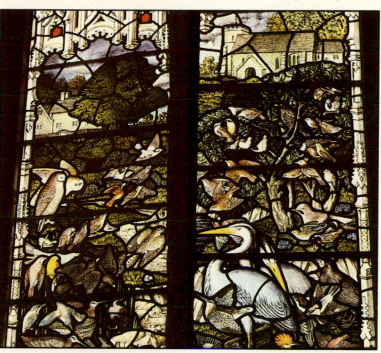

the priest, Radfred, who served it. A century after its foundation Selbourne church was rebuilt and its fabric is consequently Transitional and Early English. Both nave and chancel (5) date from 1180, and their outstanding features are the Romanesque pillars with their simply carved capitals and solid base plinths.

Dominating the chancel is a painting of 1510 which forms the reredos to the high altar. It is by the artist Jan Mostaert, and is a Flemish triptych showing the 'Adoration of the Magi', flanked on either side by St Andrew and St George. The painting was presented to the church in memory of Gilbert White by his brother Benjamin in 1793. Of a similar date and origin is the Flemish sculpture on the north side of the chancel depicting the 'Descent from the Cross'. The ivy-covered tower was added the following century and contains five bells and an old clock (3) of c1680 which was probably made by a local blacksmith.

The south aisle (10) was rebuilt in the 13th century, and its spacious interior was sensitively restored (along with much else in the church) by Gilbert's great-nephew, William White. At its eastern end the aisle possesses a chantry chapel where prayers were said for the soul of Ella Longspee, Countess of Warwick; and at the opposite end are the Royal Arms of King George III painted upon a wooden panel. The practice of displaying the Sovereign's Arms resulted from the break with Rome in 1536, when the Pope's jurisdiction in England was repudiated. King Henry VIII declared himself Head of the Church of England, and the inclusion of the Royal Coat of Arms within churches was made compulsory. In the 19th century the practice fell into disuse.

■ 7: The lovely rural church at **Elsted** in West Sussex.

ST MARTIN'S CANTERBURY/FAIRFIELD

St Martin's Church, Canterbury (1 and 4) is said to be the oldest church in England still in use. At the time of St Augustine's mission it played a unique role in the establishment of Christianity in these Isles – a service to the Faith which is reflected by the thousands of pilgrims who visit the church each year, and who regard St Martin's as the cradle of Christianity in England. The Saxon church occupies an ancient Christian temple forsaken since Roman times, but rebuilt by the heathen King Ethelbert – the 'Bretwalda' – for his French Queen, Bertha. Their marriage had been

agreed upon condition that she was allowed to practise her faith; and it was to the early-Saxon chapel of St Martin that the Queen, accompanied by her chaplain, Luidhard, came to worship. The chancel thus predates the arrival of St Augustine to Kent in AD 597, and the nave (4) was raised shortly after Ethelbert's conversion to Christianity. Such was the persuasion of the apostle's message that the King and most of his thegns were baptised into the Faith – a ceremony of far-reaching implication, which is traditionally associated with St Martin's ancient font. Although much altered, it was probably made especially for the occasion and would originally have been much smaller that it is now – so that adult supplicants could stand in a shallow bowl and have the holy water sprinkled over them. The subsequent addition of further carved stone bricks to heighten the font (with carvings of a later date) suggests that after the era of adult baptism, a higher font was required for infant baptism.

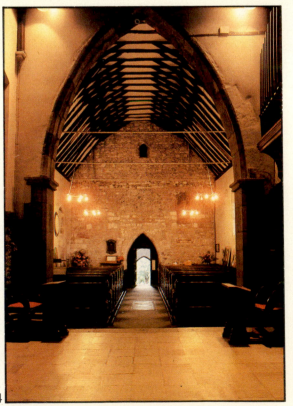

■ At **Fairfield** (2 and 5), also in Kent, the tiny, barn-like church of timber and plaster with red brick walls is dedicated to St Thomas of Canterbury. It stands in a lonely field on the Romney Marshes, surrounded by ditches and sheep – the forlorn plaint of the peewits seeming to emphasise the remoteness of the church's position.

■ St Peter and St Paul's at **Northleach** (3) in Gloucestershire, is one of the premier Perpendicular wool-churches of the Cotswolds, and its beautiful south porch (3) is widely acclaimed as the finest in all England, with its tall pinnacles and

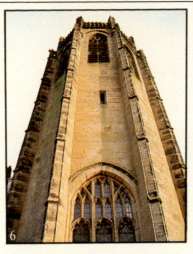

6

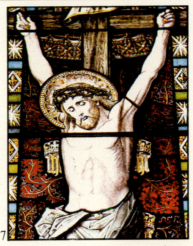

7

stone. The church itself is chiefly memorable for its regional features which at once leap to the eye. The octagonal shape (6) of the tower, the fringe-like pattern of the parapet, and the unusual form of the buttresses of its proud 15th century exterior, are all northern characteristics.

Inside Coxwold church the 17th and 18th centuries have left their own distinctive marks – in the plasterwork of the nave, in the box pews, in the west gallery and in the Jacobean pulpit. The chancel was rebuilt in 1777, and the elongated horseshoe shape of the altar-rail was necessary to provide more

8

9

10

statue-filled niches. The doorway is surmounted by an ogee hood-mould supporting a seated image of Our Lady and Child under a canopy; above this is a niche displaying the Trinity. Panels on either side contain statues of St John the Baptist and St Thomas à Becket. An unusual feature is the sanctus bellcote, and a niche near the porch entrance which was used as a stoup for holy water. The church itself has a tall clerestory with a very broad window over the chancel arch, built by John Fortey, who died in 1458 and has his brass under the north arcade.

■ Another stately Perpendicular church – that of **Coxwold** (6,7,8,9 and 11) in the North Riding of Yorkshire – possesses a fine south porch in the local honey-coloured

space for communicants – to compensate for the area taken up by monuments to the Belasyse family. The largest of these tombs is nearest the altar, dedicated to Sir William Belasyse (9) and his wife, who died in 1601 and is to be seen, along with his spouse, in life-size effigy surrounded by a wealth of armorial bearings. The windows of the nave are filled with painted glass by William Pechitt (7), raised as memorials to members of the Wombwell family. As with similar stained and painted Victorian glass at **Astbury** (10) in Cheshire, it is colourful and well draughted, yet lacks the zest and intense conviction that makes medieval glass so memorable.

Thaxted Church (1-6) is one of the most magnificent parish churches in the country, and its great size – 183ft long, with a spire (2) of almost equal height – indicates the prosperity of the Essex town in earlier days. It was in fact a centre of the wool trade, and in the mid-14th century was a famous cutlery town. This period saw the beginning of the rebuilding of the church which lasted for over one hundred and seventy years.

Thaxted church rises magnificently above the plastered and half-timbered cottages of the old town and the Guild Hall of the Cutlers. It is dedicated to St John the Baptist and consists of a narrow nave with much wider aisles – the arcade (6) was built in 1340 – a crossing with north and south transepts (1), and two porches, each with a parvis room above. Over the northern porch is the chapel of Blessed John Ball, the priest martyr and instigator of the Peasants' Revolt of 1381. At the east end of the church, occupying the site of the original Saxon foundation, is Thaxted's spacious chancel (3) in which hang the banners of St Brigid, St Catherine, St James, St Lawrence (Patron Saint of Cutlers), St Thomas of Canterbury and Our Lady. The

latter two saints have side chapels dedicated to their memory flanking the High Altar – the northern Becket chapel being renowned for its painted ceiling and Tudor glass.

The interior of the church – due to its large windows, its clerestory and the use of white paint – is full of light and air (4 and 5). This feeling of spaciousness is further enhanced by the absence of pews and by its 'walls of glass' – where only buttresses and mullions serve to break the glazing. There are good fragments of medieval stained glass remaining, but in general the glass is clear. Overhead, the roof timbers date from c1510 and are vigorously carved with figures of angels and heraldic emblems, whilst on the nave arches are some fine portrait heads wrought from stone. Good craftsmanship is also apparent in the splendid 15th century font-cover, and in the Jacobean pulpit.

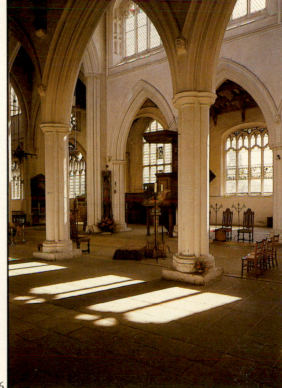

TICKENCOTE

St Peter's Tickencote (1,2,3,4, 5,8 and 9) – described in verse as *'this church, hard by Ermine Street, where three Counties meet'* – is one of England's finest Norman churches. The solid little building, planted in the lovely Rutland countryside soon after the Conquest, has a fascinating eastern front richly ornamented with corbels (8), Romanesque window mouldings – of dog-tooth and chevron – and arcading of interlaced round arches (9). Its exuberance is more than matched within the church, for the interior of Tickencote features a quite remarkable quintuple Norman chancel arch which is like a visual explosion, filling the tiny church with its massive, exotic presence.

This compressed horseshoe arch (4) was probably built about 1140, and displays six orders, each differentiated by rich ornament (2). For size, elaboration and wealth of

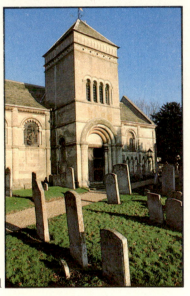

curious detail it is unique. The outer moulding has a peculiar, square-cut foliage enriched by a band of billet moulding. The next order is of chevron, whilst the third has foliage alternating with grotesque heads (3) – including such favourite Norman devices as muzzled bear's, fox's and cat's heads, semi-human monster heads, and the unusual motif of two crowned heads formed as one, but looking in opposite directions (King Stephen and Queen Maud, the rival claimants to the English throne, are probably intended by the Janus heads averted one from the other). These weird carvings may be derived from the garlanded ox skulls of Roman cornices or from Norse sources – once the floodgates of fancy were opened,

the full tide of grotesque imagery poured through. The fourth order of the arch has embattled moulding on the wall plane and double zig-zag on the soffit. The fifth displays birds' heads grasping the roll moulding of the sixth, and innermost order, with their elongated beaks.

Passing beneath the arch to enter the chancel (5) one is again confronted by a remarkable example of Norman craftsmanship – the chancel's magnificent sexpartite vault. It is a feature unique to Tickencote, for such vaults are almost unknown to Romanesque architecture, the only

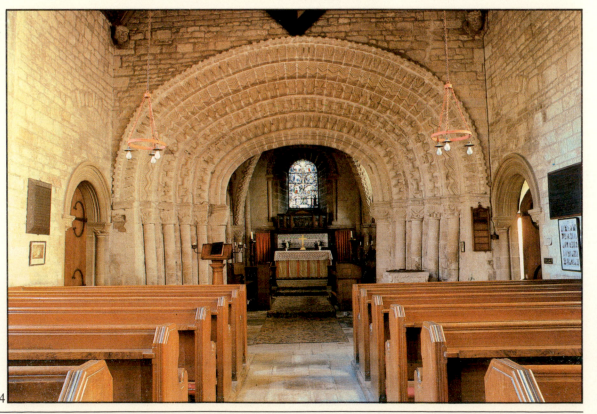

MARSTON MORETAINE/MAIDS' MORETON

other of its kind being introduced at Canterbury by William of Sens in 1175. Norman bosses are therefore extremely rare, and that of St Peter's is of exceptional interest, showing a monk's head held between two bears. In the south wall of the chancel is an interesting wooden effigy of a knight dressed in the armour of King Edward III's reign. It is probable that the timber figure was originally covered in brass and surmounted a tomb. It represents Sir Ronald le Daneys, who fought alongside his leige in the French wars, and was knighted at Carcassonne in 1355.

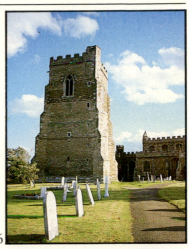

6

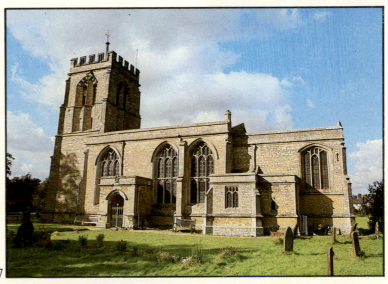

7

■ The Early English bell-tower of St Mary's at **Marston Moretaine** (6) in Bedfordshire is one of thirty-six detached towers in Britain. It has sturdy diagonal buttresses, a stairway encased within its massive walls and once possessed its own well – all of which point to its original use as a place of defence, or as a refuge against the flood-waters of the Marston Valley.

■ The Perpendicular church of St Edmund, at **Maids' Moreton** (7) in Buckinghamshire was built in 1450, and all its fine design and workmanship are of this date (save for an addition to the vestry in 1882). The church is said to have been the gift of two daughters, and a 17th century painted inscription over the northern doorway records *'Sisters and Maids of the Daughters of the lord Pruet the Pious and Munificent Founders of this Church'* – the village continues to honour the 'Maids' by perpetuating their memory in its name.

5

8

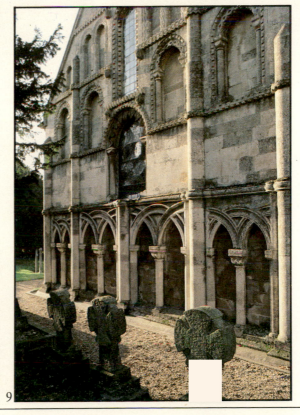

9

LINCOLN CATHEDRAL

The profiles of **Lincoln Cathedral's** (3,4,5,6,8,9,and 10) three towers majestically complement the high limestone ridge on which they stand. They are visible for miles around,

The Normans under Bishop Remigius built at Lincoln, but their cathedral was reduced to ruin by an earth-tremor in 1185. The task of its reconstruction befell Bishop Hugh of Avalon, who raised the choir in one of the earliest pure Gothic designs and – with its eccentric arrangement of arches – certainly one of the most idiosyncratic. Twenty years after his death he was canonised and the cult of the veneration of St Hugh began.

Pilgrimages enabled work to continue apace during the period 1215-1255, and under the authority of Alexander the Architect, the long, somewhat low and typically Early English nave (5) and magnificent vault (9) were constructed. Its Purbeck marble shafts and subtle arcading along the aisle walls (10) represent the culmination of the lancet style –

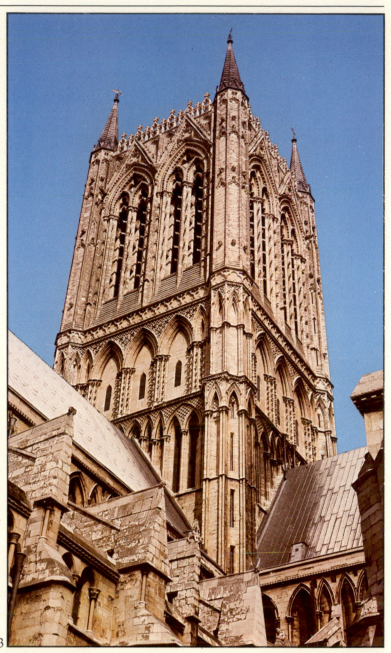

dominating the city and flat landscape of the surrounding countryside. In medieval times its central tower (3 and 8) – at 271ft the tallest in England – carried a spire of lead-encased timber said to have reached the almost unbelievable height of 525ft, a quarter as tall again as that of Salisbury. The grand conception of Lincoln, completed by the year 1280, is generally regarded as England's finest Gothic cathedral and wonderfully encourages that sense of special mission handed from one generation of masons to another. Judged from its position, strength and wealth of decorative feature it recalls the words of the 78th Psalm: *'and he built his sanctuary high as the heavens, founded to last forever'.*

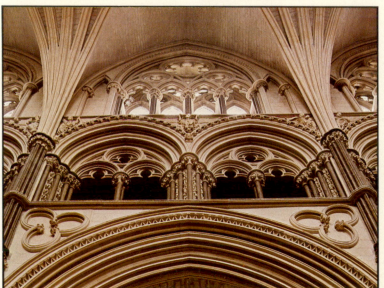

SHILLINGSTONE

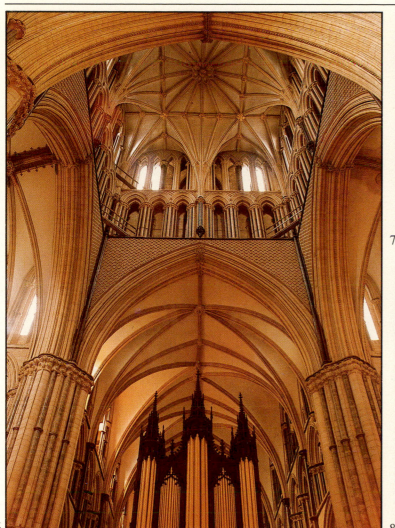

often referred to as the 'Springtime of the Style' – whose fresh and almost severe simplicity predate the arrival of bar tracery.

The lantern of the central tower (6) dates from the 14th century and is positioned at the crossing. The four bays east of the high altar are occupied by the Angel Choir - whose architecture, when it was raised, reflected the new doctrine of the 'Principle of Order', which intimated that cathedrals should exist to proclaim the unseen harmony of God's plan for the universe through the perfect proportions of its visible structure. Similarly, light had a profound

influence, enabling Lincoln's Bishop to speak of it as *'the mediator between bodiless and bodily substances, a spiritual body, an embodied spirit'.* Thus, through such ideals, the quality of luminosity pervades the Angel Choir – so named from the twenty-eight celestial beings that adorn the spandrels of the triforium (4) – constructed by Simon of Thirsk to accomodate the ever-increasing volume of pilgrims flocking to St Hugh's relics for blessing.

■ The 12th century church of the Holy Rood at **Shillingstone** (1,2 and 7) in Dorset (the dedication indicates a Saxon foundation) demonstrates how well the dignity of modern brasswork – its lectern of 1906 (1), and crucifix of the high altar (2) – blends with medieval ashlar masonry and banded flintwork. Its Purbeck marble font (7) is Early English and stands beneath a belfry which houses a bell cast in the 13th century – two hundred years older than the tower itself.

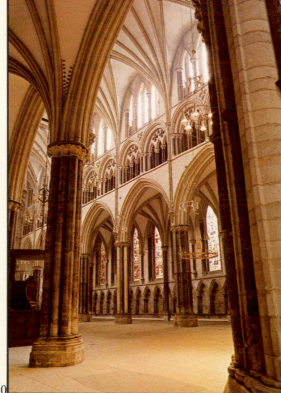

NECTON/SILCHESTER

The church at **Necton** (1,5,6 and 8) in Norfolk, dedicated to All Saints, was built mostly in the 15th century, but the nave arches are from the previous century. The oldest part of the church is St Catherine's chapel on the north side of the chancel: it was founded in 1326 by Lady Maud, widow of Sir Robert de Tony, on condition that a Chantry priest said daily prayers and masses for the soul of her husband, herself and of her father and mother. The medieval idea underlying this was the belief that the time spent in purgatory could be shortened by the prayers and intercessions of the faithful.

Necton's great possession is its fine hammer-beam roof in the nave. The colouring is original and was discovered beneath thick layers of plaster in 1908. The principals are supported by angels (6) with their wings expanded and under them, on pedestals, stand the twelve Apostles with the instruments of their martyrdom in their hands. In the midst of the six on the north side of the nave are effigies of Christ with St Peter, whilst the Virgin Mary stands with St John the Evangelist on the south side. The medieval colouring of the nave vault finds faithful echo in the chancel, where a copy of Sebastian del Piombo's 'Raising of Lazarus' (8) on the reredos adds richness to the high altar.

■ At **Silchester** (4 and 9) colour forms the basis of the church's unique charm, where mellow brick and tile seem to merge as natural forms into a landscape haunted by memories of the lost Roman city of *Callera Atrebatum.*

■ The parish church at **Wisborough Green** (3) in West

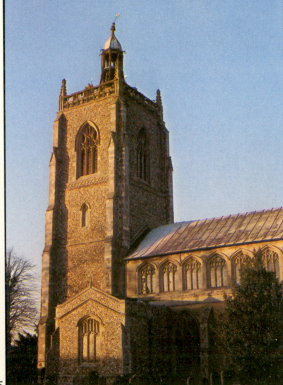

weighing more than a ton. It is a contemporary of those at Stonehenge and may originally have been associated with pagan rites. The 'holy stone' was consecrated by the Normans, but was nearly destroyed during the zeal of the Reformation when we read that, '*at the order of Henry VIII St Peter Ad Vincular gave up a crucifix with a drop of the Virgin's milk set in crystal in it; the hair shirt, comb and bones of St James; relics of the Holy Sepulchre and the Mount of Olives; hair of St Peter, stones from St Stephen's martyrdom; and other relics of St Edmund of Canterbury, St Giles, St Sebastian and St Silvester*'. To see such treasures the pious came from far and wide (and bear witness to the general importance of the church in medieval times), but all 'papist shams' were destroyed – 'cleansed' from the church – save for the altar stone which was hidden, and not discovered until 1901.

■ The Lord of the Manor was usually responsible for building the original Norman or medieval

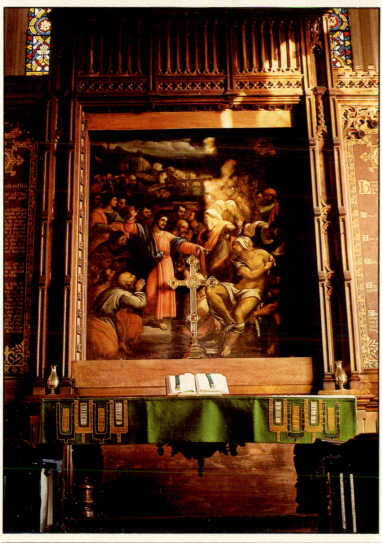

Sussex has a rare dedication to St Peter Ad Vincular (St Peter in Chains) – the same dedication as the chapel abutting the execution ground in the Tower of London. This adds weight to the suspicion that the building was formerly the keep of a castle or stockade. The doorway is 13 feet high and would admit a mounted warrior, whilst the 5 feet thick walls are strong enough to withstand a heavy assault. High on the hill, the church itself suggests an ideal lookout point above the River Arun.

The 13th century chancel has a most unusual altar – a stone

parish church, and at **Corbet** (2) he did so on his own land and near his own house. However, Victorian benefactors were responsible for the present building of St Andrew's at **Okeford Fitzpaine** (7) which was almost entirely rebuilt in 1866. Using the materials of the earlier 14th century church, St Andrew's copied its predecessor's plan and it is thus a fairly faithful and praiseworthy 19th century reproduction of a late-medieval church.

ABBEY DORE

1

crossing is striking, and their walls are painted with texts and other designs, including David with his harp, 'Time' with his scythe, the Lord's Prayer and – in the north transept (7) – the Royal Arms of Queen Anne.

Later, when the abbey had become wealthier, a more splendid presbytery was built, which serves to throw the earlier simplicity of the rest of the church into greater relief. The cathedral-like grandeur of this 13th century addition is lit by a clerestory pierced by deeply splayed lancets.

The monastery was destroyed at the Dissolution, and it is thanks to

2

3

Surrounded by the orchards of the Golden Valley, the parish church of the Holy Trinity and St Mary at **Abbey Dore** (1,2,3,4,5 and 7) is one of the finest examples of Cistercian-inspired Early English architecture in the country. The abbey at Dore was founded in this once remote and wild region of Herefordshire in 1147 by Robert FitzHarold. All traces of his first church have disappeared – save for Robert's own full-size effigy (3) which shows him as a knight, his legs crossed, his shield drawn closely to his chest, and his hand frozen in stone for all time in the act of drawing his sword.

The rebuilding of Abbey Dore between 1175 and 1200, reflects the discipline of the Early English style. Upon entering the church one is at once impressed by the restrained beauty of its architecture. The columns supporting the roof are decorated with simple foliage, and the bays of the arcade (1) are ornamented with dog-tooth moulding. The lofty appearance of the transepts and

4

5

6

the good offices of the First Viscount Scudamore that the church was rescued from being used as a cattle shelter. In 1633 he engaged John Abel to restore the abbey as a parish church. It was he who carved the fine oak screen (4) and surmounted it with the three armorial bearings of Stuart, Scudamore and Laud. Able was also the architect of the roof – rebuilt with 204 tons of Herefordshire oak – and was responsible for restoring to the church its large *mensa*, or altar-table (5) which had been used since the Reformation as a slab for salting fish.

■ The lord of the manor was frequently responsible for building the parish church, and he usually did so upon his own land and close to his own house. A splendid example of this relationship exists at **Sandford Orcas** (6) in Dorset, where the 13th century church stands alongside a beautiful, stone-built manor house.

■ Projecting from the parapets of **Warsop Church** (8 and 9) is a series

7

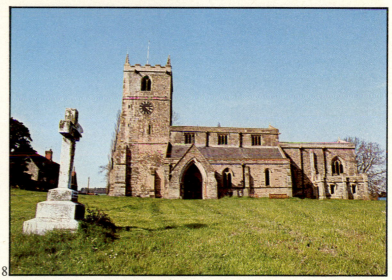

8

9

of gargoyles. These grotesquely carved water-spouts are built outwards from the gutter in order to throw water clear of the masonry. Apart from their purely functional aspect, gargoyles appear to have served a second, almost subconscious, purpose. Although the Christian Church would not accept the divinity of pagan gods, it had a lively fear of their dark malevolence, and even well into the Middle Ages it sought to defend itself against them. Thus, gargoyles were given their horrific forms in order to frighten away pagan spirits – on the medieval assumption that evil combats evil.

Raised almost entirely in the Decorated style, the elegant church of **Trumpington** (1,2 and 3) in Cambridge, is a fine example of a building dating from the first half of the 14th century. Its clerestory set above piers of the lofty nave arcade is particularly noble – as is the western tower (1) of local clunch with flint battlements. The church's greatest treasure is its memorial brass of Sir Roger de Trumpington – *'a noble knight and brave soldier'* – dated 1289, which is the second oldest brass in the country (the oldest, at Stoke d'Abernon, is twelve years its senior). It is probable that Sir Roger was the church's original benefactor and at his instigation the present building was erected. The brass (3) rests on a slab of Purbeck marble, and is in the north chapel on a tomb chest over which rises a canopied arch (2). His brass depicts him cross-legged in chain-mail; the shield he bears displays two trumpets – the family rebus.

■ A fall of snow, and the intense light that it engenders, highlights

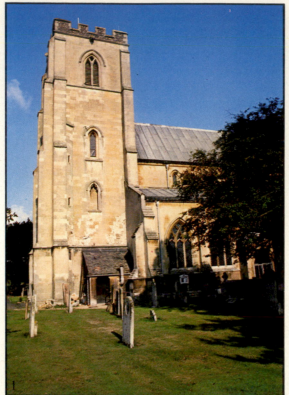

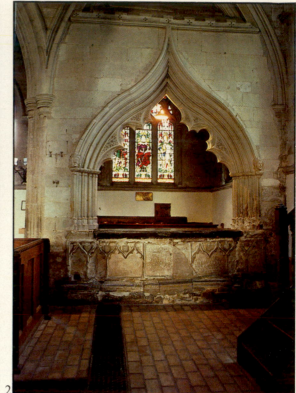

the mellow stonework and Tudor brick of the 14th century church at **Earls Colne** (6) in Essex. At All Saints', **Bisham** (5) snow throws into contrast the dark flint fabric of the medieval church. It is much restored, apart from its Norman tower, and 16th century Hoby chapel with its remarkable monuments, the most beautiful of which is an Elizabethan obelisk surmounted by a heart guarded by four swans.

■ **Ottery St Mary** (7) in Devon, is a Collegiate Church of great fame and interest, modelled upon Exeter Cathedral by Bishop Grandisson, who reconstructed the

OTTERY ST MARY/ST ENDELLION

(by the movement of a golden sun) and of night. An inner circle bears thirty discs marked with Arabic numerals to represent the days of the Synodic month. A moving star shows the age of the moon, and an orb in black and white – which revolves on its own axis – indicates the precise phase of the moon as it travels round, completing its

church in the period 1338-42. Its rather squat exterior is more than compensated for by the interior – a blaze of light and colour – which offers much detail for study. There are canopied tombs of Ortho Grandisson and his wife, stone vaulted ceilings with fascinating roof bosses, carved choir-stalls, a minstrel's gallery, and a superb medieval clock (7) – the gift of the Bishop of Exeter. It is one of the oldest surviving mechanical clocks in England. Based upon the Ptolemaic theory, whereby the earth was regarded as the centre of the universe, the wooden clock-face indicates the hours of the day

revolution once in every twenty-four hours.

■ Another Collegiate foundation, that of St Endellion at **St Endellion** (8), stands alone on a Cornish hilltop. One steps down from the lichened, granite exterior into an airy building (8) touched by the blue light of its unstained glass and the reflected hue of the slate floor – an effect of atmosphere held shimmering beneath the elegant simplicity of the nave's wagon-roof.

■ 9: Projecting stone conduits, in the guise of angels, at **Welbourne** in Lincolnshire.

■ 4: Victorian heraldic glass at **Garston**.

SALISBURY CATHEDRAL/STOCK/MELLS

2

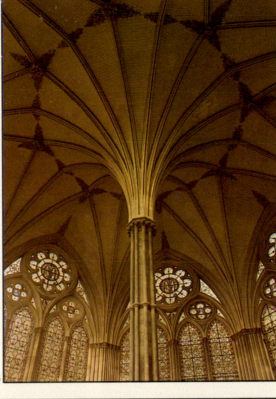

3

4

Early English architecture – the first phase of the Gothic – is fresh, and characterised by a restrained sense of classical simplicity. Nowhere is this feeling of light and elegance more apparent than at **Salisbury Cathedral** (1,3 and 5), the purest example of the style. The building is without rival, for it is the only Gothic cathedral wholly constant in both design and construction – no other has achieved such a pinnacle of unity. It was planned by Bishop Richard Poore in 1220 as a single conception, built upon a virgin site; thus it was neither influenced by the architecture of a previous age, nor was it a piecemeal of styles. From the laying of the foundation

5

stone in the watermeads of the River Avon – where grew *'lilies, roses and violets among the many crystal springs, as pure as gold'* – to the completion of the cathedral in 1258, took but thirty-eight years – a surprisingly short period of time for such a monumental task. Having been raised to the glory of God, the geometrical shapes of its masses culminated the following century in the erection of the famous cathedral spire. It is Salisbury's most splendid feature, and its exceptional height expresses a combination of strength and the ascetic striving of the peculiarly medieval desire to lay claim to heaven.

The nave, transepts, Trinity chapel and choir (5) were all completed by the year 1258. In comparison with the grace of Salisbury's exterior (1) the cool, balanced cathedral interior may appear slightly 'remote': the watchwords, however, are 'clarity', 'simplicity' and 'harmony'. The idea of using Purbeck marble (one of the hallmarks of Early English architecture) was inspired by the crusaders' reports of the Holy Land's *rich marbled halls*. Its use quickly came into vogue and dark columns of marble appear throughout the building – the only touch of luxury the Salisbury Master allowed himself. There is virtually no naturalistic carving within the cathedral – only severe rounded moulding – and no tracery, merely lancet windows glazed with monochrome grisaille.

After its dedication in 1258 there were but three major additions to Salisbury Cathedral. The period 1263-84 saw the erection of the grandest cloisters in England, and the building of the magnificent chapter-house; both are among the finest of their kind. The latter (3) is 53ft in diameter and has a beautiful vault rising from a slender central column. In 1334, Richard Farleigh raised the cathedral's culminating feature – the crossing tower, crowned by a 404ft high stone spire (the loftiest in England, and the second tallest in Europe) – which acts as a centralising point for the main body of the cathedral.

■ Two other distinctive towers are to be seen at **Stock** (2) in Essex, and at **Mells** (4) in Somerset. The former is a remarkable example of an early tower which supports a timber belfry and spire; whilst the latter is one of the loveliest of the great Perpendicular stone towers.

CLIFFE

The church of St Helen's at **Cliffe** (1,3,4,5,6,7,8 and 9) in Kent, stands remote and large among trees above the marshes of the Thames estuary on the Hoo Peninsula. It is Early English in style and cruciform in plan; with aisles and long transepts. The twelve sturdy pillars in the nave have distinctive chevron markings (7 and 8) painted in bands of colour upon them and uphold an ancient oak tie-beam roof. There are traces of wall paintings in various other parts of the church – notably in the north and south transepts – where the subjects include the 'Martyrdom of St

Stations of the Cross. On the opposite wall of the chancel is the sedilia (4), which incorporates a double piscina: the beauty of the tracery and elegance of the pinnacles surmount a perfectly proportioned vaulted roof. A fascinating feature of the decorative stonework is the number of small faces carved on the level of the capitals, each one expressing either disdain or heavenly bliss. The sedilia was used by the celebrants, deacon and sub-deacon as seating during the singing of the Creed and Gloria.

The church plate at St Helen's (9) is another of the church's

Edmund', the 'Last Judgement', the 'Virgin and Child' and the 'Execution of St Margaret'.

The nave is divided from the Decorated chancel by a 14th century screen (6) which in the Middle Ages served to partition the secular and social affairs taking place in the nave from the Sacramental Presence and worship east of the divide. Here, in the chancel, are two of Cliffe's great treasures – its Eastern Sepulchre and magnificent sedilia. The former (3), is a large, tomb-like recess to which the Blessed Sacrament was brought in procession following the Maundy Thursday Eucharist. It was surrounded by spring flowers and set with candles burning before it. This signified Christ praying in the Garden of Gethsemane. The faithful kept watch (as His disciples were bidden to 'watch and pray' in the Garden) until dawn the next morning – the time when Jesus commenced His journey to Golgotha – the faithful then proceeded on the rounds of the

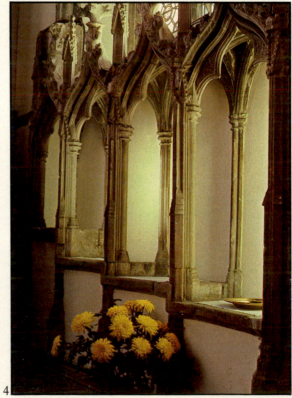

memorable possessions. It includes a silver chalice; a silver flagon, dated 1735, and the famous 'Cliffe-at-Hoo-Paten', a pre-Reformation gilt plate with the Latin inscription *'Let us bless the Father, and the Son, with the Holy Spirit'.*

The churchyard overlooks a landscape of grey marshland, but contains some fine monuments (5) and a flint-built 'watch box' (1) – an interesting feature of life in the 18th century. It is a small hut in which armed men took guard at night to foil the activities of the 'Resurrection Men' or body-snatchers, who reclaimed corpses from recently dug graves to sell to

medical students for dissection.

■ The parish church at **Goathurst** (2 and 10) is one of the few dedicated to the young Saxon King, St Edward the Martyr, murdered on the orders of his stepmother, Elfrida, in AD 978. The building as it now stands is mainly of the Perpendicular period and dates from the second half of the 15th century. The tower (2) is plain for Somerset and belongs to an older church of the 14th century: there is stylistic evidence for this in the rich moulding of the tower archway which is distinctly of the Decorated period. The Halswell family were closely

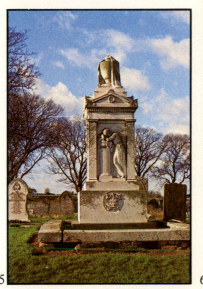

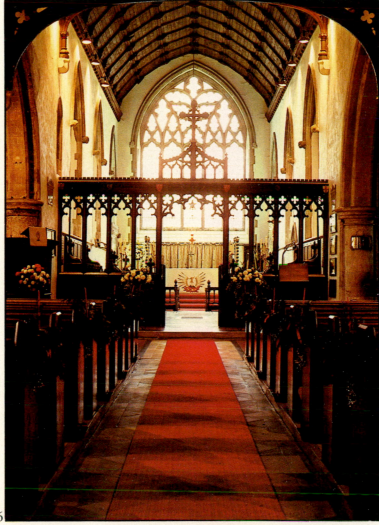

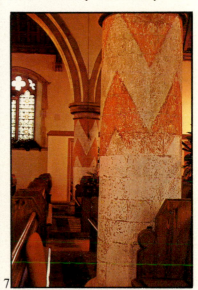

associated with Goathurst for many centuries, and their private chapel on the north side of the chancel was added to the church in the early-17th century. The chapel is dominated by the splendid monument to Sir Nicholas Halswell, whose heraldic device (10) surmounts the tomb.

ASHPRINGTON/STEVENTON

The parish church of **Ashprington** (2,3,4,5,8 and 9) is one of the few outside Wales dedicated to St David. It is of the Perpendicular period, built of dunstone with red sandstone dressing. The tower dates from 1350 and is peculiar in that it has no buttresses, and batters or diminishes upwards, making it appear curiously thin. The interior of St David's is in the tradition of fellow Devonshire churches, being tall and light; its white pillars looking majestic against pale-brown woodwork. Much of this carpentry is modern, yet the ornately carved pulpit (3 and 9),

the pews of the nave (8) and the eagle lectern (4) are all of the highest craftsmanship – in accordance with Ashprington's legacy of medieval excellence.

In the north wall of the church is a blocked up doorway – in times past provided for the use of men, while women entered by the south door. In the Middle Ages the sexes were divided for divine worship, and the line of demarcation is indicated by the capitals of the pillars in the nave (5): the western two are perfectly plain, whilst those nearest the chancel are adorned with foliage. The font (2) is also ornamented with foliage, being

1

2

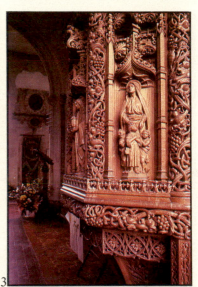

3

4

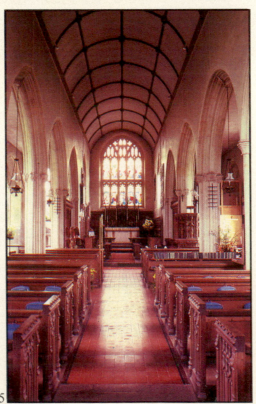

5

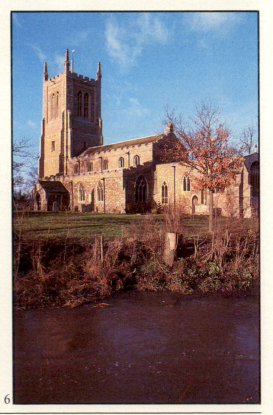

6

very large and hewn from red sandstone. Tradition states that it was made locally in South Devon by a 12th century monk. The Ashprington chalice is another remarkable survivor from an earlier church which stood upon the site. It is the oldest in use of any parish church in England. Experts have dated the vessel to c1275, and it is heartening to reflect that for over six hundred and fifty years successive generations of the faithful have received the Holy Sacrament from the same chalice.

■ The church at **Steventon** (1 and 11) has seen little alteration since its first recorded mention in the

■ St Oswald's, **Widford** (7) in Oxfordshire is a tiny church which once stood amid the Royal Forest of Wychwood (until it was cleared in the 1860s) in a countryside dotted with deserted medieval villages. The church itself was raised during the late-12th and early-13th centuries by the monks of Gloucester.

■ The Cambridgeshire church of **Great Stoughton** (6) dates in its entirety from the 13th to the 16th centuries.

■ The altar of **Gorway** (10) ably demonstrates that lack of ornamentation places no restriction upon dignity.

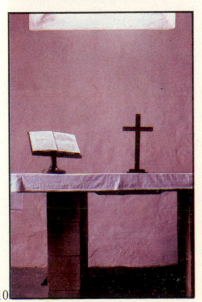

12th century. Despite being small and simple in structure, it is both interesting and full of unexpected charm. The west door has an elegantly carved medieval face (1) below the hood-mould, and nearby is a 'scratch-dial' or mass-clock, which must previously have been positioned within the south wall to catch the sun. The shadow cast by its gnomon indicated the hour of mass. In later years the church became associated with the Austen family who, for three generations, were rectors here from 1761 until 1873. Jane Austen, daughter of the Reverend George Austen, was born at Steventon in 1775 and is mentioned in both the parish register (which dates from 1603) and in a commemorative tablet within the church.

SOMPTING/ST MARTHA-ON-THE-HILL

The Anglo-Saxons first came to Britain as pagan raiders about AD 400. Three centuries later they had peopled and tamed much of England. During this period the Saxons embraced Christianity, and although still divided into many kingdoms, they established a united Church. Their faith was to be the inspiration for their finest works of architecture. The tower of **Sompting Church** (4) in West Sussex has survived for a thousand years as evidence of their skill. The 100ft high tower is unique in England – being the only remaining example of the style known as the 'Rhenish Helm'. The

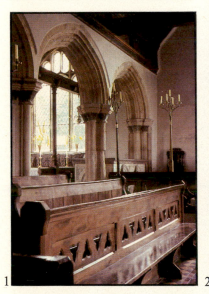

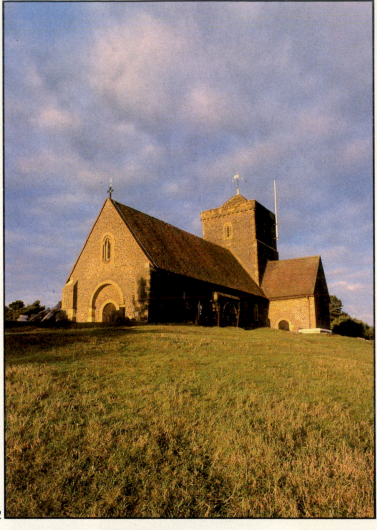

use of Roman bricks in the masonry at Sompting shows how Saxon England grew out of the ruins of Roman Britain.

■ Although a Norman church, **St Martha-on-the-Hill** (2) above the Pilgrim's Way in Surrey, is a Saxon foundation, raised upon the site of four 'Druid Circles' buried beneath the bracken on the south side of the hill. The church's dedication is a corruption of 'St Martyrs' – for upon this spot six hundred Christians were put to the sword in early Saxon times. In the centuries that followed the massacre prayers were raised for the souls of those slain, and in 1463 Bishop Waynflete of Winchester granted an indulgence of forty days to *'all those who came for devotion, prayers, pilgrimage or offering to the chapel; and should there recite the Paternoster, Angel's Salutation and Apostles' Creed'.* Still to be seen are the pilgrims' votive crosses incised into the stonework of the old nave doorway.

■ Similar medieval graffiti (although infinitely more extensive

and interesting) exists at the magnificent 14th century church of **St Mary's, Ashwell** (3 and 5) in Hertfordshire. On the north wall under the tower is a scratched Latin inscription (3) of great historical importance, *'M. CT. Expente miseranda ferox, violenta MCCLL'.* Translated into English, these tragic words mean *'1350 miserable, wild, distracted, the dregs of the people alone survive to witness...'* referring to the Black Death which swept through England killing one man in three. Another inscription alludes to the Magna Carta – *'Let the Church of England be free'.*

6

7

8

9

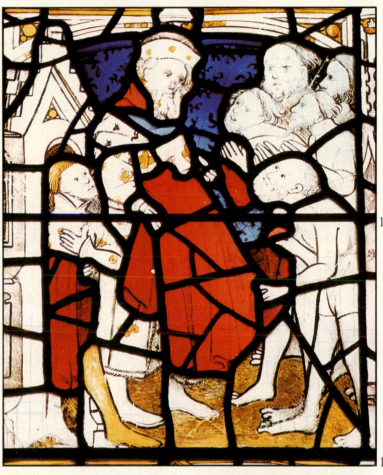

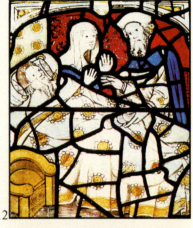

12

13

10

11

The richness of stained glass is an indication of the prosperity of a city or town in the Middle Ages. Florence, Chartres and York are typical of Italian, French and English cities that acquired their wealth of stained glass when their merchant classes were at their most affluent. The latter, a great wood centre, still has nineteen medieval parish churches, many rich in coloured glass – which is not surprisng since York was famous for its stained glass workshops. The most exciting windows (some eleven in all) are in **All Saints' Church, York** (6 -14). A particularly fine one, dating from 1410, depicts the 'Corporate Acts of Mercy'. Six of the compassionate deeds: giving drink to the thirsty (9), feeding the hungry, housing the stranger (10), clothing the naked (11), tending the sick (12) and visiting the imprisoned (13) still survive, but the seventh, burying the dead, is missing. Death dominates another of All Saints' famous windows. This is based upon a poem, *'The Prickle of Conscience'*, written in Northumbrian dialect by the mystic, Richard Rolle. The theme covers life, death, Purgatory, Doomsday, the pains of Hell and the bliss of Heaven. The window is

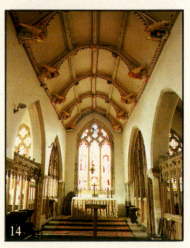

14

intended as a warning of what is to come and concentrates on the last fifteen days of the world. The macabre scenes are most vividly evoked, and include monsters emerging from the seas to overrun the land (7), the sea and trees on fire (8), the ground giving up the bones of the dead (6), men hiding in shelters to pray for help, death coming to claim all mortals, and finally, earthquakes and flames devouring everything on the last day.

■ 1: The north chancel of **Mottistone** church on the Isle of Wight.

CHILLINGHAM/SHREWSBURY

Set on a gentle elevation sheltered from the north by oak and beech woodland, the simple stone church of **Chillingham** (1,3,5,7 and 8) is a much restored building of Norman origin. Its font and cover date from 1670, its pulpit is Jacobean, there are fine box-pews in the nave, and its chancel (1) is elevated above a crypt. St Peter's chief object of interest however, is its monument to Sir Ralph Grey (3) who died in 1443, and his wife Elizabeth. Their alabaster effigies (5) lie on a

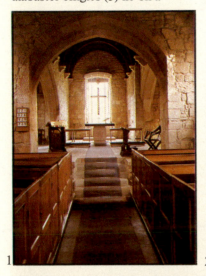

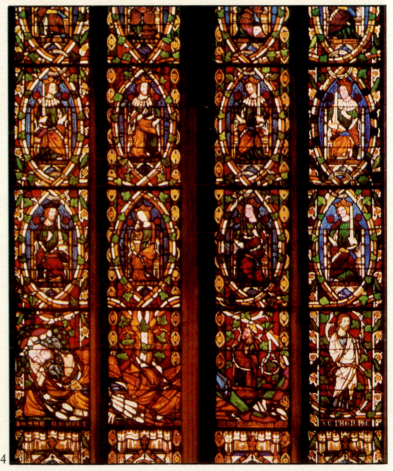

sandstone altar-tomb, its side richly carved with niches and canopies enclosing the figures of saints (8) alternating with angels bearing shields. Unlike many others of its kind, this tomb escaped injury during the Reformation and the iconoclasm of the Commonwealth.

■ Some of the finest medieval glass to survive the turmoil of religious upheaval in the 16th and 17th centuries is to be seen in St Mary's, **Shrewsbury** (4). The Great East Window is filled with superb English 14th century stained glass and is one of the largest representations of the 'Tree of Jesse'. The glass was originally commissioned by Sir John de Charlton and his wife, Lady Hawis, for the Grey Friars. It was transferred to St Chads in Shrewsbury after the Dissolution, but in 1788 the tower collapsed and destroyed the church. Only the Lady chapel and the Jesse Tree's stained glass

survived – whence it was again removed and rehoused in St Mary's.

■ Two delightful country churches noted for the beauty of their settings are **Troutbeck Church** (2) in Cumbria and **Uffington Church** (9) in Oxfordshire. The former has a marvellous east window by Burne-Jones, and lies in a wild and remote valley, dominated by the lofty Kirkstone Pass to the north, and by Lake Windermere to the west. The large cruciform, stone and pebble-dash church of St Mary's at Uffington stands among willows, at a corner of the chalk and thatched village, within sight

6

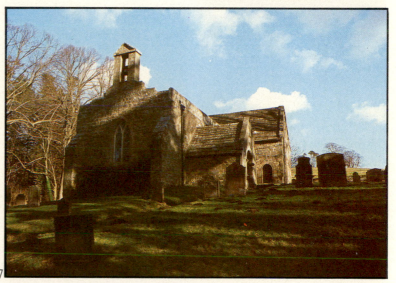

5

7

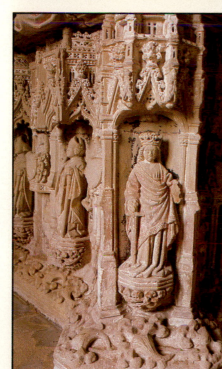

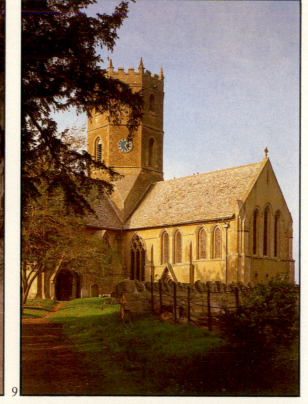

8

9

of the prehistoric White Horse of Uffington whose sinuous form is incised into the greensward of the nearby down. The church – with its unusual octagonal tower, once topped by a spire – is often referred to as the 'Cathedral of the Vales'. It is one of the finest examples of early Gothic architecture, and possesses an impressive rib-vaulted south porch with a door fastened by elaborate ornamental hinges. Each of St Mary's three transept chapels has its own piscina and is lit by unusual lancet windows.

■ The medieval parish church at **Westerham** (6) in Kent, has a three-gabled east end and a squat western tower, within which is a rare timber spiral stairway leading to its upper chamber. The tower has stood for nearly seven hundred years – the record of time written visibly yet without sign of weakness and decrepitude – its desert flanks of rough-hewn masonry, full of puttock holes (now abandoned to nesting jackdaws) and fissures, enclosed within the grip of its massive buttresses.

EYE/CLOPHILL/UFFORD

Once surrounded by water, and named after the old Saxon word for 'island', the church of St Peter and St Paul, at **Eye** (2 and 3) in Suffolk, is well known for its splendid 100ft high, 15th century west tower, panelled in flint and stone, with octagonal buttresses. The main body of the church predates the tower by one hundred years, and upon entering one is surprised by its lightness. The effect is mainly due to the clear glass of the clerestory, the relative simplicity of which is augmented elsewhere by the richness of modern stained glass (3). The pre-Reformation screen is the greatest

statues, and terminates in a carved pelican pecking its own breast (6) – the mystical symbol of Christ's sacrifice for mankind upon the Cross. It was carved in 1450 and the elaboration of the pinnacles, canopies and tabernacle work is an astonishing triumph of medieval art, made even more impressive by the fact that the whole work is telescopic, so that when raised the lower parts slide up over the superstructure.

The Ufford font cover was once '*all gilt over with gold*', and enough of the gilding and gesso-work remains to convey some idea of its original appearance. The hammer-

treasure at Eye, having fifteen painted panels of saints and kings, and a magnificent rood (2) supported on either side by figures of the Virgin Mary and St John the Baptist, nobly restored by Sir Ninian Comper.

■ Another of Suffolk's famous village churches is the Norman and Perpendicular church of St Mary, **Ufford** (5,6,7 and 8), raised in the typical East Anglian fashion of elaborate flushwork with a pleasant warming relief of well-carved stone (8). As at Eye, it can show incomparable woodwork, and Ufford possesses the finest medieval font cover to be seen. This great Gothic masterpiece is said to be the most beautiful cover in the world – Nuremburg runs a close second. The font itself is plain by comparison, carved with Tudor roses, grotesque faces and heraldic shields of the influential Suffolk families of Willoughby and Ufford. Above the stone font, the cover (5) rises for a staggering 18ft, soaring in graceful receding tiers of canopied niches which once held

beam roof of the nave – with its carved angels – and the chancel's tie-beam vault also possess much of their original colouring, and in their rafters the sacred monogram 'IHS' and 'MR' (the cypher of Our Lady) are repeatedly painted upon the boards. The chancel roof (7) is unusual in having the arched bracings intersected by pendants halfway up: they bear shields upon which the instruments of Christ's Passion are vividly evoked.

■ The purpose of medieval font-covers – however elaborate – was to protect the holy water of the font from being stolen by witches who used it in their magic rites.

Fantastic as the idea of black rites might appear to the modern mind there are still those who take the opportunity to practise the art. One notorious incident occurred in March 1963 amid the gaunt ruins of St Mary's, **Clophill** (1), whose eerie remains crown the brow of Dead Man's Hill. In this sorry Bedfordshire church, which has been deserted for centuries, the tomb of an apothecary's wife was torn open, and her bones arranged in a circle about the gutted nave. The desecration supposedly served some part of a Black Mass, and an attempt at necromancy.

■ 4: The church at **Beddingham** upon the South Downs of Sussex.

LAPFORD

The hilltop church of **Lapford** (1-6) above the River Yoe in North Devon can trace its foundation back to a Saxon fane, yet the present parish church was built largely at the instigation of one man – Earl William de Tracey. He was one of the four knights to strike down Archbishop Thomas à Becket in his own Cathedral church at Canterbury – the most heinous of medieval deeds, and one that gave England her greatest saint. For his part in the martyrdom, the Earl's property was forfeited and he was ordered to build a certain number of expiatory churches, of which

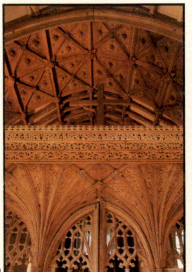

1

2

right across the building, separating the nave (6) from the chancel (4), and divides the north aisle into two portions. Local craftsmen were responsible for the extremely ornate screen, erected in the early years of the 16th century. The outline resembles many of its fellow Devonshire screens, but the enrichments – especially those of the spaces between the ribs of the groining, and the running patterns of foliage and flowers – are perhaps the greatest specimens to be seen anywhere. To add to the splendour, there is a canopy of honour over the Calvary – crossed-ribbed with *roses-en-soleil* in the panels. Where

3

4

5

Lapford was one. Construction commenced in the 1170s and the church was naturally dedicated to St Thomas of Canterbury. By an interesting twist of fate, three hundred and seventy years later King Henry VIII tried to blot out all memory of Becket (who was seen to represent the supreme victory of Church over State), and foundations bearing his name were rededicated – generally to St Thomas the Apostle. Despite intense pressure, however, Lapford and its people courageously refused to bow to royal command: thus the church is one of the rare medieval survivors to have continually honoured the martyr's name.

Lapford church shares with Atherington the reputation of possessing the finest rood screen (1 and 2) in the Kingdom. It extends this ends, the vault of nave and aisle is taken over by a typical 'Devon Cradle', or wagon roof. The church's wealth of carved detail spills over into the magnificently carved bench-ends which display a great variety of devices.

SWINBROOK

St Mary the Blessed Virgin at **Swinbrook** (1,2,3,4,7,9,10 and 11) is a Transitional Norman church, with Perpendicular additions, built in the mellow local stone of the Windrush Valley. It is famous for its extraordinary 17th century storied tombs of the Fettiplace family, who flourished with great wealth and influence in Tudor and Stuart times – one even married a Portuguese princess and brought her to the chillier climes of Oxfordshire. The tombs stand before the high altar (3), resting against the northern wall of the chancel. They are of immense size, adorned with innumerable shields

and family arms (11). The two adjoining monuments each produce a fascinating trio of reclining figures. The earlier monument (4), erected in 1613, was ordered by Sir Edmund Fettiplace I for his grandfather, father and himself, whilst the later of the two was carved in 1686 at the behest of Sir Edmund Fettiplace II to honour his uncle and his father as well as its patron. It is interesting to compare the rigid Tudor style of the earlier, armoured effigies – which stiffly recline on one elbow – with the more realistic Stuart style of the later tomb, whose figures are relaxed and casually loll upon their shelves with one knee slightly bent (2).

Narrowly separating the two monuments is a fine altar-rail. These were gradually introduced into English churches after the Reformation to protect the altar when rood screens were disappearing. They became popular at the time of Archbishop Laud in the 1630s to prevent the altar being

moved into the body of the church (as desired by the Puritans) and to stop stray dogs from profaning the holiest part of the building. Above the communion table rises Swinbrook's 15th century Perpendicular east window whose tracery of strongly veined mullions is seen to best advantage from the churchyard (7).

■ The Norfolk church of St Peter, **Weasenham** (6 and 8), possesses some interesting and lovely panels of pre-Reformation glass in the lofty north windows of the nave. One of the panels shows a feathered angel (6) with a pair of golden wings on his back, a

feathered body, legs and arms, but with graceful human hands and bright, curly hair. Another light depicts St Margaret (8) with a book in her left hand and a crozier piercing a dragon at her feet.

■ The present church of the Holy Trinity at **Long Sutton** (5) dates almost entirely from the end of the 15th century; Bishop Fox having granted a licence in 1493 to 'consecrate and bless the Parish Church of Long Sutton lately rebuilt and made new'. It is this church that we see today, a spacious and impressive fabric in the best Somerset manner, with tall west tower and clerestoried nave. The

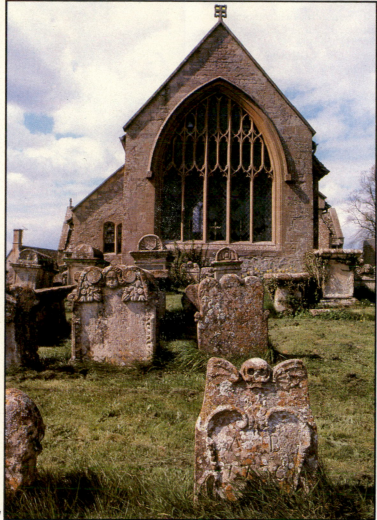

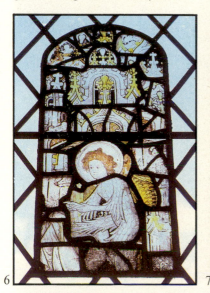

6

7

8

11

church is built in lias stone with Ham stone dressing. Its beautifully painted, medieval wooden pulpit (5) of sixteen sides is the greatest treasure of Holy Trinity and dates from the reign of King Henry VI.

9

10

PATRIXBOURNE/WAREHAM

St Mary's at **Patrixbourne** (2,3,4,6 and 9) is a small but very fine late-Norman church of flint and Caen stone. It lies in the Kentish countryside a mile away from the old Roman road linking Canterbury with Dover and the Continent. It dates from the time of Becket's murder (1170) and comprises a nave, chancel, a very narrow south aisle (sometimes referred to as the Bifron chapel) and a north aisle added in 1827. The chancel (6) has three recessed Norman lancets, above which is a noble wheel-window in the form of a marigold. The lancets and the windows of the Bifron chapel

the Lion'.

The church of Patrixbourne is renowned for the Early English craftsmanship of its exterior (2), which shares with nearby Barfreston the distinction of having extraordinarily beautiful carvings above its south door (3) and priest's door. The former has five orders to its sculptured arch (4). The outer moulding is carved with a knot of foliage with human heads (one has a long moustache and wears a hat) alternating with birds and beasts framed in it; the next order bears a looped cable design, and the third has floral crosses alternating with semi-humans and

1

2

3

contain Swiss glass of exquisite delicacy – both in design and colouring. The enamelled glass (as distinct from stained glass) dates from a period extending from 1538 until well after the Thirty Years' War in 1670, and embraces a wide variety of subject matter, including 'Pyramus and Thisbe'; the 'Murder of St Meinrad'; Samson holding the jaw bone with which he slew the Philistines, and 'Samson and

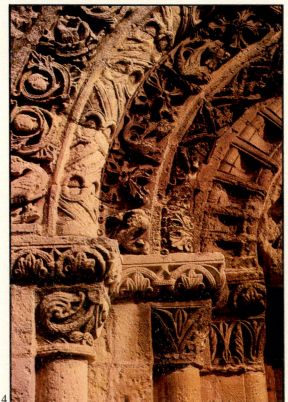

4

5

winged monsters with foliaged tails – known as wyverns. The next order has a chevron pattern and the last, innermost moulding has straps laid across it, and encloses the tympanum carved with a seated figure of Christ surrounded by apocalyptic creatures and angels. The priest's doorway (9) leads into the south chancel and is equally ornate with mouldings of ribbon chevron, beaded cable and nail-head design, surmounted by one of the earliest representations of St Thomas of Canterbury – a stone figure with mitred head and right hand raised in benediction.

■ The Perpendicular church of All Saints, **Godshill** (5) is the least restored of all the churches on the Isle of Wight, and boasts a unique (to use a much abused word correctly) mural on the east wall of the south transept. It is a Lily Cross (5) dating from the 15th century, and was discovered by chance beneath layers of Reformation whitewash. The painting depicts Our Crucified Saviour nailed to a three-stemmed lily: the theme is rich in symbolism; suffering is linked through the image of the plant to rebirth, and the Cross of Christ is associated with the lily, symbol of purity and of the Virgin Mary.

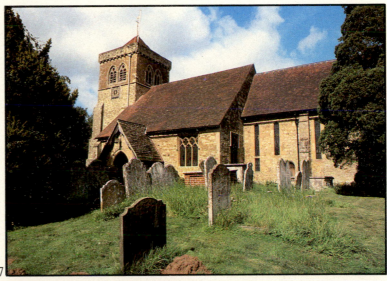

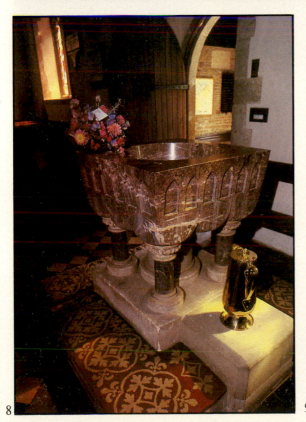

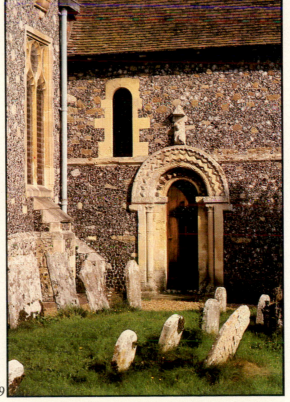

■ Well sited upon massive earthen ramparts, St Martin's Church at **Wareham** (1) is mainly Anglo-Saxon, of c1030 and is the oldest church extant in Dorset. It was enlarged in the 13th century and doubtless benefited from medieval homage paid to the site of Edward the Martyr's shallow grave at Wareham. The 'boy-King' had been treacherously murdered at Corfe, and his body hastily concealed by the wayside. Miracles were reported at the burial-site, which led Dunstan, Archbishop of Canterbury, to send men to investigate: the boy's body was found to be incorrupt – a sure sign of holiness – and was subsequently transferred to Shaftesbury. '*Men murdered him*' comments the Anglo-Saxon Chronicle, '*but God glorified him. He was in life an earthly King; he is now after death a heavenly saint. Those who would not before bow down to his living body, now bend humbly on their knees in front of his lifeless bones.*'

■ 7 and 8: The early-Gothic church of **Chiddingfold** in Surrey.

BRISTOL/BOUGHTON

Bristol (2-8) was one of six abbey churches that King Henry VIII elevated to cathedral status in 1542. Up to the time of the Dissolution it had been an Augustinian foundation of Black Canons, founded in 1140 by Robert FitzHarding, Provost of Bristol and ancestor to the Earls of Berkeley. Of the abbey church's earliest days little now remains – save for the Romanesque chapter house (one of the finest Norman rooms in the country) and its vestibule of 1150-1168 with stone vaults and richly decorated arcading and mouldings.

What declares the originality of

Germany, Bristol Cathedral can claim to be the first great church of its kind in Europe. The roof – the earliest lierne vault (8) in the country – extends the whole length of the building and is enriched with cusping from the high altar westwards. In the games of surprise that all great medieval architects played with space, the hall church is a splendid development, and reveals another facet of the Gothic spirit – shafting and over-arching of light, which combine to present the effect of a forest in stone – always leading the eye to expect further prospects ... further glades beyond.

The Lady chapel extends

the Cathedral church – and reflects the international importance of Bristol as a premier port of late-medieval England, and one of Europe's richest cities – is the magnificent sanctuary (3) and its soaring aisles which, together with the attendant Lady chapel, were begun in 1292 and completed with the remodelling of the central tower piers (2) in 1330. The aisles, ambulatory and eastern Lady chapel all rise to the full height of nave and chancel – which at fifty feet makes it the tallest interior in the country; higher even than Westminster Abbey.

This type of building (in which all main features rise to the same height) is known as a 'hall church', and although the style is more usually associated with late-Gothic

behind the chancel – with its grandiose reredos (4) restored and rebuilt over its ancient foundation – and here, at the eastern extremity of the cathedral, one can gauge something of the glory of the Middle Ages. Almost everything about the Lady chapel must have seemed a startling novelty in the 13th century when it was raised. The arches are enormous and the window tracery unique. The stone reredos (6) is contemporary with the chapel, its medieval colouring restored in strict accordance with traces of the original, and proudly displays the shields of Clare, Berkeley and the

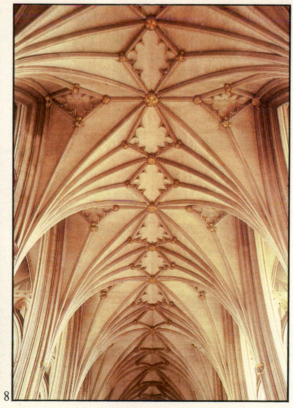

heraldic leopards of England (7). Around the walls are stellate tomb-recesses, ornately carved with abbots' heads, and abbesses in wimples (5). The interned appear in effigy, each wearing the habit of a bishop, with mitre, pastoral staff and ring. They are Abbot Newbury who died in 1473, Abbot Hunt his successor, who erected the vaults of the transepts, and Abbot Newland (1481-1515) under whom the rebuilding of the nave was started and much work undertaken on the monastic building.

■ 1: The Kentish ragstone church at **Boughton** is set typically amid the county's apple and cherry orchards (a particularly lovely site at Eastertide when the surrounding area is engulfed in a white and pink haze of blossom) around which are dotted the dazzling white wind-cones of oast houses. The attractive exterior of the church possesses an octagonal stair-turret at the south-east corner of the tower. Within, much remains from the church's medieval past.

ST PETER, MANCROFT

Norwich is reputed to have more medieval churches – thirty-two in all – than any other city north of the Alps. Of these **St Peter Mancroft** (1,2,3,4,5,6,8,9 and 11) is incomparably the finest. Indeed, it has few rivals among the parish churches of England for its unity and beauty. Even John Wesley – with his preference for an open-air altar – wrote of St Peter's in his diary, '*I scarcely remember ever to have seen a more beautiful parish church; the more so because its beauty results not from foreign ornaments, but from the very fine form and structure of it. It is very large, and of uncommon height, and venerable look, and at the same time surprisingly cheerful*'.

Upon entering the splendid Perpendicular church one is immediately aware of the nobility of its proportions and the unity of its design; a legacy of its completion within a single period, 1430-55. The whole 180ft length of its interior (1) is quite staggering in size, but all can be taken in at one glance; there is no chancel arch to

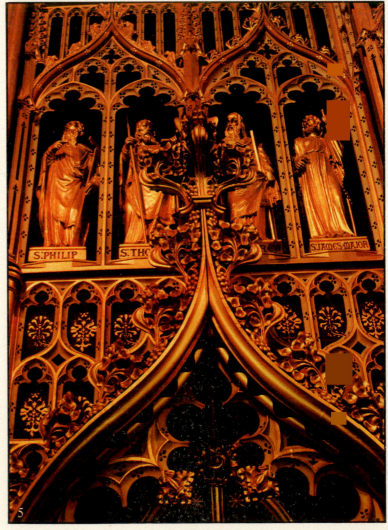

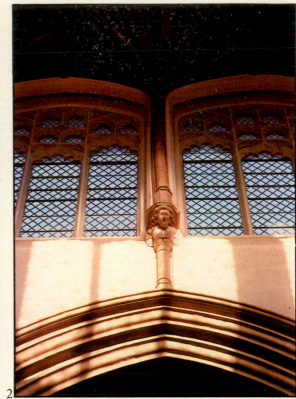

break the vista eastwards (6) and the eight bays of the aisle arcade march from end to end. Looking at this elegant arcade one wonders that such piers, so tall and widely spaced, can support the great arches, with their walls above – pierced by continuous rows of clerestory windows (2) – and crowning all, the heavy vault of chancel and nave which one knows to be topped with lead. It is a hammer-beam and arch-braced roof (8) – one of St Peter's greatest glories – but the hammer-beams are concealed under the beautiful fan-like groining (9); this in turn rests on long wall posts supported

S:PHILIP S:THO S:JAMES MAJOR

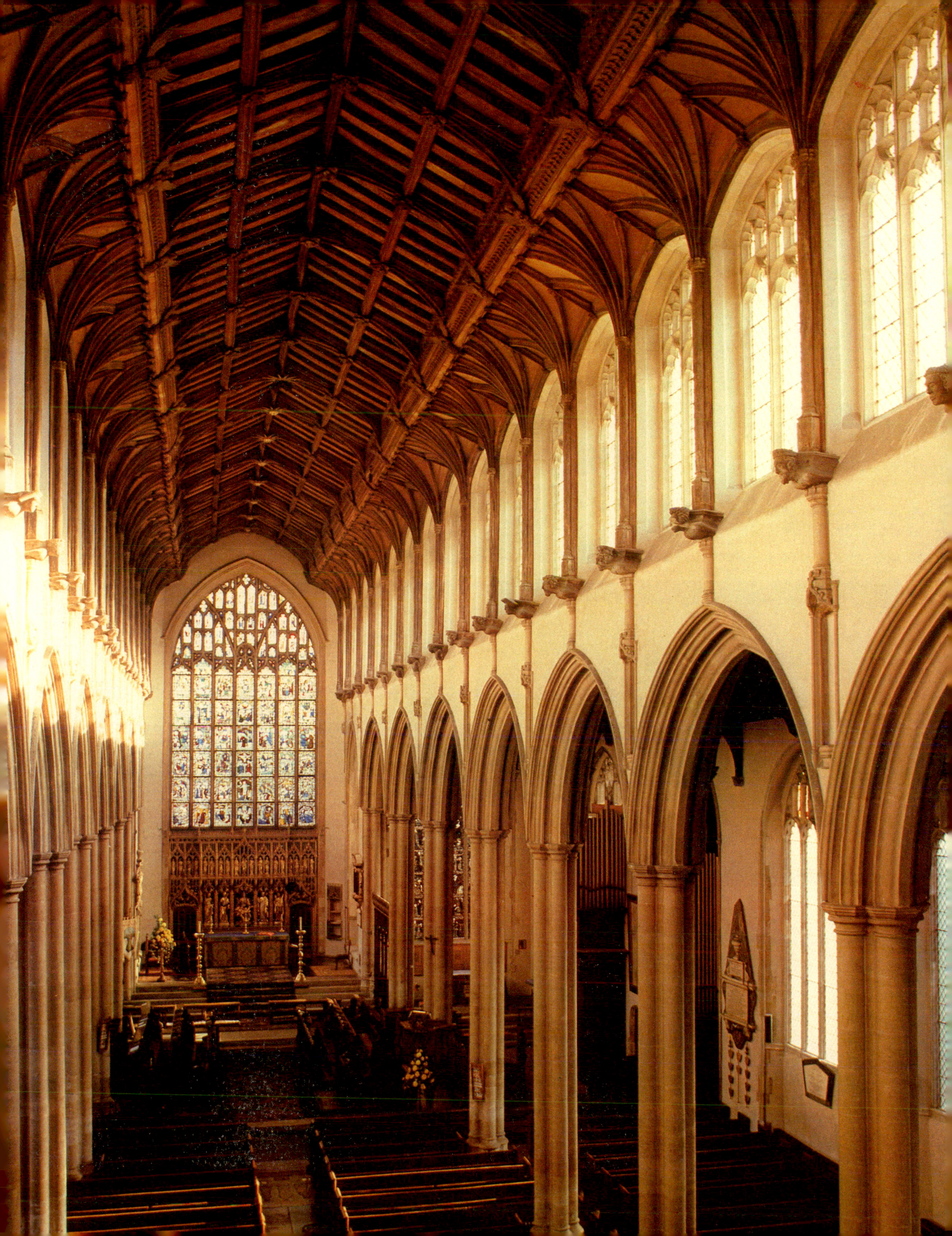

by carved heads. There are angels at the end of the hammer-beams and Tudor flowers at the main intersections.

The windows of the aisle and clerestory flood the place with light; especially the chancel (1) which glows with medieval glass and the richness of its gilded Victorian reredos (3 and 5). It was designed by J. P. Seddon in 1885 and coloured by Sir Ninian Comper, who also added the central figure of Christ in Glory seated on a rainbow. Behind the reredos rises the magnificent east window (11), which contains the finest and most extensive collection of the work of the celebrated 15th century school of Norwich glass-painters. On close examination these sparkling panels transport one back to a world of refreshing simplicity, with all the natural humanity, humour and pathos of the medieval mystery plays – a nativity scene shows an angel removing thatch from the roof of the stable to allow the star's light to fall upon the Christ-child;

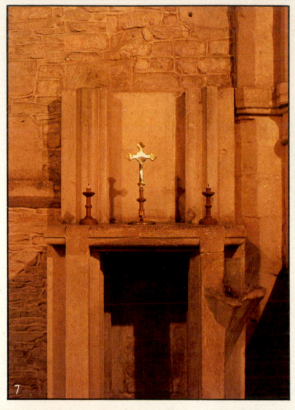

7

8

9

another angel stands ready with a fresh bundle of straw to repair the damage. Herod is made to accept responsibility by joining in the Massacre of the Innocents and a frantic mother tries to strangle an armoured knight who has impaled her child. The artist of the window was a keen (and courageous) satirist, for it is not only soldiers who mock Christ and dice for his robe, but also nobles and merchants such as those who sat in the Norwich church. Nor do the ecclesiastics escape his irony; as Jesus is humiliated the High Priest, in bishop's mitre and robe, exchanges a congratulatory

10

11

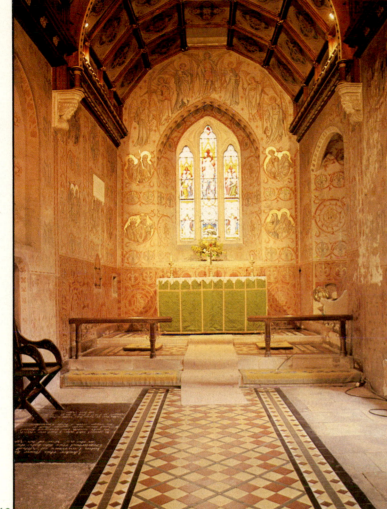

handshake with a monkish scribe.

■ The fine trans-Norman church at **Asthall** (7,10,12,13 and 15) in Oxfordshire is architecturally of great interest and beauty, retaining portions from each of the main medieval building periods. The nave and its arcade pillars (supporting bold arches) are of the late-12th century; the corbels have faces of men, women and angels and, in the north aisle, bird-beaks – a rare feature, The Norman bird-beaking also decorates the chancel

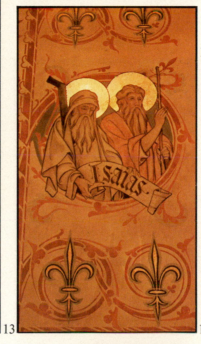

arch, whilst the chancel itself (12) was raised in the Early English style and has murals of 1892 showing figures from the Old and New Testament (13) and the sacred IHS monogram of Our Saviour. The north chapel is divided from the chancel by a stone parclose screen, and was once a chantry chapel served from Burford Priory. The chapel has a touchingly simple altar (7) built into a piscina – believed to be unique – and an effigy of a woman in a wimple, veil and flowing robes (15) claimed to be Lady Joan, wife of Edmund, Earl of Cornwall. The churchyard has a fine 'banded' tomb (10).

■ The church at **Keswick** (16) is dedicated to St Kentigern, who fled from the pagan Morken to erect his cross in the Cumbrian 'thwaite'. The churchyard – where he planted his missionary cross – is a splendid feature, especially in springtime when it seems to possess a remote and almost magical quality, lying below the towering Bulk of Lakeland's Saddleback and Skiddaw mountains.

The Cornish church of **St Mawgan in Pydar** (2 and 4) dates from the 13th century and originally comprised a sanctuary, chapel, nave and northern transept. The Lady chapel was added the following century and the building was completed by the addition of the south aisle and the upper section of the tower (2) in the 15th century. Also from this latter date is the churchyard Lantern cross (4). Before the Reformation every graveyard had such a cross, which acted as the only memorial to the departed in the days before individual headstones; a practice which had a lot to recommend it,

incorporated into the parish church of St Mary and St Botolph which was restored by Inigo Jones. However, medallions of medieval stained glass (5) within the chancel depict a time when the Abbey flourished and pilgrims flocked to Thorney to visit the shrines of St Botolph (one half of his body rested here, and his head at Ely); the holy Benedict Biscup, the tutor of the Venerable Bede; and the high, marble tomb of Baldwin de Wake, founder of Deeping Priory. Other relics were brought here for veneration, obtained both by fair means and foul – the monks were not above stealing, and in this

for belief in eternal life with God is more important that the desire to be remembered in the sight of men.

■ The most northerly of the Fenland isles' houses **Thorney Abbey** (5), the 7th century monastery founded by hermits, which grew to become one of England's great Mitred Abbeys. Sadly, all that now remains is the tall west front and the nave,

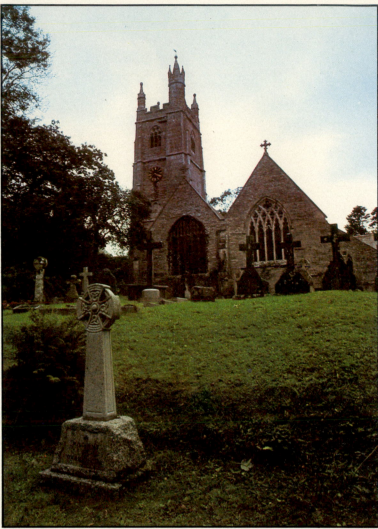

6

magnificence may be gauged: the Romanesque sculptures of the south porch, which are the finest in England. The outer portal has eight orders of arches filled with biblical figures and scenes, whilst inside the porch is the 'Last Supper', with six Apostles on either side and angels flying above (6).

■ The Norfolk church of St Nicholas at **Potter Heigham** (8) has a thatched nave and chancel, and a round Norman tower with an octagonal top added at a later date (when the nave clerestory was inserted) to give the tower better proportion. Another East Anglian church, that of **Graffton** (1 and 3), possesses a calm dignity in its lovely Decorated south chapel(1), and nave lit by deep-splayed clerestory windows (3).

■ The Easter Sepulchre at **Heckington** (9) in Lincolnshire has a beauty which remains unsurpassed. Its carved stone depicts the Risen Lord, the women at the Tomb with the Angels, and Roman soldiers asleep at their posts.

7

8

underhand manner Thorney acquired the body of St Huna.

■ Sharing the same fate as Thorney, the Abbey of **Malmesbury** (6) in Wiltshire now casts but a shadow of its former glory. The present parish church incorporates fragments of the original abbey, which once had transepts, a tall central spire and a western tower: all that is now left are the aisles and nave, of Norman work with 14th century lierne-vaulting. As if to atone for the loss of so much, the existing south porch possesses a unique treasure which acts as a measure by which Malmesbury Abbey's past

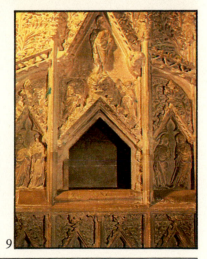

9

SOPLEY/STRATFORD-UPON-AVON

Sopley Church (1,2 and 3) in Hampshire is raised upon a small knoll – claimed to be a site of pagan worship – overlooking the watermeads of the lower Avon Valley (a common river name in Celtic Britain). It dates from the Early English period and is built to a cruciform plan in ironstone rubble, probably obtained from neighbouring Hengistbury Head. The church looks as if it grew where it stands, but ironstone – magnificent in colour though it is – is clumsy and intractable to work, and many other materials have been utilised in the walls: Isle of Wight limestone and brick among

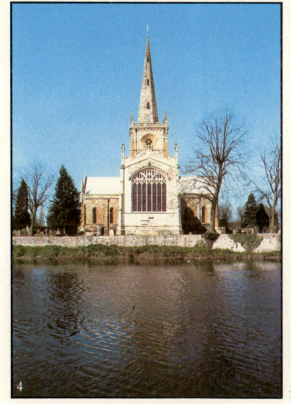

to 1330, and in 1415 King Henry V conferred the privileges of a chantry and a college, thus entitling Holy Trinity to be styled a 'collegiate' church. A further period of medieval embellishment at the end of the 15th century saw the building – in Warwick stone – of the chancel, the Great West Window, the north porch and the clerestory (5), which floods the nave with light.

The church is, of course, at the heart of a famous place of pilgrimage, and Holy Trinity can claim to resemble fairly closely the building that William Shakespeare knew, and was baptised in – but

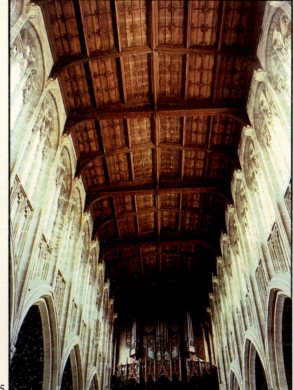

them. Sopley church possesses a good Jacobean pulpit and some attractive linen-fold panelling. An interesting chair in the sanctuary, which is now used by the Bishop at confirmations, bears the date 1604 and the arms of the Abarrow family (3) who were considerable landowners in the 16th and 17th centuries. Another local family, the Wyndams, donated the fine brass lectern with its three attendant angels at the base (2). Upon the eastern wall of the nave, above the chancel arch (1) is a mural depicting the Crucifixion, by John Emms.

■ The Collegiate Church of the Holy and Undivided Trinity, at **Stratford-upon-Avon** (4.5.6 and 8), is a splendid example of Early English and Perpendicular architecture. It stands beside the waters of the slowly flowing River Avon (4) surrounded by lime trees, yew, and cedars from the Garden of Gethsemane. The tower, the north and south aisles, and the piers of the nave were all constructed during the period 1280

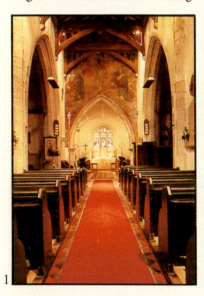

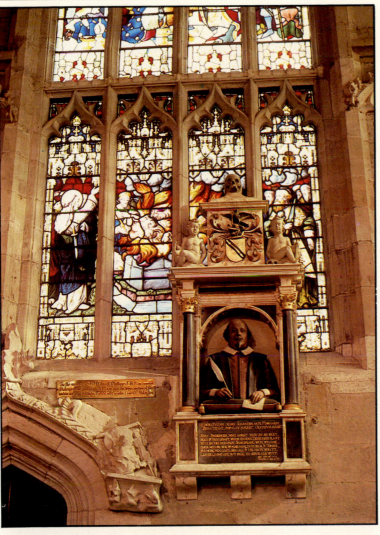

6

7

8

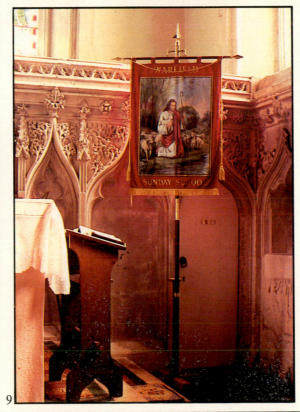

9

with one notable exception. In the north wall of the chancel, close by the poet's monument (6) and the Elijah window, there is a walled-up doorway which gave access to the charnel-house. This 'bone-house' fell into decay and in 1799 was demolished. It was a three-storey building; on the ground floor was a crypt where bones collected from the churchyard and chancel vault were stored. Shakespeare must have witnessed the removal of mortal remains from the vaults and never forgot the event. Later he became a lay rector, a post that gave him the responsibility of helping to keep the chancel in good repair during his lifetime, and bestowed the privilege of burial within the chancel vault. He composed the immortal lines which can still be seen on his tombstone (8):

Good friend for Jesvs sake forbeare
To digg the dvst encloased heare;
Blest be ye man y spares thes
stones,
And cvrst be he yt moves my bones.

Thus, undisturbed, the remains of the great poet and playwright have rested since 1616.

■ Another attractive riverside church – that of St Mary at **Hecton** (7) in Berkshire – was part of an old monastery consecrated in 1086 by St Osmond, Bishop of Sarum. It stands amid the ruins of a quadrangle charmingly named 'Paradise'. The nave of the parish church is of Saxon origin, and King Edward the Confessor's sister, Edith, is said to be buried here. She held the manor at Warfield, and in 1086 the advowson became part of the endowment of the newly formed Benedictine monastery at Hurley. The prior, as patron of **Warfield Church** (9), caused it to be raised in its present spacious and stately manner. Much work was carried out during the mid-14th century when it seems that the chancel (an excellent example of the Decorated syle, with its east window a masterpiece of curvilinear tracery) was used by the monks of Hurley as a private chapel whenever they came to Warfield to escape the floods that plagued their Thames-side monastery.

ZENNOR/EARLS BARTON/EVESHAM

In the northern half of the gale-swept Penwith peninsula, **Zennor Church** (1,2 and 4) has its village huddled closely around it, in an almost treeless landscape (2) of boulders and dry-stone-walled fields. The nave was built in the

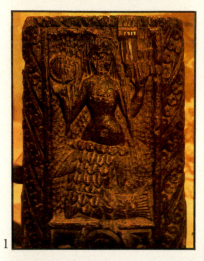

■ The Northamptonshire church of **Earls Barton** (6,7,8 and 9) is built upon the site of a Roman signal station and possesses one of the finest Anglo-Saxon towers in England (6). It is built of stone and rubble with external plaster, in four stages, each with its own distinctive pattern, making the whole look strong and massive, with an overriding air of permanence. The tower dates from the reign of King Edgar the Peaceful, (959-975) and incorporates wooden-looking pilaster strips arranged to resemble the timber buildings of the time. They run from ground level to the belfry, with rounded arches occupying the second stage, pointed arches the third, and culminate in the top floor windows of fine baluster shafts admitting light and air. An old tradition suggests that when raiders threatened, the local inhabitants fled to the comparative safety of

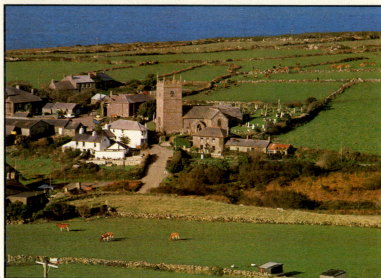

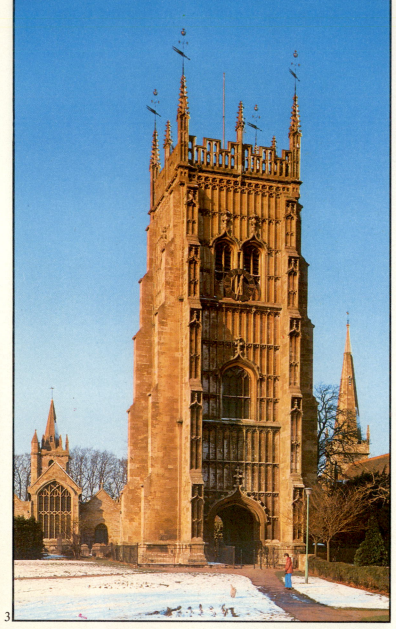

12th century, and the chancel raised some two hundred years later (4). The church is dedicated to St Senara, and was originally cruciform in shape, but in the 15th century it was enlarged and an aisle replaced the northern transept. In the side chapel is the famous mermaid chair, formed from two medieval bench-ends which depict a mermaid (1) combing her hair. The carving relates to a local legend concerning a chorister, Matthew Trewella, who sang in Zennor church. Such was the sweetness of his voice that a mermaid was attracted from the sea. Using all her charm she lured him back to her deep domain. His voice, so the story tells, can still be heard rising up from beneath the waves.

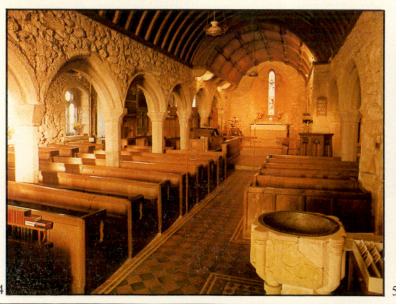

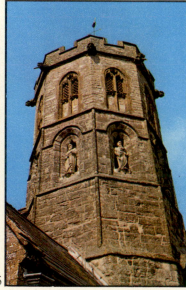

6

the tower's first storey, reached by a rope ladder: the entrance is located beneath the present clock. The plastered face of the tower is in contrast with the rubble fabric of the rest of the building, just as the tiny Saxon openings contrast with the ogee windows of the aisles. Later work includes a tastefully restored 15th century rood screen (8) with much intricate medieval carving (7), and a fine Jacobean oak pulpit (9).

■ If the Saxon late- period – exemplified by Earls Barton – represents the foundation of church tower building in England, then its climax must be **Evesham's**

7

8

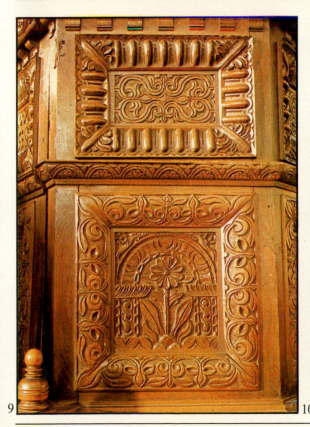

9

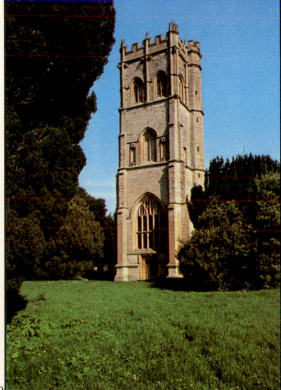

10

(3) beautiful, 110ft high bell-tower built in 1539 by Abbot Lichfield – the last of a succession of fifty-five abbots, for the Dissolution of the Monasteries occurred in the same year that this masterpiece of late-Perpendicular art was completed. Its superb panelled faces, ogee arches and the elaborate decoration of its buttresses, together with its delicate, pierced parapet and ornamental pinnacles, place it among the greatest treasures of English architecture.

■ Contemporary with Evesham, the grand Perpendicular towers of Somerset are unrivalled for composition and exquisite detail. They number about sixty and occur mostly in groups within particular districts. The tower of St Peter and St Pauls' at **Muchelney** (5) is a splendid example of the genre, with two belfry windows abreast. The church of **Stoke St Gregory** (10) is also in Somerset, yet its tower is of an earlier age: some three hundred years older than that of Muchelney.

AYLESFORD/WIGGENHALL

The lofty situation of **Aylesford Church** (2) – seen towering above a perfectly grouped Kentish village lying behind the grey span of its medieval bridge – suggests a very elderly foundation. The present building of St Peter's has a Norman base to its tower, but is otherwise substantially of 15th century workmanship, tidied up excessively in Victorian restoration, and is full of interest. Immediately facing the

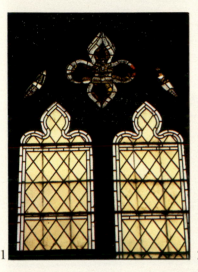

entrance are the Royal Arms of William and Mary – not painted, but magnificently carved – and the font, although modern, is nevertheless a most successful exercise in the Gothic style.

■ Wood-carving of great quality also marks out St Mary the Virgin at **Wiggenhall** (4,7,8,9 and 10) as the church with the finest collection of sculptured bench-ends in the country. The building itself (8) was raised in c1400; the windows throughout are Perpendicular with elements of the Decorated style – confirming the church's construction to the transitional period between the styles. Contemporary with the window tracery is that of the benches on the south side of the nave (7), which are beautifully pierced with carvings and traceried backs displaying the motif *Virgo Regina Ave* (Hail Queen of Virgins). Their most important feature are the 'poppy-heads' (a corruption from the French word *poupee*, a 'figurehead') on the bench-ends, accompanied on either side by small, seated figures (9 and 10). The benches which lie

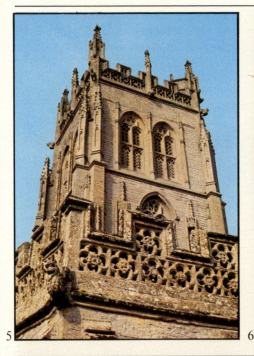

5

6

The little railed-in oval churchyard looks out over the gentle landscape of Normanton Park – now, alas, without Sir Gilbert Heathcote's Great House. It was as a chapel to serve the manor that St Matthew's was originally built in 1764. A dignified west portico and tower were added in 1826; the latter being a copy of St John's at Smith Square, Westminster. Unfortunately, the Georgian nave and chancel were demolished early this century and replaced in a style thought to be more in keeping with the dignity of the tower.

■ The stately Perpendicular tower of **Isle Abbots** (5) rises from the Somerset flats through which the river Isle meanders. It is considered to be one of the finest in a county famous for its towers, and still displays ten ancient statues within niches. Among their themes are found 'The Risen Lord

7

8

to the north follow a similar pattern, but were created about one hundred years later.

The legacy of craftsmanship at Wiggenhall is also apparent in its medieval eagle lectern (which originally possessed silver talons); in its parclose and rood screens; in its Jacobean pulpit, and in its dole cupboard (4) that stands opposite St Mary's pre-Reformation font (with a cover surmounted by a pelican vulning itself).

■ Standing entirely alone, the church of St Matthew at **Normanton** (3) in Leicestershire, appears to sail like a white ship upon the surface of Rutland Water.

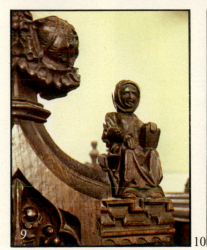

9

10

stepping from his sarcophagus', and 'St Michael' with a star as his sole armour. Isle Abbots is a place of great beauty: around the base of its tower the lichen and the sunlight add ever-new tones to the golden surface of its churchyard box-tombs, to the buttresses and to the niches with their medieval saints; all else is but the stillness of the centuries.

■ 1: The quatrefoil head of a 14th century two-light window at St Peter and St Pauls', **Bilsington** in Kent.

■ 6: The altar-cross at Christchurch, **Virginia Water**.

WIDECOMBE-IN-THE-MOOR/ST GERMANS

Sited high up on Dartmoor, the church of St Pancras at **Widecombe-in-the-Moor** (1 and 2) overlooks a vast panorama of moorland. It is a setting of incomparable loveliness in all seasons; the distant hills shading to green in spring (1), shimmering purple under summer heather, or enfolded in the white of winter snows. The large, late-14th century church has one of the noblest towers in Devon (2). It is granite at its most glorious and rises for 135ft. Dating from the early-16th century, it was raised at the expense of prosperous tin miners keen to manifest their newly

Germanus and part of the shroud in which his body rested, from the Abbot of St Germains' Convent in Auxerre. The fabric of the church is a lovely, dappled, rust-coloured stone, and the interior has at various times been altered. Much of the recent restoration work has been with a fine sense of the dramatic, and the interior retains a grandly baronial air.
■ The tower and south porch of St Mary's, **Boxford** (5) in Suffolk. The former houses a fine peal of medieval bells, whilst the latter is elaborately carved in stone with the 'Annunciation' at its centre.

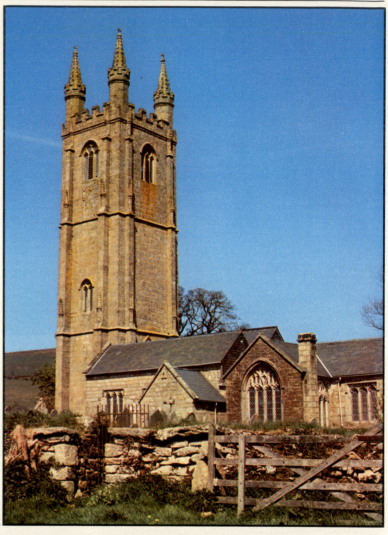

acquired wealth. The tower has an interesting story associated with it. In 1638, in the middle of Divine Service, a bolt of thunder – '*with lightning, hail and fire*' – struck the tower, toppling one of its pinnacles, and a great, fiery ball passed right through the choir, killing four people and injuring sixty-two, some of whom died later. One survivor recalled seeing a mysterious traveller at the service who smelt of sulphur and in an unguarded moment exposed a cloven hoof!
■ In 1162 a priory of Augustinian canons was established at **St Germans** (3 and 4) in Cornwall, and it is their monastic building which forms the present parish church. Its west face is Norman, and at its centre is a magnificent, cathedral-like doorway. Through the Romanesque door, looking east, is a lofty nave 25ft wide, and an aisle of equal proportions on the south side, divided by an arcade of six arches (3). It was built in such splendid manner to receive a gift of one small bone of the arm of St

CROWHURST/BRAMPTON

In the graveyard of **Crowhurst Church** (1,4 and 5) in East Surrey, is a vast, hollow yew famed for its girth and great age. In all probability the tree is older than the church itself, which, as its dedication to St George suggests, must have been founded after the miraculous intervention of the Saint in aid of the Crusaders at

inspiration – William Morris and Edward Burne-Jones produced stained glass that is now accepted as the best of the 19th century. Among their outstanding commissions were the windows of St Martin's Church, **Brampton** (7 and 9) in Cumberland, rebuilt in 1878 under the patronage of George Howard, the 9th Earl of

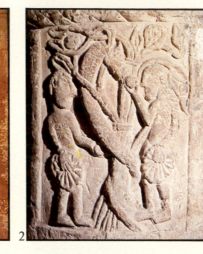

1

2

3

4

Antioch in 1198: St George was made Patron Saint of England after the Third Crusade. The nave is basically a 12th century structure, but with a 15th century west window. The chancel was largely rebuilt during the Perpendicular period, and the tracery of the Great East Window strictly adheres to the style. In 1882 the east wall of the chancel was 'restored and beautified', with the lovely figures of the Blessed Virgin (1) and St John (4) set against gilded mosaic work on either side of the high altar, which has an elegant reredos of kneeling angels (5).

■ In a similar vein – with reflective glances back to the finest days of the Middle Ages for their

5

6

the central light is filled with a 'Pelican in her Piety' – the bird baring her own breast to feed her young – this legend from the bestiaries having made the Pelican one of the types of Christ. On the south side of this symbol stands first St Dorothy clad in purple and blue, and next St George in golden armour; on the north side are the

In a lovely window of three lights (9) are the cardinal virtues: 'Hope' is in blue on tiptoes, 'Faith' is dressed in red with a tiny flame in the surrounding darkness, whilst 'Charity' is in a glorious golden-pink with a stronger flame and children around her.

■ **Breamore Church** (6 and 8) on the edge of the New Forest in Hampshire, boasts one of the few practically complete examples of a Saxon building dating from the late-10th century. It lies in parkland beside splendid cedar and yew trees. The church is exceptionally long – 96ft – consisting of a chancel and aisle-less nave (8) separated by a square, central tower from which opened a chapel on each side. The northern chapel no longer exists, but over the archway of the south transept (6) is an inscription – a rare and precious survival from the reign of King Ethelred II (979-1016). It reads as follows: 'HER SWUTELATH SEO GECWYDRAEDNES THE': which may be translated as *"Here is made plain (is manifested) the covenant to thee".* This would appear to be a quotation from Titus i,3: *'But God hath in due time manifested to us His Word'.* Among other contemporary features are the double-splayed windows and a great Saxon stone rood over the south door.

■ Dating mainly from the 14th century, the church of St Peter at **Langtoft** (2 and 3) contains a massive Norman font sculpted to depict Adam and Eve in the Garden of Eden (2), and the martyrdoms of St Lawrence, St Margaret and St Andrew.

Carlisle. The glazing was executed by Morris, while Burne-Jones was responsible for the stained glass design; reproducing in it the unearthly atmosphere and languid beauty of his paintings. The church's greatest treasure is the east window (7) which incorporates three rows of figures. The upper third contains a representation of Christ as the Good Shepherd, surrounded by angels who bear scrolls inscribed with verses from the 23rd Psalm. The lower part of Virgin Mary dressed in varying shades of blue, whilst next to her St Martin divides his cloak with a beggar. The whole background of the window consists of a mosaic-like pattern of vivid-coloured flowers.

BRENTOR/BURNHAM

The church of **Brentor** (1 and 2) in Devon is perhaps the most striking English example of a church on a height – standing 1,100ft above sea level on what is believed to have once been a volcanic cone. Perched on the very summit (2), it is encircled by the gorse-tangled ramparts of an Iron Age hill-fort; a position described in 1625 as '*full, bleak, and weather-beaten, all alone as if it were forsaken*'. It is still bleak, weather-beaten and alone, but in summer it is not forsaken, for every Sunday evening people flock to the church known to seamen for centuries, for the church '*serveth as a mark to sailors, who bear with Plymouth haven*'.

■ **Burnham Norton** church (3 and 7) also stands on elevated ground, overlooking the Norfolk coast. By tradition its round tower (3) was a lookout post manned by Saxons against Viking marauders, but the facts do not support this popular theory. The round, flint tower was raised at a later date (c1090) and the original Norman church to which it belonged would also have possessed a rectangular

for evensong, and it receives some twenty thousand visitors a year. Its dedication to St Michael is in common with many churches raised on high rocks. On a fine day it commands a truly magnificent view over half of Devon, Cornwall and Somerset (1) and has been nave and small chancel. Now only the tower and font – carved with scenes depicting 'The Seasons' – remain from this period. The nave and chancel were rebuilt, and the aisles added in Transitional and early-Gothic styles. The church took on its present form during the Perpendicular period when the clerestory, chancel and north porch were raised, and late-Perpendicular windows with steep, crenellated transoms were inserted into the aisles. The greatest glory of Burnham Norton, its famous wineglass pulpit (7), also dates from the mid-15th century.

■ The church of St Mary and All Saints at **Ockham** (4,5,6 and 8) in Surrey, stands among the tall trees of Ockham Park. It is one of only two churches to possess a seven-lancet east window – described as one of the loveliest features to be

5

found in any village church in England. The window dates from the 13th century and has arches of dog-toothed moulding. On a chancel window nearby, re-glazed at a much later date, is to be found an intriguing comment scratched into the glass with a diamond (4). It reads: '*W. Peters new leaded this in 1775 and never was paid for the same.*'

A noble feature of Ockham church is the memorial to Peter King, the first Baron King of Ockham, which dominates the family's brick-built mausoleum. He died in 1734 and his white marble monument (5) is the work of the Flemish sculptor Rysbrach. It depicts the deceased in the robes of the Office of Lord Chancellor, with his wife Ann seated beside him. The sculpture is as magnificent as it is lacking in reverence; the emphasis placed upon self-glorification is an all too common feature of the period that coincided with the low state of the Church of England.

Beneath the King chapel is its crypt – measuring about 15ft square by 6ft high – in which

6

7

8

twenty members of the noble family were laid to rest from 1734 until 1862. Since that date the crypt has remained sealed, but permission was granted by Lord Lytton to reopen it in order to examine the tomb. Having crawled through a 1ft wide gap into the crypt, torch-light illuminated the brass plates that identified each coffin. These fell away from the rotten wood at the slightest touch and with a little dusting the names could clearly be seen. Originally the coffins had been stacked upon racks, but these had long since collapsed and the coffins now lay sprawled over the floor (8). It was possible to see the inner lead boxes of the coffins, and a few of the older lead boxes had caved-in, revealing the occupant. The contrast between the splendid marble monuments of the chapel and the reality of the grave seemed to echo the spirit of a medieval cadaver tomb; where alabaster bishops, nobles and kings are displayed in all their finery, whilst their worldly treasures are mocked by the carved stone corpse beneath.

BOSTON

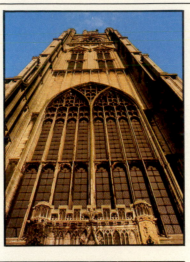

Across the Lincolnshire Wash stands the unmistakable tower (or 'Stump') of St Botolph's Church, **Boston** (1-10) – one of the loftiest in England – whose medieval beacon-light shining from the octagon was visible to ships forty miles out to sea. Boston is one of the largest and, in some respects, the grandest of all parish churches. Raised entirely during the 14th century, it is an unrivalled example of late-Decorated architecture. Its size and grandeur speak of the medieval prosperity of Boston's lost port – which was second only to that of London and, indeed, at the end of the 13th century, paid more

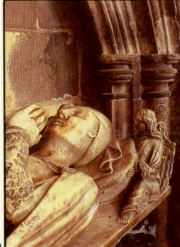

in customs duty than did the capital. Fleeces from the backs of three million sheep were exported annually; the finest wool that Europe produced. The present church was built during the port's mercantile peak between the years 1309 and 1390, when trade with Flanders fashioned St Botolph's church somewhat in the manner of Bruges or Antwerp.

The story of Christianity in Boston goes right back to the 7th century, when an Anglo-Saxon missionary monk named Botolph preached here and established a chapel. The place was known as 'Botolph's Stone', later shortened to 'Boston'. His relics are spread as far afield as Norway and Denmark, and there are eighty English churches dedicated to him, of which Boston is the most remarkable, with its Stump (3,7 and 10) soaring 272ft above the River Witham. The foundation stone of this elegantly ornate tower was laid in c1430 by Dame

Margaret Tilney, who lies buried in the Founders' Chapel (now known as the Cotton Chapel) beneath a splendid alabaster effigy (4). The tower took ninety years to complete and required the services of four successive architects to oversee the building programme. Its enormous windows (1) are in the great tradition of Lincolnshire curvilinear tracery, and the interior walls are panelled and rise to a vault 137ft above the floor (2). Such delicacy, however, is not without its price, and the tower is much too fragile to carry a stone spire.

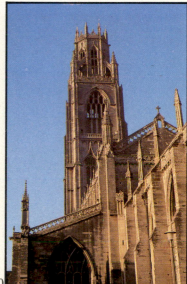

The interior of Boston Church is 282ft long (9), stretching from the 18th century wrought-iron screen beneath the western tower (which has the civic arms as its centrepiece, surmounted by a woolsack), past a Victorian font designed by Pugin, and a pulpit (5) made in 1612 and decorated with the Prince of Wales' feathers, on through the nave and into the chancel (6) with its sixty-four carved choir-stalls incorporating hinged *miserere* seats of c1390 and, at the farthest end, the high altar and reredos which covers much of the Great East Window. The glass in this window was described by Nathaniel Hawthorn as '*the richest and tenderest I have ever seen*'. Later generations disagreed, and in 1906 the window received a coat of greenish paint to tone it down. People are now beginning to appreciate it again, and to rejoice that the paint is wearing off. In the south aisle, recessed into the wall, is the tomb of a knight of St John (8) dating from the 14th century.

EAST MEON/IGHTHAM

The church of All Saints, **East Meon** (1,4,5,6,7,8 and 9) is set in one of the loveliest river valleys in Hampshire – at a place where Izaak Walton once cast for trout in the local Meon stream – which rises in the green downs behind the church and gradually gathers strength as it flows on its twenty mile journey to the Solent. The striking cruciform building of All Saints is a boldly-massed church (4) with a burly, enriched Norman tower at it centre (6) capped by an overlapping lead spire. The nave and south transept (9) are mostly Norman. In the late-15th century the chancel (8) and south chapel

1

2

3

face (7) shows the flat world upheld by pillars and arches, upon whose soil and water teem many forms of newly created life, all encompassed within the composite, dragon-like creatures that represent fish, fowl, reptile and animal all in one. The second panel depicts the serpent offering Eve the forbidden fruit from the Tree of Knowledge. The third side of the font (5) shows the Gates of Paradise (represented as a Romanesque palace) barred by an angel holding a sword; but in compassion he teaches Adam how to dig and Eve how to spin flax. The world upheld by pillars is

4

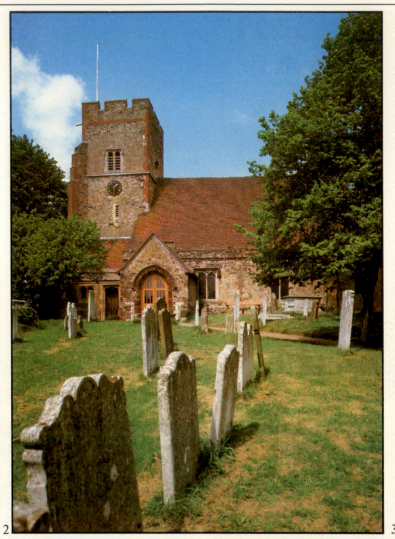

5

were rebuilt by Prior Hinton of St Swithin's Monastery, and later reglorified by Sir Ninian Comper, who was also responsible for the stained glass (1) above the altar.

East Meon's greatest possession is its rare Tournai font, created by the famous Flemish sculptors from

their local black marble. In c1150 it was shipped the five hundred miles from Tournai down the Scheldt, across the North Sea and English Channel, up the Ichen and, finally, laboriously hauled overland for the last few miles. The font was probably the magnificent gift of

Bishop Henry de Blois (William the Conqueror's grandson), who is known to have donated many rich works of art to his Cathedral at Winchester, which also possesses a Tournai font. Its four sides depict the theme of the 'Creation', the 'Fall', and 'Re-creation'. The first

again depicted in the final panel, upon which fierce dogs chase doves: representing the wicked persecuting the faithful after the Fall of Man.

■ The fine Kentish ragstone church of St Peter at **Ightham** (2) was mainly built during the 14th

6

7

and 15th centuries, but with some Norman work remaining. It possesses a magnificent example of medieval craftsmanship in the life-sized effigy of the knight, Sir Thomas Cawne. The tomb is exactly contemporary with the well-known monument of Edward, the Black Prince, in Canterbury Cathedral, and the armour is in the same style of mixed chain-mail and plate.

In Ightham's churchyard the oldest gravestone still legible bears the date 1703. This stone, and others nearby, are of interest as being peculiar to Kent – made of thick ragstone shaped like a head and shoulders. The well-carved moulding and letters contrast with the crudely incised faces. The style gradually deteriorated from facial features into grotesque skulls – the emblem of mortality. The representation of skulls was widely used upon headstones throughout the 18th century, as at **Escomb** (3), where it has accompanying crossbones.

■ The delightfully named church of **Melbury Bubb** (10) is one of the most rewarding small churches in Dorset. Its exceptional, Anglo-Saxon font is carved with wrestling animals, all of which are upside down. The reason for this would

8

9

10

appear to be that it originally formed the base of a churchyard cross. The church's glass is medieval, made by a school of local craftsmen at Sherborne, and contains a graphic panel of the thorn-crowned Christ (10).

The church of St Mary, **Hunstanton** (3,5,6 and 7) is a notable example of the early-Decorated style of architecture prevalent in the first quarter of the 14th century. It possesses a fine

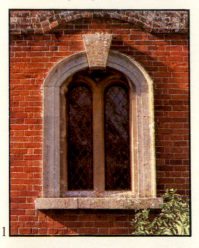

1

2

5

chancel screen with Tudor panels showing painted figures of the Apostles (6), and a Victorian pulpit (3) of white stone and alabaster, dedicated to the memory of Henry le Strange. Indeed, throughout its history this Norfolk church has been closely associated with the le Strange family, who have lived at the nearby moated mansion of Old Hunstanton for over nine hundred years. Their monuments crowd the church; the finest being the tomb-slab portrait in brass of Sir Roger le Strange (7) in an unusual attitude with hands uplifted and outspread, as if contemplating the '*wonderment of heaven*', and in full knightly panoply, including a tabard with an intricate coat-of-arms. Another brass (5) of 1490, depicts Edmund and his wife, Agnes, in civilian costume. His tight, upper garment resembles a

3

6

pelisse or surtout with fur around the wrists, whilst his wife wears a head-dress consisting of a perfectly plain bonnet with a veil.

■ In its assured Wren manner the noble, red brick tower of St Catherine's, **Wolverton** (1,2 and 4) contrasts with the low-built church beneath it. Both tower and church were raised in 1717. St Catherine's consists of a nave and north and south transepts – with gracious windows (1) with distinctively pronounced keystones – and a chancel (4) with wrought-iron altar-rails and wooden, carved reredos; both displaying splendid, 18th century workmanship.

BOSHAM

Sited upon a Roman basilica, the historic Saxon church of **Holy Trinity, Bosham** (1,2,3,4,6 and 8) lies at the head of a creek, on the rim of Chichester harbour. This is the ancient church of the missionary Dicul; of King Canute; of Earl Godwin; of King Harold and of the Bayeux Tapestry – and the oldest site of Christianity in Sussex. The first to worship Christ here were Irish monks led by Dicul in the late-7th century, and their original monastic cell probably occupied the crypt – located beneath the lovely Gothic chapel of All Hallows (3), and unusual in the fact that it is raised 5ft above,

buried within the church nave: she now rests beneath a stone monument placed over her grave by the children of the parish in 1906, upon which the black raven of the House of Denmark is emblazoned (6).

In 1954 the nave floor was re-laid, and an apsidal-headed coffin was discovered. It contained the bones of a strong man, which led to speculation that they were the remains of Earl Godwin of Wessex. His son Harold, the last King of the Saxons, is known to have prayed in the church prior to his fateful voyage to Normandy in 1064, where he was tricked into swearing

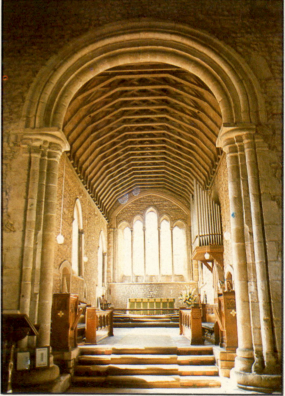

and shrinks a similar distance below, the level of the floor of the south aisle (1).

There grew out of Dicul's church a larger building of the early-11th century, comprising a nave, chancel and sturdy tower. The latter (2), now surmounted by a shingled broach spire, was originally developed as a watchtower, built as a defence against seaborne Viking raids. The Saxon lookout was able to scan all approaching waterways and when an attack was imminent the women and children fled to the church tower for safety. Canute – the sovereign of both Denmark and Norway – won the throne of England in 1017, and the new king soon began to restore the ecclesiastical buildings that he and his father, Sweyn Forkbeard, had injured or destroyed in the course of their military incursions. It is probable, therefore, that Bosham church was raised by Canute in c1020. Indeed, he is believed to have had a residence in the village, and his eight year old daughter lies

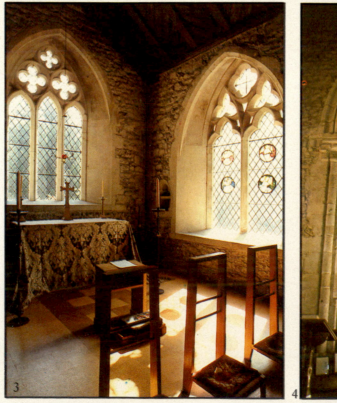

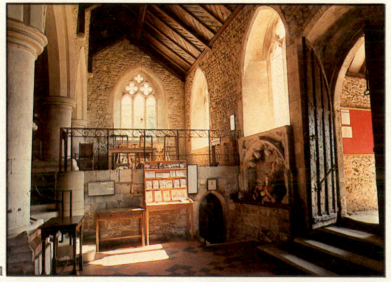

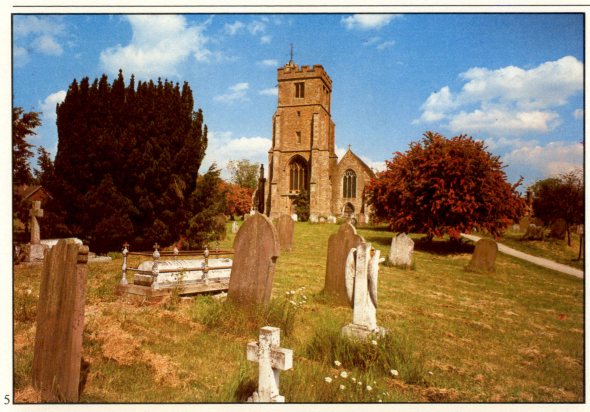

5

pre-Conquest work, the mid-section of the chancel incorporates the herringbone masonry of the Normans, and the far sanctuary is Early English, displaying a magnificent five-light east window of 1180.

Of the many interesting features of the church, the rough-hewn crosses in the stonework of the porch are particularly poignant. They were cut by the 'Lionheart's' Crusaders before departing from Bosham quay for the Holy Land – intending to complete the crosses on their return. Another reminder of days long-past is the touching inscription upon the gravestone (8)

8

of James Shepard, who died in 1720 aged 9 months and 15 days: '*for I was my father's son, tender and only beloved in the sight of my mother*'.

■ It is known that an Anglo-Saxon church existed at **Otford** (7) in Kent, and the core of the present building dates from the mid-11th century, superseding an earlier timber one. A western tower was added in c1170 and, in the first quarter of the 14th century, the chancel was built. A massive monument to Charles Polhill dominates the northern wall of the chancel (7). He was a great-grandson of Oliver Cromwell, and the memorial dating from 1755 represents one of the major works of the sculptor Sir Henry Cheere. A most unusual and delightful feature of Otford Church is that it is lit by candles, some of which occupy chandeliers over two hundred years old.

■ 5: The lovely Decorated and Perpendicular exterior of All Saints church at **Biddenden**, Kent.

6

7

allegiance to Duke William; an oath that was to prove so fateful for the English at Hastings. The Bayeux Tapestry records '*Udi Harold Dux Anglorum et sui milites equitant ad Bosham*', and shows Harold and his soldiers entering the Sussex church to offer up a prayer before sailing. Although the embroidery stylises the church, the representation of Bosham's chancel arch is unmistakable, and it even depicts the unusual 'horseshoe' shape. This fine Saxon arch (4) includes stone from the original Roman basilica and introduces the onlooker to the glories of Bosham's chancel. The first section contains

IFFLEY

The church of St Mary at **Iffley** (1-10) in Oxfordshire is one of England's most famous Norman churches. It dates from the late-12th century, and was built by the Norman family of St Remy in the reign of King Henry II. It is a Romanesque showpiece, and rightly so, for a wealth of superb Norman ornamentation adorns both the exterior and the interior fabric of the church. It comprises a Norman nave, tower and chancel (probably based upon a two-cell Saxon church). The sanctuary (3) in which the high altar (10) now stands is an extension of the Romanesque chancel. It is a very fine example of 13th century workmanship, with its three single-light lancet windows and slim vault-mouldings springing from compound filleted shafts, in striking contrast to the heavier and more ornate Norman choir (5). The boss at the centre of the choir's multi-chevron (zig-zag), carved ribs of the vault has a *seraph* (7) surrounded by grotesque heads. This fabled creature is one of the

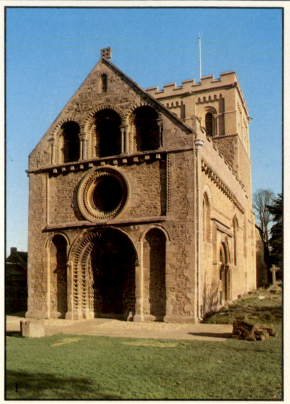

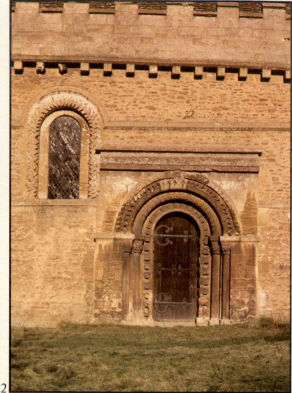

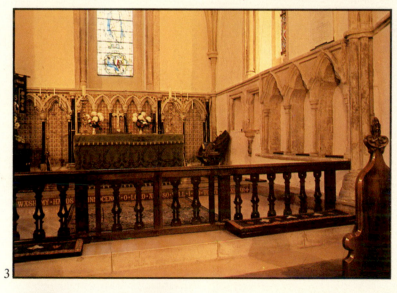

Seraphim; the living creatures with three pairs of wings seen in Isaiah's vision as hovering over the throne of God.

A similarly lively theme is enacted in the moulding of the south doorway (2), whose Romanesque carvings have weathered well because a porch protected them from the 15th century until 1807. On the right hand side of the door are symbols of Good – a knight encouraging his weary companion, and Samson slaying the lion – whilst the left side of the portal shows warnings of Evil – wild beasts overpower tame; King Henry II (among the

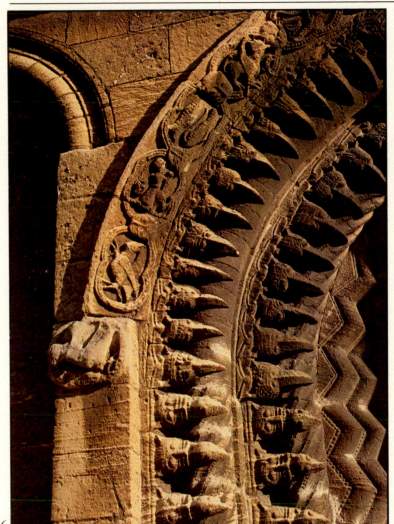

6

7

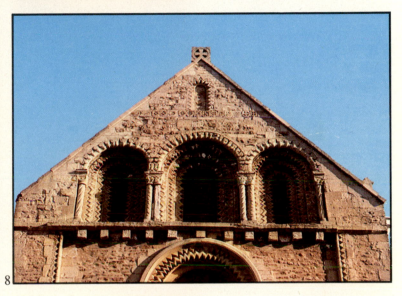

8

9

10

'monsters' for his role in Becket's martyrdom) and a centaur suckling its young (9). The latter, half-human, half-horse, were seen by the Church as pagan figures. Epona's children, they pulled the chariot of the solstice sun.

Iffley's Great West Front (1) displays a most impressive array of Norman decoration, with its deeply-recessed doorway of six superimposed orders without capitals: four are of chevron pattern and two columns are adorned with one hundred and ten beak-heads (6) surmounted by a semicircular hood-mould of medallions linked by lions' heads, among which symbols of the Evangelists and signs of the zodiac can be identified; all seasons being subject to the Gospels. The richness and originality of this craft is extended to encompass the three top windows of the western gable (8) and the centralised 'Eye of God' window.

Some exquisite fragments of medieval glass remain in the nave and in the southeast window can be seen the arms (4) of John de la Pole, Duke of Suffolk, and great-grandson of Geoffrey Chaucer. A little further along is a blocked up arch which was probably the window through which Annora, a noble anchoress, viewed the altar. The extreme degree of religious observance involved the hermit being walled-up for life within a small cell, which had but one aperture to the high altar, and another prepared in readiness for the grave. Annora lived in her cell at Iffley for nine years, until her death in 1241, during which time she received gifts of clothing and firewood from King Henry III.

ST NEOT

The church of **St Neot** (1-10) dominates the pretty slate and granite village in one of the last pockets of luxuriance before the bleakness of Bodmin Moor. The finest of all Cornish Celtic crosses stands in the churchyard, and nearby is a holy well – dedicated to St Neot after the area's conversion to Christianity – whose waters were highly revered for their curative properties. Pilgrims came here on the eve of the Saint's feast-day and spent the night watching or *waking* here. Small objects, such as bent pins or crooked coins, were 'offered' to the depths, and the

Cain and Abel. It is full of delightful things: God with His mathematical instruments planning the universe; a newly created bird flying from the tip of His finger, and the Cornish folk-legend of Seth placing in Adam's mouth the seed from which the wood of the cross will eventually spring. One panel representing the Fall of Man (4) shows an unusually bloated serpent with a man's head, twined around the Tree of Knowledge. The distended coils and male (rather than female) face suggest that the image was inspired by a theatrical serpent in a mystery

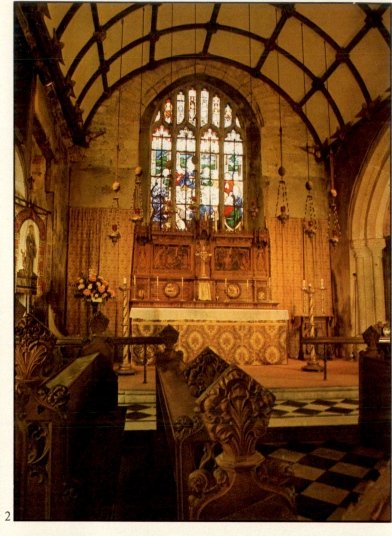

local wise woman was paid to interpret the bubbles that rose to the surface. Such practices, however, reflected deeper, pagan beliefs involving the mythology of the head-hunting Celts.

St Neot's list of vicars is complete from 1266, but no trace remains of the original church. The chancel (2), nave and south aisle (1) date from the 15th century, and the tower from the Decorated period. The glories of the church are its fifteen windows of medieval stained glass whose glowing frames of colour impart to this remote place a legacy of supreme beauty. The glass dates from the late-15th and early-16th centuries and was produced locally in the last period of English craftsmanship before the traditional style of the Middle Ages was submerged and diluted by the Renaissance. The earliest is the 'Creation Window' at the east end of the south aisle. The tracery lights are occupied by the different degrees of angelic powers, and the body of the window presents the Creation, the Fall and the story of

5   6   7

8   9   10

play, performed by an actor in an elongated green sack. The smug satisfaction on Eve's face when she receives the apple from the snake is nicely contrasted with her look of weary despair in another panel after she is driven out of Paradise.

The glass in the Motton window depicting the Evangelists is particularly fine, and that illustrating St Matthew the Apostle (3) shows him holding the winged figure of a man, which emphasises the human aspect of Jesus, whose

genealogy opens St Matthew's Gospel. However, the most famous of all St Neot's windows is that of the north aisle, presenting with a charming simplicity a series of incidents (5-10) from the life of the Saint to whom the church and village are both dedicated. Neot relinquished his crown to his younger brother and became a monk. He is seen reading a psalter (5) with his feet immersed in the water of the holy well – a common penitential practice among Celtic

saints – and an angel instructs him about three fishes in the well: he was to take one only each day, and the supply would never diminish (this, of course, is common form in Celtic hagiography). Neot falls ill and commands his servant to bring him a fish to eat. The servant, thinking that his master needs 'building up', catches two fish from the holy water (6) and cooks them for the saint's meal. Realizing that he has broken the angel's instructions, Neot rebukes the

servant and sends him back to throw the two fishes into the well (7), whereupon they are both miraculously restored to life. In another story, robbers steal Neot's oxen (8), and a man and a boy are seen ploughing the glebe with stags (9) that offered their services in answer to the Saint's prayers. In the final panel St Neot receives the papal blessing (10).

CULLOMPTON/HINTON ST GEORGE

From whichever direction one approaches **Cullompton** (2,4 and 5) in East Devon, the first glimpse is likely to be of the red tower of St Andrew's, seen through trees, or set against the back cloth of the Culm hills and it is a pointer to the beauty enfolded in what ranks as one of the finest parish churches in the West Country. The present structure, dating from 1430, is built entirely in the Perpendicular style, with both the tower and the Lane Aisle being later additions. The exterior is embellished by carvings of ships, sheep shearers and even a Jack-in-the-Green, with foliage and fruit growing from his mouth.

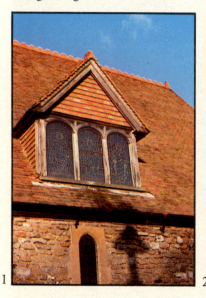

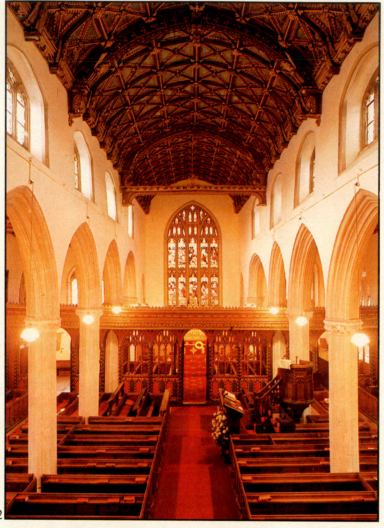

fans on either side constitute the chapel roof, and twelve attendant angels hold various emblems, including a shield crossed with spears and a crown of thorns; the five wounds of Christ; John Lane's merchant marks, and a pair of sheep-shears and a teasel-holder to indicate the importance that wool played in erecting so fine an example of Gothic Art.

■ The church tower of **Hinton St George** (7) is raised in attractive stone quarried from Ham Hill. It dates from the 15th century, having been erected by Sir Amyas Poulett, whose remains – along with others of his line – lie within the church.

Within, the magnificently coloured roof runs unbroken throughout the entire length of the church (2), and a splendid, coloured and gilt rood screen extends across its entire width. The roof's elaborately carved quatrefoils are highlighted by blues and reds, and the screen's tracery (which mirrors that of the aisle windows) and orders of vine trail, set against the white background of the Beer stone arcade, impart upon the onlooker a sense of the lush colour and majesty that must have filled the medieval church at the height of its glory.

Cullompton has a treasure greater even than that of its timber roof and screen, for in the Lane Aisle (named after its benefactor, a wealthy wool stapler), is a magnificent example of the most beautiful and purely English form of vault, known as the 'fan vault'. This was raised in stone (4) in 1526. The piers have half-shafts with small, separate capitals from which springs the fan vaulting (5). Four complete fans and two half-

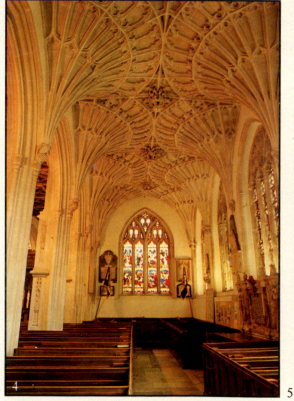

6

7

the pre-Norman tower and commenced the new church several yards to the north, reassembling the south doorway of the old church in the newer 'pointed style' of Early English. Inside St Andrew's is a circular Norman font with carved medallions of a sturdy nobility.

■ **Edith Weston** (3 and 10) takes its name from Edward the Confessor's queen, Edith, and is dedicated to St Mary the Virgin. It dates in part from the 12th century and is raised in local Rutland limestone. On its external walls are gargoyles interposed with the mitred heads of bishops (3); and within are many

9

8

10

The 'Somerset tower' contains many fierce-looking gargoyles and is surmounted by a handsome, gilded weathercock dated 1756. By way of contrast, the graveyard at **Autingham St Mary** (6) contains the ancient ruins of a previous church whose flint-built tower is now overrun with bramble and ivy.

■ Also raised in flint, the Norfolk church of St Andrew at **Little Snoring** (8) shares with its neighbour, Great Snoring, one of the most delightful of the many quaint names with which East Anglia abounds. Indeed, the mood of the surrounding countryside is almost as tranquil as the name

suggests: corn slowly ripens to gold and the hedgerow flowers of poppy, scabious and camomile lazily tilt their blooms to follow the arc of the harvest sun. Architecturally, Little Snoring is a curiosity. The present church must have replaced an earlier Saxon one and made use of its flint fabric. The builders left

fine monuments to the Heathcote family (10).

■ 9: **Ibberton Church** in Dorset was built between 1380 and 1400, and is one of only three English churches dedicated to St Eustace.

■ 1: A stained glass dormer window at **North Mundham**.

EXETER CATHEDRAL

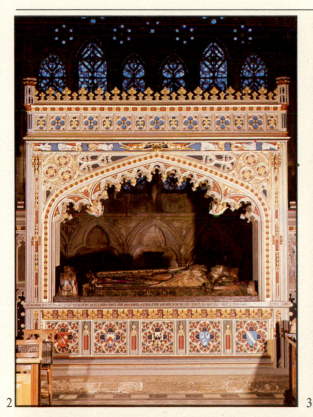

once said *'to view the nave on a day when the sun is shining through the windows of the clerestory is like looking at a forest in springtime'.* The harmony and balance of this massive vault produces in the spectator that particular and miraculous 'singing of the mind' which only the greatest of architectural effects may achieve. It embodies the sense once described by Schlegel, that the purest forms of medieval architecture are in themselves 'frozen music'.

The founding of Exeter Cathedral can be traced back to the year 1049 when its first bishop, Leofric – whose effigy (3) is now in the south niche of the Lady chapel – was granted royal permission to transfer the government of his diocese from the defenceless village of Crediton downriver to the walled city of Exeter. Leofric also founded the cathedral library, bequeathing a collection of manuscripts, among which is the famous *Exeter Book*; the largest single source of Anglo-Saxon verse. It was written between AD

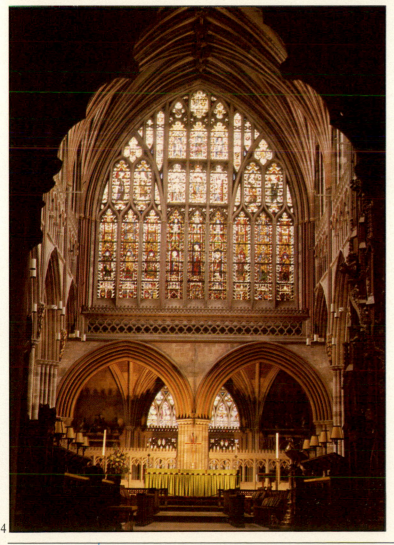

Exeter Cathedral in Devon (1,2,3,4,5,6,7 and 9) – the realm's finest example of the Decorated style – echoes to a mysterious 'ringing of song' seemingly frozen within its stonework. The effect is evoked by one of England's architectural glories – the cathedral choir and nave (1) – which, at nearly 300 ft in length, comprises the largest uninterrupted stretch of Gothic vaulting in the world. It took nearly one hundred years to complete, and its cones of descending stone ribs, supported by thirty soaring Purbeck marble columns, give the effect of graceful, curving branches. A former dean

950 and 985 and includes 'The Wanderer', a poem reflecting the sorrows of banishment, *'oft a solitary mortal wishes for grace, his Maker's mercy. Though sick at heart he must long traverse the watery ways, with his hands must stir the rime-cold sea, and tread the paths of exile'.*

The tithes from flourishing Cornish tin mines gave the bishopric substantial revenue, and through the personal munificence of Bishop Walter Bronescombe the old Romanesque church was gradually transformed into the Gothic masterpiece we see today. Bishop Bronescombe inspired the creation of the rectochoir (4) with its Great East Window glazed by Robert Lyon, and the Lady chapel – which houses the Bishop's canopied tomb (2), one of the finest and most elaborate of its kind in the Kingdom. His successor, Bishop Peter Quivil, directed much of his wealth towards converting the twin Norman towers (5) which flanked the main body of the church, into transepts. Thereafter, each bishop added his own distinctive improvements. There are several fine chantry chapels, where prayers were offered for the souls of their benefactors. Adjoining the south choir aisle, a particularly fine example was raised to house the tomb of Bishop Oldham (7), dedicated to St Saviour and St Boniface.

John Grandisson received the bishopric in 1327, and during his forty-two year reign was to realise the successful conclusion of the long and difficult work begun by Bronescombe. The construction of the nave was entrusted to Thomas

6

7

Witney, and the roof vault executed by Richard Farleigh, the architect of Salisbury's spire. His glorious 'palm vaulting' (9), with its multiple tiercerons, extends (unbroken by a central tower) along the entire length of nave and choir (6). This vault – the most poetic in the country – together with exuberant stone carvings and elaborate window traceries, combine at Exeter to present English Decorated Gothic at its very best. Indeed, so pleased was Bishop Grandisson with his mason's craft that he wrote to Pope John XXII: *'the cathedral at Exeter, now finished up to the nave is*

8

9

marvellous in beauty and when completed will surpass every church of its kind in England and Wales'.

■ The tumbledown and quite unrestored 12th and early-13th century church at **Old Romney** (8 and 11) stands apart from its scattered village in a most attractive setting. Like all churches of Kent's Romney Marsh it was built on a mound to lift it above flood water – the landscape's many dykes indicating that this is land reclaimed from the sea. Old Romney's dedication would thus seem appropriate, for it is one of only four churches in the country to have chosen St Clement as its patron. He was a successor of St Peter in Rome and was martyred for the Faith by being cast into the sea with an anchor fastened around his neck.

■ Between castle and priory, the church of St James at **Castle Acre** (10 and 14) in Norfolk, possesses a fine Perpendicular font cover and a magnificent pre-Reformation pulpit (10) with four original painted panels representing the Latin Fathers of the Church – St Augustine of Hippo, St Gregory, St Jerome and St Ambrose. At the base of each panel is the projected figure of an angel (14).

■ Church furnishings of a later

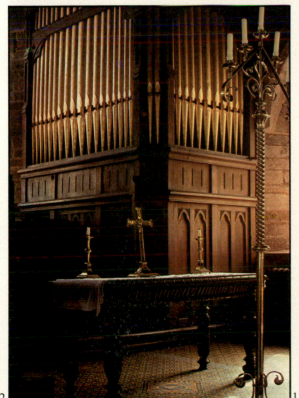

date may be seen in the chancel of **Abbotsbury** (13) in Dorset, which was remodelled in the Classic style in the 18th century, and has retained its plastered barrel ceiling and handsome stucco reredos (13) which has the Ten Commandments inscribed upon it. Notable work also remains at St Luke's, **Hodnet** (12) whose organ, communion table and noble brasswork are all of similar date.

CHESTER CATHEDRAL/DUNSTER

A Saxon Minster, a medieval Abbey, and a Cathedral since 1541 – the great red sandstone church at **Chester** (1,2 and 4) has been all three; yet Chester Cathedral is principally known for the inventiveness and sheer exuberance of its many images exquisitely wrought in the wood of bench-ends and misericords. There is hardly a legend, fable or Bible story that has not contributed a theme – angels remove the stone from Christ's tomb whilst Roman guards sleep; herons preen their feathers; a curious lion with two serpentine bodies breathes fire (2); lovers meet beneath a tree haunted by the pagan fertility spirit of the 'Green Man' (4); marshals watch over a wrestling contest; a porcine man drinks ale whilst a child licks

the spillage from his beard; devils leer out (1), and innumerable scenes from the life of St Werburgh fill the 13th century choir.

■ From the 12th until the 16th centuries St George's church at **Dunster** (5 and 6) in Somerset was shared between the Benedictine Priory which stood to the north of the church, and the laity. The sanctuary and high altar (5) were the domain of the monks, and the splendid parochial rood-screen running right across the aisles and nave – claimed to be the largest in England – acted to define the easterly limits of the church over which the congregation had jurisdiction. They rebuilt the nave during the Perpendicular period and raised its magnificent wagon-roof in c1500.

■ Also of monastic foundation, **Christchurch** (3) in Hampshire, is the largest parish church in the

country. At the Dissolution, the Augustinian priory buildings were destroyed, but its church was retained to serve the parish. The nave is 118 ft long and seven massive Romanesque arches still remain. Its chantry chapels are perhaps Christchurch's chief

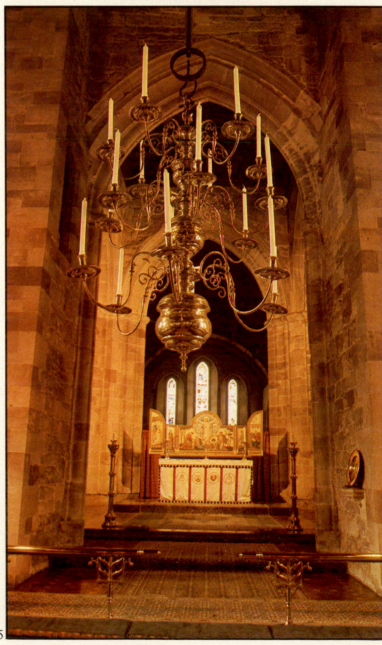

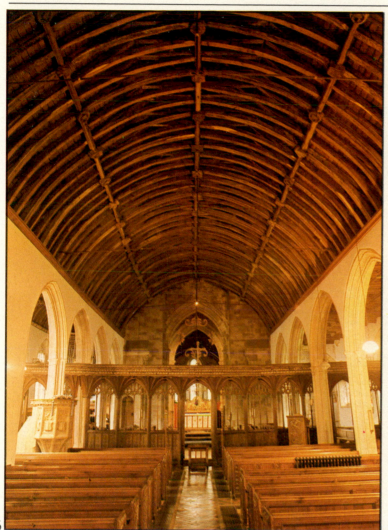

6

glories, and of these the Salisbury chantry is the most beautiful. It is built of Caen stone which is so hard that even today every detail of the carving remains sharp. The chantry has, however, a sad story attached to it, for Margaret Plantagenet, the Countess of Salisbury and niece of King Edward IV, lost brother, son, father and grandfather either in battle or to the axe and, in her seventieth year, was herself butchered on the orders of King Henry VIII. Her dying wish was to be buried within her beloved chapel at Christchurch, but even this last kindness was denied her.

■ In marked contrast to the enormity of Christchurch, the small, reduced church of **Southease** (7) in East Sussex is tiny by comparison. It is set on a slope in the Ouse Valley, with flint rubble walls of a pleasant texture, a hipped roof and a round tower with a shingle spire.

■ Also in the county of Sussex stands **Herstmonceux Church** (8 and 9) on rising ground surrounded

7

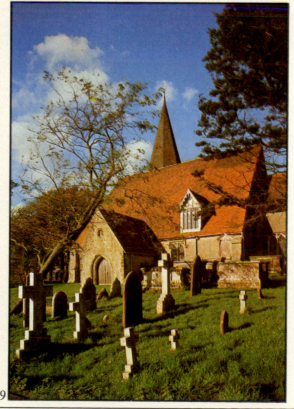

8

9

by trees, and opposite a medieval moated castle. The church dates from between the 12th and 15th centuries, but its dedication to All Saints is indicative of a Saxon foundation. It is famous for its memorials to the Fiennes family. On the floor of the chancel lies an almost perfect brass – dating from 1402 – to the memory of Sir William Fiennes whose son, Sir Roger, built the castle in 1440.

About 1450 the Dacre chapel was added to the original church building and is one of the earliest examples of brickwork in Sussex. It contains the Gothic monument (8), erected in 1534, of Thomas – Lord Dacre – and his son, Sir Thomas Fiennes, who predeceased his father. On the tomb lie the effigies of the two men in Milanese armour, beautifully carved in Caen stone. Their hands are held in an attitude of prayer, their heads rest on Brocas helms and their feet lie upon animals – the Bull of Dacre, and the Alant (wolfhound) of the Fiennes.

ST BARTHOLOMEW-THE-GREAT

The Norman church of **St Bartholomew-the-Great** (1,2 and 4) West Smithfield, is actually the choir and transepts of a monastery whose nave was on the site of the present tree-hung graveyard; the battered 13th century West gate (1) survives, together with one side of the cloister. With the exception of the Chapel of St John in the Tower, the church is the oldest in London, and both it and the nearby hospital of St Bartholomew were founded by the worldly and eccentric courtier of King Henry I – Rahere, who had a vision of St

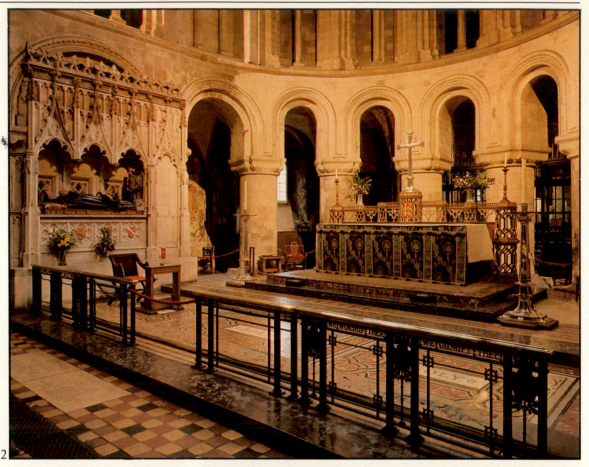

Bartholomew on his return from a pilgrimage to Rome. The Apostle told him to raise a priory on the Smooth Field (Smithfield) where the horse fair was held outside the city wall. This he did in 1123, for the Augustinian Canons, with himself as their first prior. After the Reformation the church became parochial.

The building is vast and dark – of substantial solidity, admitting light as if under sufferance. The grand march of great plain columns and rounded arches, with the gallery over – all Norman work, although the clerestory above is Perpendicular – to the rounded close of the apse (4) is one of the most satisfying sights in London. It is interrupted in the gallery on the south side, as if by a grace note, by a delicate oriel bay inserted just before the Reformation by Prior Bolton, and is marked by his punning device – an arrow *bolt*, transfixing a barrel *tun*. The church is rich in monuments, and none is

finer than that of its founder, Rahere (2) – retrospective, for he died in 1143 and his tomb north of the sanctuary dates from c1500. It is a canopied tomb-chest inserted between rugged Norman columns, painted and set with kneeling monks holding books inscribed with verses from Isaiah.

■ The little church of St George, set in a Hereford orchard at **Brinsop** (5,7 and 8) allows its unprepossessing exterior to hide a gem of a church within. The building itself was raised between 1300 and 1350, and it houses a Norman tympanum, two beautiful pieces of medieval stained glass and some modern glass portraying the Nativity in memory of Wordsworth and his family. The gilded oak chancel screen (5), with golden angels holding tapers, dates from the 14th century, as does the magnificent Christ in Majesty reigning from the cross. Even modern additions like the St Hubert and St Francis windows, and the alabaster reredos, have been achieved with sensitive taste. Above the reredos, and on either side of the east window, are gilded statues of St George and the Dragon, who, as patron of the church, adorns its banner – (8) and St Martin (7) seen cutting his cloak to share with a naked beggar. The traditional story relates that half the cloak was given, but the Brinsop statue is probably nearer to the truth when it portrays St Martin cutting but a fraction – the fragment which held a precious, jewelled buckle.

■ Also in Herefordshire is All Saints, at **Brockhampstead-on-Ross** (3), designed by W.R. Lethaby in 1902. The church has a central tower and a charming thatched roof. It is a temple of the Arts and Crafts Movement with work by Burne-Jones, Morris and Whall.

■ The fine local church at **Whiston** (6) in Northamptonshire, was built in 1534. Its richly pinnacled tower rises in two stages, and is built of contrasting ashlar and ironstone. Gargoyles leer down from the parapet and the walls are decorated with a wealth of stone carvings of men, animals and angels.

TEALBY/WINKFIELD

The much restored trans-Norman to Perpendicular church of All Saints at **Tealby** (2,3 and 11) is noted for the beauty of its setting – on the western scarp of the Lincolnshire Wolds, and the finely wooded slopes of the valley of the River Rase. The view from the church porch down over the stone-built cottages of the village, and across the Lincoln Plain to the great Cathedral away on the horizon, is one of never failing beauty and fascination. The church (2) is of the local golden-red ironstone quarried at Walesby, and much of the medieval fabric has been retained in restoration work

1

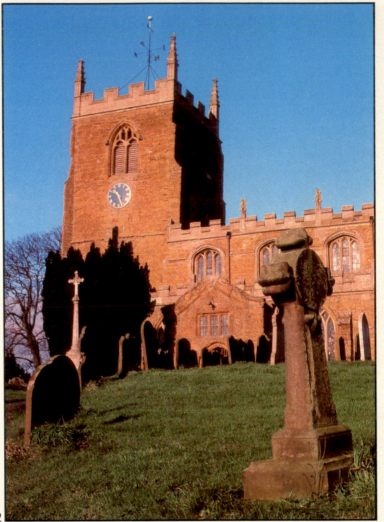

2

3

Venetian altar frontal of bead tapestry in a pattern of flowers and leaves on a silver field.

■ St Mary's church, **Winkfield**, in common with Tealby, is much restored, and although the nave dates from c1300 and the brick tower from 1629 (designed and built solely by the artisans), the overriding impression is one of Victorian sumptuousness. Nowhere is this feeling more apparent than in G.E. Street's restored chancel (9) with its sculptured reredos of the Last Supper (6), its painted tilework (5), and its east window of 1728, glazed with a depiction of 'Christ in

4

5

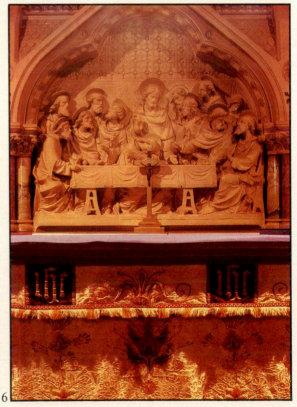

6

of the mid-19th century: one particular single-light window (11) is in the best Norman tradition and incorporates an ancient carved head at its apex. Tealby possesses much colourful glass (3) originating from the refurbishment of the Victorian era, and the chancel contains a notable 17th century

Majesty' (7) surrounded by an almond-shaped aureole illuminating the whole Host of Heaven. Another church displaying impressive examples of Victorian stained glass is St Peter's at **Finsthwaite** (1 and 4) in the Lake District, where there is a particularly tender study of the Virgin (1) holding a single stem of lily flowers.

■ The parish church of **Chartham** (8 and 10) also owes its restoration to the eminent Victorian architect G.E. Street. It was originally a gift of King Alfred the Great to the monks of Christ Church, Canterbury, after the Danes had plundered and burnt their monastery. The present church (10) was built at the end of the 13th century and the chancel's grandeur suggests the importance attached by the monks to their Chartham manor. The chancel windows are filled with medieval pattern glass (8) displaying curious 'bat-like' angel heads sprouting wings in the upper tracery; and the cusped cinquefoils enclosing the four-

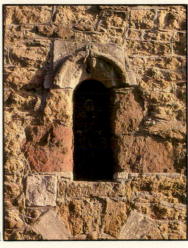

leafed symbols of the Evangelists, with a ruby-red grape-trail surround. The vault overhead is perhaps Chartham's most glorious feature, and is certainly one of the most imposing roofs in Kent. The original 14th century rafters are exposed and at the crossing, long scissor beams in the manner of stone vaulting are joined by a splendid carved boss. This boss is very similar to those of the Angel Choir of Lincoln Cathedral, and has naturalistic oak leaves with a primrose at its centre – the whole represents a triumph of carpentry over six hundred and fifty years old.

St Peter's at **Barton-upon-Humber** (4) in Lincolnshire, is an example of the curious Saxon plan in which the tower forms the body of the church, with a tiny chapel projecting towards the east. The noble pre-Conquest tower (4) dates from the 10th century, with earlier foundations which may go back to the original missionary church of St Chad, built in the 8th century. The general impression made by the tall, square, unbuttressed structure, so delicately patterned by its rows of arcading – the lower round-arched, the upper triangular-headed – is emphatically linear. The windows are small and occur in pairs, both lights being divided sacred monogram I.H.S. – *'Iesus Hominum Salvator'* (Jesus the Saviour of Mankind) – to indicate the mural's former glory.

■ The City of London's church of **St Mary Aldermary** (2) was first mentioned in the 11th century, and was rebuilt after the Great Fire by Wren – the money being donated on condition that the new building echoed the architectural principles of the old, medieval church. Thus, the aisles and nave are charmingly roofed in Wren's own version of late-Perpendicular fan vaulting (2), consisting of circular saucer domes and semicircles with the spaces in between filled with quatrefoil panelling.

by a heavy, central shaft.

■ Noted for its ornate, 133ft high tower and Northamptonshire broach spire, the Early English church of St Peter at **Raunds** (1,3 and 5) possesses an elegant and well-proportioned nave (3) famous for its vigorous 15th century wall-paintings that adorn the northern arcade below the clerestory. The murals depict the 'Three Living and the Three Dead', a mortality picture on the vanity of life – three kings in rich robes encounter skeleton kings who mock earthly 'treasures'. There is also a fascinating study of a saint harried by demons (1), and an excellent example of the theme of the 'Seven Deadly Sins'. Above the chancel arch (5) a painting of Calvary prepared medieval worshippers for the sanctity of the Mass. Sadly the crucified figure of Christ and the supporting witnesses to His suffering, the Virgin Mary and St John the Baptist, are defaced, but enough remains in the representation of the Evangelists and the repeated

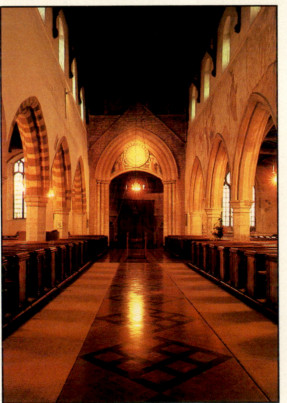

GLOUCESTER CATHEDRAL

Gloucester Cathedral (1,2,4, 5,7 and 8), one of the Great Mitred Abbeys of medieval England (cathedral status was bestowed by King Henry VIII in 1540), owes its present splendour to the valiant decision of Abbot Thoky in 1327 to bury the remains of King Edward II at his abbey church. The mystique surrounding kingship, allied to an association between sudden, violent death and sanctity, made this ineffectual sovereign a strange candidate for impromptu canonization. The gruesome manner of his murder –

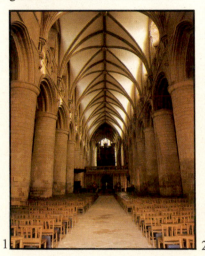

said to be reflected in King Edward's alabaster effigy (2) modelled on his death mask – promoted this political victim to the status of kingly martyr. The hitherto rare display of acumen, financed by offerings from the vast crowds of pilgrims that swarmed to his ornate limestone tomb (5), led to the rebuilding of Gloucester Abbey in the then little-known Perpendicular style – transforming the original Norman church into the birthplace of English Perpendicular Gothic architecture. Indeed, Gloucester was to hold its place in the vanguard of fashion by beautifying its cloisters (7) with the earliest example of fan vaulting.

St Peter's at Gloucester, like so many Saxon abbeys, was reformed after the Norman invasion and the Conqueror's chaplain, Serlo, was installed as its new Abbot. At his instigation the building of the existing church commenced in

5

1089. It comprised a crypt, a choir, two transepts, a central tower and a splendid Romanesque nave (1).

Few buildings demonstrate the fundamental contrasts between Romanesque and late-Gothic architecture better than Gloucester Cathedral. The former, characterised by the massive, cylindrical columns of the nave, appears to have been planned from the foundations upwards; whilst the latter, exemplified by the flying arches which carry the springing of the 14th century vault (4), seem to have been designed from the topmost roof bosses downwards.

The later work was started in

1331, only four years after King Edward's body had been received. To permit more light and air into the dark, shadowed abbey, William of Ramsey was commissioned to advise on the new design of the transepts and choir. The solution adopted was not to pull down the existing Norman work, but to clothe it with a skin of masonry in the Perpendicular style. The old roof was removed, the east end pulled down and a vast, stone screen taken up the inside of the Romanesque arcade. Windows were inserted into the screen and a great lierne vault, 92 ft high, erected over the whole. The final

6

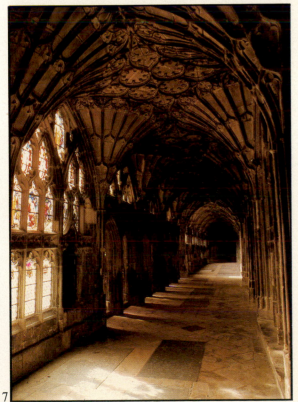

7

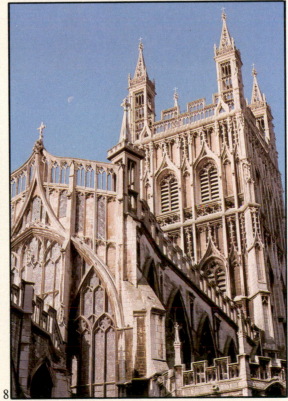

8

flowering of this most uniquely English of styles can be seen in the Lady chapel of 1499, whose entire wall surface seems to be filled with tall, pointed glass, and the 225 ft high central tower (8), raised in 1450 to replace its Norman predecessor. On a clear day it is a glorious sight, the sunshine beaming through its lattice parapets and spires shining white against the deep Cotswold sky.

■ The church of St Leodegarius at **Ashby St Ledgers** (3) in Northamptonshire, is situated in close proximity to the Manor House. Abutting the churchyard is a gateway leading to the Manor. In the half-timbered room above, the conspirators of the Gunpowder Plot are alleged to have met; and it was through this gateway that Robert Catesby and four fellow conspirators fled once the news had broken that their plot had been discovered.

■ 6: **Barbon Church** in Cumbria is set in the remote and lovely countryside of the Vale of Barbondale.

NORTH ELMHAM/BLISLAND

Near the site of the parish church of St Mary at **North Elmham** (1,3,4 and 5) stand the ruins of a Saxon cathedral founded in the 7th century. The diocese covered the whole of East Anglia, but the bishopric was removed to Thetford in 1071, and from there transferred to Norwich in 1095. The bishops continued to cherish their link with North Elmham and such was their love for the little village, which had once been the centre of their See, that they endowed it with a magnificent medieval church.

St Mary's was raised by the first Norman Bishop of Norwich,

on her head, and carries a garland of flowers in her hand.

■ **Blisland Church** (2) in Cornwall – dedicated to St Portus and St Hyacinth – is celebrated for its coloured and intricately carved rood-screen, the work of F.C. Eden in 1894. As a restoration (even improvement) of a medieval church this can hardly be bettered. The screen, with its 10ft high Calvary carved in Oberammergau, Bavaria, is how most of the West Country and East Anglian medieval rood-screens would have looked in their youth.

■ **Kilpeck** (6 and 7) in Herefordshire, owes its universal

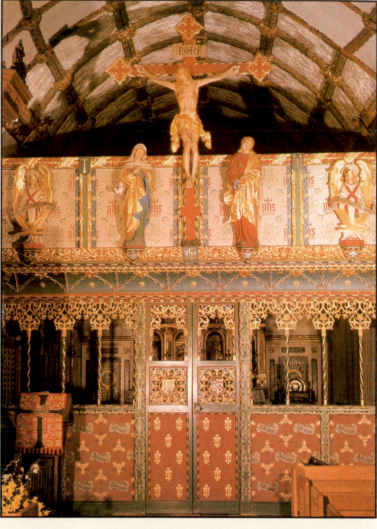

2

1

Bishop de Losinga, at the beginning of the 12th century, and substantially remodelled one hundred years later when the Romanesque arcade was replaced by the present alternating round and octagonal piers and capitals of the early-Gothic style. The chancel (5) dates from the late-13th century and the impressive square tower from c1400. The tower walls differ from the rest of the church (1) in that they are faced with rough flintwork, in contrast to the knapped flints used elsewhere.

Within the church, North Elmham's chief features are its bench-ends with poppyhead carving, and the surviving lower part of its early-14th century rood-screen, containing some of the best and earliest screen painting in the country. The faces of the sixteen panels have been scratched, but the saints can be identified from the symbols they bear: St Thomas (3) holds a spear – the instrument of his martyrdom – and St Cecilia (4), the patron saint of music, wears a wreath of roses and lilies

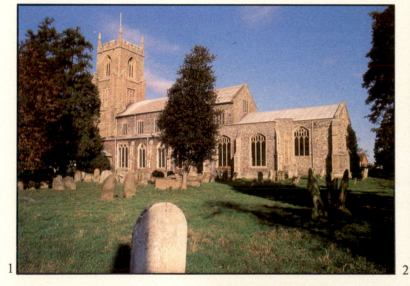

3

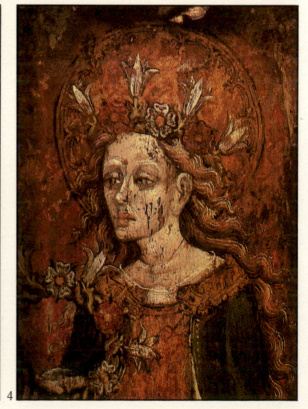

4

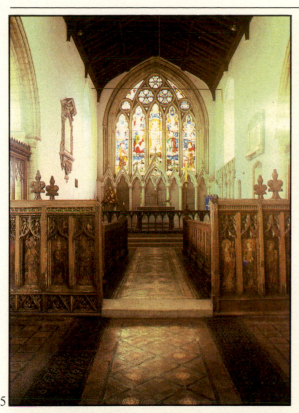

In the tympanum is a formalised Tree of Life bearing thick grapes. The outer arch of the portal has linked medallions of mythical monsters, fish, birds, a lion with a man's face, a phoenix in flames, and dragons swallowing each other with such abandon that the final dragon is swallowing itself. Two Welsh warriors – wearing mail jerkins and Phrygian caps – on the left-hand column, are said to represent both Church and State.

A corbel table embraces the whole building with a wealth of carvings, and over the portal is depicted the 'Holy Lamb of God', the only religious sculpture, for the rest of the eighty figures are symbols of the chase – falcons, harts and wild boar heads. Other motifs include a dog and rabbit, wrestlers, a sheila-na-gig, a muzzled bear and a ram's head: evidently some of these figures were considered too erotic in detail and were removed during Victorian restoration work.

Many widely differing influences have come together at

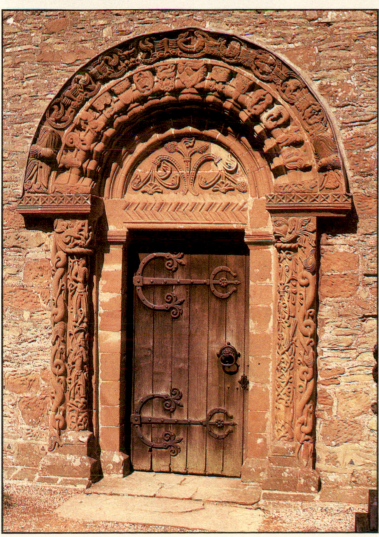

acclaim to its small **Norman** church – the most perfectly preserved and, architecturally, the richest example of its kind in England. Apart from a corner of the nave, which is Saxon, and some late-medieval windows, everything in the church dates from the third quarter of the 12th century. The whole exterior is rich in Romanesque decoration, yet the gem is without doubt the sumptuously carved southern doorway (7). Here is depicted 'Eden', the Temptation and the Fall of Man who, on the right-hand jamb, is represented as being tempted to eat the forbidden fruit of the knowledge of good and evil.

Kilpeck. The arches of the portal and the beakheads of the corbel table are said to have drawn their inspiration from manuscripts kept in the great Benedictine Abbey at Reading: the figures of warriors are clearly Celtic (Kilpeck was very much in Wales during the 12th century) and the long, twisting *dragons*, or serpents, are purely Viking – like nothing so much as figureheads of wooden ships, they could have been lifted straight from the prow of a Viking longship.

■ 8: The remote country church at **Leckhampstead** in Buckinghamshire, dedicated to the Assumption of the Blessed Virgin.

EWELME/SEVENOAKS

Standing in a flint and brick village in the Chiltern foothills, St Mary the Virgin at **Ewelme** (1,2,3,4 and 5) is a distinguished Perpendicular church built (apart from its 14th century tower) to a single design. It is castellated – with some amusing carved faces peering down from the parapet (1 and 3) – patched with brick, stone and flint, rising above the attached almshouse, cloister and school. These foundations were the gift of Alice de la Pole, Duchess of Suffolk, and her husband. She was the granddaughter of Geoffrey Chaucer, and the chapel of St John contains her magnificent alabaster

Anglian one.

■ The church of St Nicholas at **Sevenoaks** (6) in Kent, developed from a Saxon chapel sited in a lonely position deep within the ancient forest of Andred, but abutting the strategic London to Rye road. Beneath the church eaves was held a market which grew in size and importance to form the nucleus of a prosperous medieval town. St Nicholas' acquired an Early English nave – raised during the rectorship of Henry de Grandavo – and a century later, a northern aisle with Decorated windows built as an enlargement to the nave. In the

1

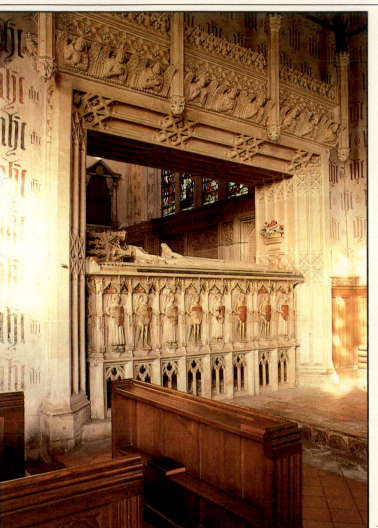

2

3

4

5

tomb. This is one of the finest monuments of medieval Europe (2) and was raised shortly after her death in 1475. The tomb stands under an elaborate canopy of panelled stone (surmounted by wooden angels), and consists of three tiers – firstly, the recumbent effigy of the Duchess (4) wearing a

ducal coronet on her head, and clothed in the habit of a vowess; next, the tomb-chest which contains her remains, embellished with 'weepers' of exquisite angels bearing shields (5); and below, an open space, enclosed by an arcade of eight arches on either side, within which may be seen an

emaciated figure clothed in a shroud, representing the Duchess in death. The timbered ceiling of the chapel, together with its sculptured angels, the rood-screen, and spired font cover and counterweight, give the whole interior the feel, not of an Oxfordshire church, but of an East

mid-15th century the Archbishops of Canterbury took possession of the manor of Knole and under the guidance of Archbishops Chichele, Bourchier and Morton, Sevenoaks received its striking Perpendicular tower, Great West Arch, chancel and chantry chapel.

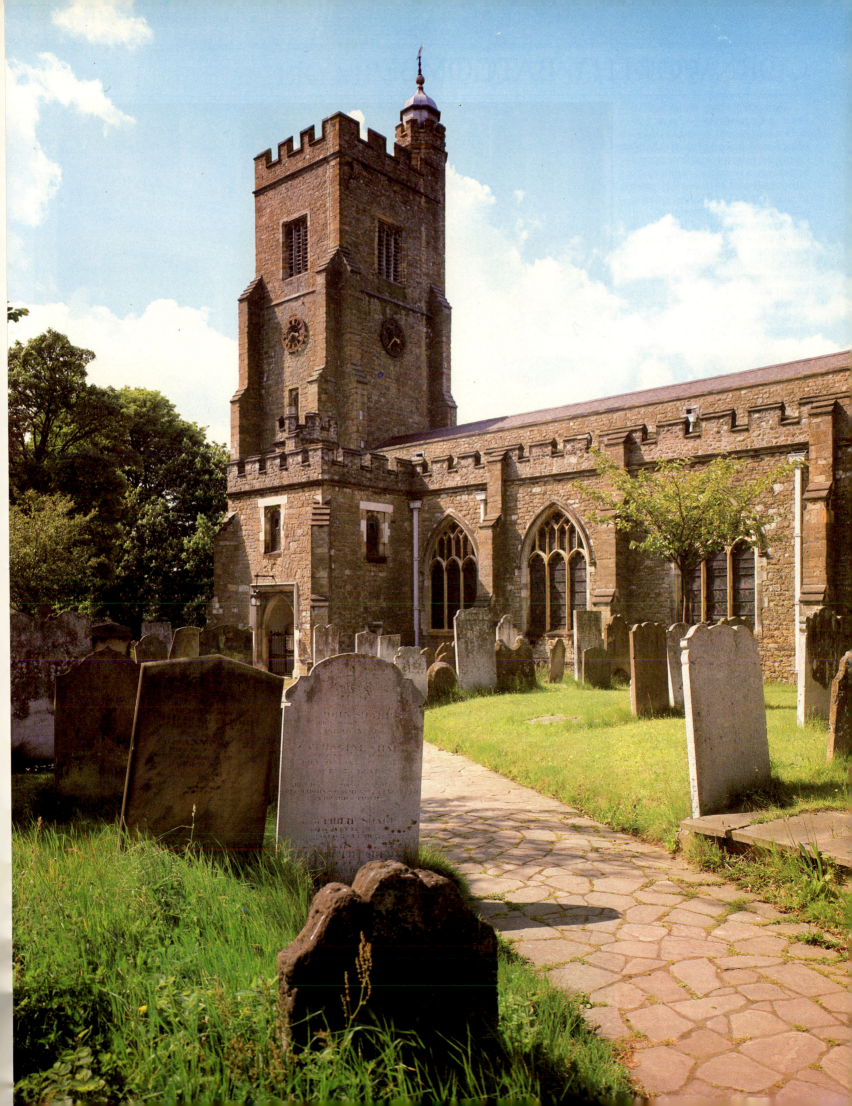

FLAMSTEAD/BERWICK

The church of St Leonard at **Flamstead** (2,4,5,6 and 8) lies in the Hertfordshire countryside above the River Ver. Its picturesque churchyard is surrounded by giant sycamores, lilacs and red and white chestnuts, above which rises the needle point of its slender, octagonal spire. This is an excellent example of a traditional 'Hertfordshire spike' and contrasts admirably with the massive Norman tower (4). Much of the church is of the 14th century, but the piers of the nave have capitals of Totternhoe stone carved with 'stiff-leaf' foliage that clearly belongs to the dawn of the Early English style.

Under one of the arches of the northern arcade is St Leonard's oldest monument – the figures of a man and woman (5) who lie side by side beneath a cusped, crocketted canopy, with simple tracery in the spandrils and a

battlemented cornice. The design, of late-14th century character, lacks the usual crispness and clarity of work of that period and has suffered severely over the years. In consequence it is impossible to say who the effigies represent – although it is likely that they are members of the House of Beauchamp who were lords of the manor. Two further monuments of note include a board bearing the arms of George Cordell (2) with an inscription stating that he '*served Queene Elizabeth and was Sergeant of the Ewry to King James and to the late King Charles, in all sixty years*'. The second memorial is a large altar-tomb in black and white marble by Stanton, which depicts Thomas Saunder's children (8).

Flamstead church possesses a notable medieval wall-painting showing, among others, St Christopher, Christ in Glory and the Last Supper – found hidden beneath layers of plaster in 1930. Also revealed was one of St Leonard's original consecration crosses (6) used to denote the exact spot anointed with holy oil by the Bishop in the ceremony of the church's dedication.

■ As witnessed at Flamstead, medieval wall-paintings were invariably limed-over or whitewashed after the Reformation; but the lovely South Downs church of **Berwick** (9,10 and 11) in East Sussex has sought to redress the balance. Here, at the instigation of the Bishop of

GREAT ROLLRIGHT/SOMERTON

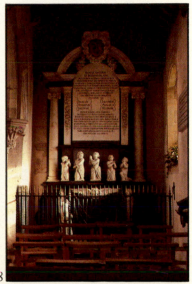

Berwick's Rector as Chaplain. The outer screen – 'While the Earth remaineth...' – is also by Grant, as is the 'Victory of Calvary' in which Christ is depicted on the Cross, but with all traces of suffering banished, His arms outstretched in the Jewish attitude of prayer. Below the east window is the reredos by Quentin Bell of the 'Supper at Emmaus' (10).

7

8

9

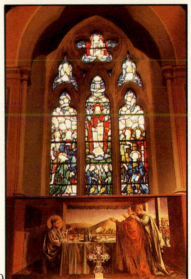

10

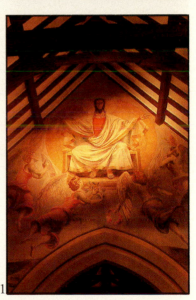

11

Chichester, the 13th century walls of the parish church were beautified with murals painted by members of the Bloomsbury Group. The work was executed during the Second World War, and over the chancel arch is 'The Glory' (9 and 11) painted by Duncan Grant. To the left are the kneeling figures of a soldier (the portrait of Douglas Hemming, who fell in combat at Caen in 1944), a sailor and an airman. To the right is the Bishop wearing a crimson cope of Spanish provenance with

■ The remote hillside church at **Colton** (7) commands impressive views of the wild sweep of Cumbrian countryside that forms its rural parish. In contrast, **Somerton's** Early English church of St Michael (1) is lulled by the gentle beauty of the Somerset landscape.

■ 3: The Norman church at **Great Rollright** in Oxfordshire possesses a 12th century tympanum upon which is incised the unusual theme of a crocodile – half-serpent, half-dragon – devouring Man.

ALDINGTON

The early-16th century tower of St Martin's, at **Aldington** (3 and 6) is a landmark for miles around. It is among the finest of the characteristically Kentish embattled towers, and has an exceptionally enriched west front, with the most elaborately decorated niches above and beside the late-Perpendicular doorway. Aldington was the scene of a rather sour comedy in 1511, when the humanist scholar Erasmus was proferred the living of rector. He was, however, of no comfort to the souls of the village, being more fluent in Latin and Greek than in English. The parishioners pressed for his

TO THE MEMORY OF
LIZABETH WILKINSON

1

2

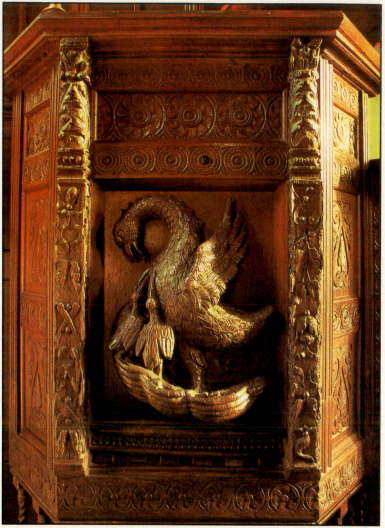

3

removal, and the great reformer at last surrendered Aldington – but took with him a pension for life of rather more than half the value of the living.

With extensive views across Romney Marsh, this handsome church (6) is of unusual interest: it possesses elaborate, though battered, wooden stalls incorporating misericords from the 15th century, and a splendid Jacobean pulpit displaying a 'Pelican in her Piety' (3). This symbol of self-sacrifice was popular in medieval ecclesiastical art. The pelican was believed to love its chicks so deeply that it pecked open its own breast and fed them on its blood. The bird became synonymous with Christ's own sacrifice upon the Cross. The Christian theme developed out of an older, pagan legend which explained that pelican chicks attack their parents, who eventually strike back and kill them. Driven by remorse, the mother mutilates herself, and her blood restores the murdered chicks to life.

4

5

tombstones and table tombs within the shade of its great yew tree (2), which is said to be over eight hundred years old. In the south-east corner is the grave of Colonel Kitchener, brother of Lord Kitchener of Khartoum (5). At **Muchelney** (8 and 9) in Somerset, the churchyard is also worthy of note, with its two magnificent cedars and other fine trees and shrubs. There is a path leading to a medieval, thatched priest's house (8) and a stone coffin (9) of 12th century date; it is likely that the coffin was originally buried in the floor of the church with its substantial stone lid forming part of the pavement. Muchelney Church is notable for its tiles – which once formed the floor of the ruined Abbey nearby – and for its rare, painted barrel roof.

■ An impressive feature of Somerset churches is the provision of niches on their outside walls, in which were set statues of saints, kings and martyrs – as at Isle Abbots (4 and 7).

6

7

8

Churchyards are often just as fascinating and beautiful as the buildings they surround. Many are readily abandoned to nature and each year bring forth a carpet of wild flowers – celandine, lady-smock, cowslip, meadow-sweet, speedwell, violets and primroses (1) – as well as the blossom of plants placed on graves in honour of the dead: country lore states that wild briars were once placed over the remains of parents – '*that the roses might grow, entangle and flower as one*'.

■ **St Mary Bourne** (2 and 5) is one such charming graveyard, which shelters some fine 18th century

9

ELY CATHEDRAL

Originally a monastery sited on an island in the midst of a vast expanse of marshy Fenland, **Ely Cathedral** (1-5) was founded in AD 673 by St Etheldreda. As mists from the now drained countryside roll in to skirt the lower fabric of the Anglo-Norman silhouette, its immense bulk, divided at intervals by the vertical forms of pinnacles, turrets and buttresses, rises up to haunt the cowled landscape like a shadowed crown against the Fens.

The Norman Abbot, Simeon, was eighty-six years old when appointed to the See in 1083, and from his vision (to create a church worthy of God's presence within it)

medieval passion for geometry created Ely's breathtakingly beautiful star-shaped vault and lantern tower – the octagon – a work of supreme genius (executed by William Hurle, the King's Master Carpenter), and medieval architecture's most original concept. Its essence of spacious boldness epitomises the spirit of the Decorated style. The octagon is a masterpiece of uplifted beauty, where dappled light shafts downwards from the highest windows and is captured within the lantern to be held like a glorious aureola (2) over the whole body of the church.

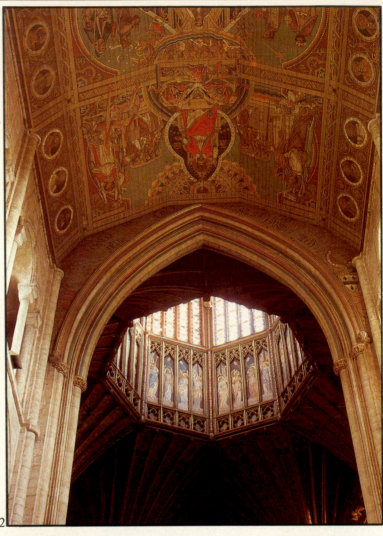

the present cathedral springs. The west front (4) is a notable survivor of the Romanesque minster – as is the magnificent 248ft long nave (5) whose feeling of soaring stonework is created by the exceedingly high triforium: the effect is no mere illusion, however, for Ely's nave is taller than any of its contemporaries. At 86ft in height the walls' tendency to bow ruled out the possibility of a stone vault, and thus the ceiling has always been of the lighter material – wood. Beyond the soaring nave, the presbytery and High Altar (3) were constructed during the period 1234-52 to provide a more sumptuous setting for St Etheldreda's shrine.

In 1322 the Norman crossing tower collapsed *'with a roar like thunder, of shock and so great a tumult'*. Faced with a gaping hole torn from the cathedral's heart, the sacrist decided against rebuilding the tower, and opted instead for the daringly experimental idea of creating an octagon. The choice was indeed fortunate, for the

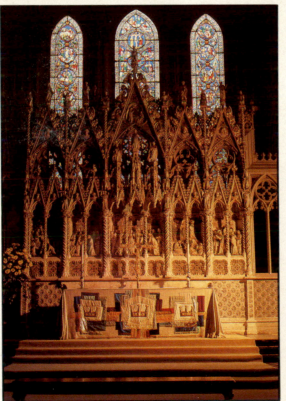

ICKFORD/LOWICK/GAYHURST

Near the grey ribbon of the Thames, in some of England's richest grazing land, is sited the church of St Nicholas at **Ickford** (7,9 and 11). The earliest parts of the building – the lower tower, the chancel and the centre aisle of the nave (9) – date from 1170-90. Characteristic of the architecture of this period are the string-course running round the chancel, both inside and out, and the narrow, round headed windows of the aisle (11) – which contain diamonds of ancient grisaille glass that is among the earliest of its kind in existence. About 1350 the tower (7) was heightened and given its distinctive saddle-back roof of red tiles. Such a gable often indicates that a medieval tower remains unfinished, but at Ickford the differing height of the 14th century windows on the north and the two tall lancets on the west prove that a saddle-back was intended from the start.

■ The interesting church of St Peter at **Lowick** (2 and 8) stands in a small Northamptonshire village,

1

3

2

5   6

dominated by the church's tower with its octagonal pinnacled lantern. There is much to savour from the Middle Ages, including fragments of 14th century glass and remarkable monuments to Edward Stafford, the Earl of Wiltshire (8) who died in 1499; and, eighty years its senior, the impressive altar-tomb of Sir Ralph Greene and his wife, Catherine.

Their alabaster effigies (2) lie hand in hand beneath intricately wrought canopies that shield their heads. The plate armour and Catherine's ornate head-dress are typical of the reign of King Henry V.

■ The present church at **Gayhurst** (3 and 4) in Buckinghamshire replaced an earlier medieval foundation in 1728, and is

acknowledged to be one of the finest examples of Georgian church architecture – its workmanship and detail being remarkable. The tower has urns at the corners, with a charming little cupola at its centre; and the interior has remained practically unaltered since the day of its completion. There are two very attractive peculiarities in the church; one is to be seen in the text of the reredos (4) – which contains the Ten Commandments, the Lord's Prayer and the Creed – it is the double negative '*Thou shalt not have none other Gods but me*'. The second is in the fact that there is no inscription carved on the monument (3) although the large marble slab which forms the front is obviously intended to have one. The two figures in period dress and wigs are the men responsible for raising the church – Sir Nathan Wrighte, Keeper of the Great Seal of England to Queen Anne, and his son George. Their splendid monument is attributed to Louis Roubiliac.

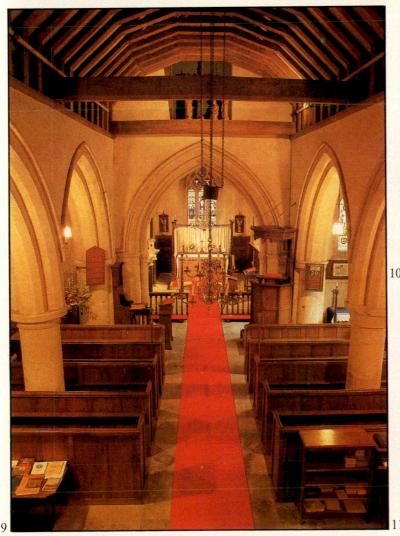

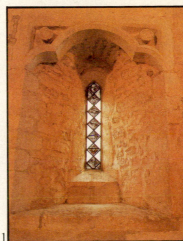

■ A noble memorial, dating from the previous century (1649), is to be seen on the wall of the north aisle of St Andrew's parish church, **Yetminster** (5 and 6). It is a mural monument (5) and depicts Bridget Minterne kneeling at a prayer desk, flanked by Corinthian columns supporting an entablature with two shields of arms. The Dorset church also possesses the upper part of a 10th century Saxon churchyard cross (6).

■ Also of interest is the early-13th century church at **Great Coxwell** (1 and 10), which possesses a fine cartouche to the Reverend John Bowle (1).

CAWSTON/HUTTOFT

The large flint church of St Agnes (5,6,9 and 10) is one of Norfolk's finest. Its freestone tower soars for 120ft, to dominate the village and surrounding countryside – with mighty buttresses reaching to the tower's summit. Its mood is sombre and starkly impressive – without parapets its austerity is relieved only by the combination of windows and doorway. The latter displays in its spandrils the carving of a dragon and a 'wild man'. The motif is repeated on the piscina within the church and bears witness to the fact that the De la Pole family – whose crest the

and is renowned for two features – its incomparable nave roof, and the rood screen. The former is of a hammer-beam construction and has carved angels on its projecting beams (6) and cherubs with outspread wings along the cornice. The bosses (5) are magnificently carved, and at the east end are the figures which formerly stood by the great rood. The screen itself (10) is in very good condition, with its original paintings by Flemish artists of the 15th century. It includes among its twenty portraits those of the church's patron saint, St Agnes, with a lamb (reminding us of the connection between

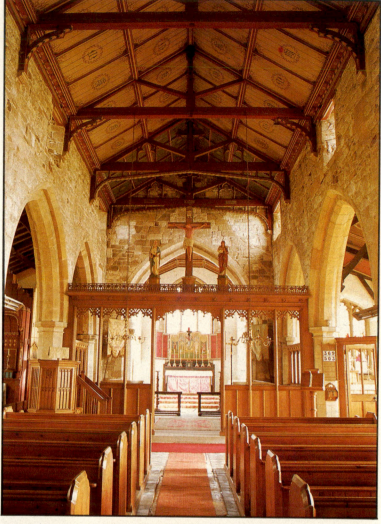

1

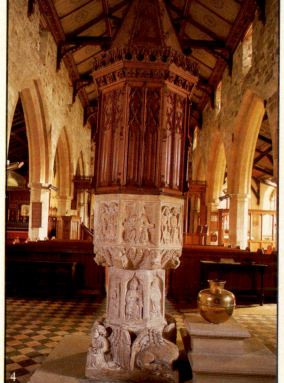

2

3

carvings represent – were patrons of the medieval church. Indeed, St Agnes' itself was rebuilt in the 14th century by one prominent member of the House – Michael, the Earl of Suffolk.

His church at Cawston displays both Decorated and early-Perpendicular styles of architecture,

4

5

6

wooden roof of the nave incorporates within its design the sacred monograms of Christ and the encircled letter 'M' of His mother, the Virgin Mary. At the west end of the nave lies Huttoft's greatest possession – its Perpendicular font (4), depicting the Madonna and Child, and the Trinity with the Twelve Apostles in pairs on the bowl, saints on the stem, and the symbols of the four Evangelists at the base.

■ **Pirton Church** (1 and 8) in Worcestershire has a picturesque example of a half-timbered Tudor belltower (1) surmounted by a pyramidal roof of red tiles. These 'magpie' towers are rare, and are only found in districts that were once thickly forested. They are invariably raised in oak with a complex framework filled with 'wattle and daub' – wooden sticks woven in the form of close hurdles and coated in clay mixed with chopped straw. Pirton's tower abuts a Norman nave containing an ancient font and many medieval tiles (8), of which there are two distinct colours – red and ochre – with a fleur-de-lis pattern predominating.

■ 7: A festival of flowers at St John's Church, **Buxton**.

7

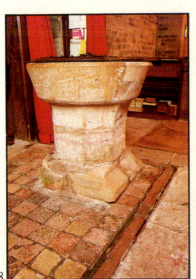

8

9

10

Cawston and the Middle Ages' wool industry), St Andrew with his saltire cross (9), and an interesting representation of Sir John Schorne removing a horned imp (symbolizing gout) from his boot – an allusion to Sir John's well at Marsham, the waters of which were much praised as a gout cure.

■ The medieval Lincolnshire church of **Huttoft** (2,3 and 4) possesses a graceful chancel and nave (2) with ancient arcade and clerestory. Contemporary with these are the robustly carved belfry windows (3) and the splendid 14th century chest – panelled throughout with tracery. The

The wonderful Norfolk church of **Salle** (1,2,5,7,9 and 10) has the best of everything that the 15th century produced. The architecture of c1420 is superb, yet its great size is out of all proportion to the size of the village it served – whose population rarely exceeded two hundred. The church's grand scale is a result of the area's flourishing weaving industry (there were no less that six trade guilds, all of which maintained separate altars within the church) and the personal munificence of three families – the Fountains, the Briggs and the Boleyns. The latter, of

yeoman stock, were destined for prominence and subsequent shame as they rose and fell with the fortunes of Anne Boleyn and the whims of her Tudor husband.

Salle's dominating tower is 126ft high, and sets the standard for the rest of the church which is 171ft long, with nave, aisle and transepts all in perfect proportion. The entire building is raised in Barnack stone and is Perpendicular in both style and emphasis. The nave (9) possesses one of the most graceful arcades of the period; slender columns rise to a lofty clerestory, and above is a roof which is a

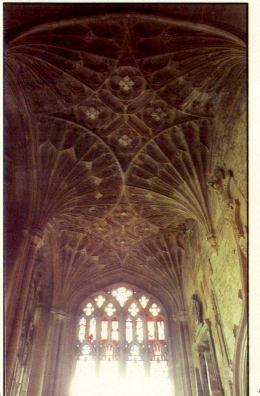

1

3

4

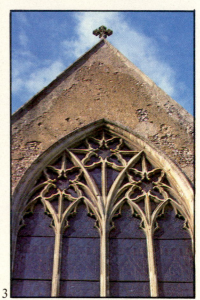

5

6

marvellous piece of medieval heavy carpentry and structural daring, with wide arch braces coming down on to wall posts which stand on corbel brackets – a venturesome construction for such a wide span. Indeed, the excellence of the carpenter's art is one of Salle's greatest attributes – be it in the functional strength of the great medieval oak door of the Lady chapel (1), in the delicacy of its beautiful 15th-century 'wine-glass' pulpit (10) complete with Jacobean tester and canopy, or in the carvings of stalls and benches with poppy-heads and misericords (5).

The church's font is one of the Seven Sacrament variety, of which thirty-nine exist, and all but two belong to Norfolk and Suffolk. This is a very good example (2): it is not over-elaborate and the sculpture is graceful. The font's pedestal is unique in having angels bearing emblems corresponding to the sacrament displayed in the panel above – an altar stone, a chalice, a chrismatory, a mitre, a scourge, a lyre, and a figure representing the soul of a sick man. Over the font – suspended by the wooden arm of a medieval crane (7) – is Salle's 12ft tall font canopy, which retains

traces of its original colouring, but has lost the carved figures that once filled the upright spaces of its three tiers.

■ Two exquisite examples of architecture contemporary to that of Salle exist at **Chartham** (3) and **North Leigh** (4). The former has an east window that is a 'text-book' example of 'Kentish tracery' (3) whose distinctive split cusps produce a beautiful star effect. At the Oxfordshire church of North Leigh the Wilcote Chapel was raised in 1442 on the orders of Lady Elizabeth Blackett for Mass to be said daily for the souls of her husband and son (killed at the Battle of Agincourt). It contains a fine example of fan-vaulting (4): one of the most notable to be found in any small parish church.

■ Views from the south-east showing St Thomas of Canterbury at **East Clandon** (6) in Surrey, and St James at **Avebury** (8) in Wiltshire.

BRIDFORD/FRAMLINGHAM

The granite, Perpendicular church at **Bridford** (1,2,3,4 and 5) lies to the west of the Teign Valley, in the Dartmoor foothills of south Devon. The gentle, time-weathered stone of its ancient fabric (2 and 5) is perhaps a last reminder of mellowness before the harsh moor landscape grips the senses with the bleakness of its grey boulders piled like ramparts and horizons topped by massive, jagged tors. The 15th century church has some late-medieval glass, a fine carved pulpit, stalls, bench-ends, wagon roofs and other notable medieval woodwork. Best of all, however, is Bridford's splendid rood screen (3) of 1508. It is exceptional in possessing small, exquisitely carved figures of Apostles and Prophets (1).

■ The church and churchyard of St Michael's at **Framlingham** (7) in Suffolk are positioned high above the market-place. The nave, with its hammer-beam roof, and the tower (7) are both fine examples of the East Anglian 15th century style.

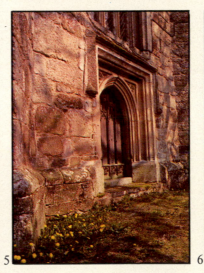

■ The parish church of **Castle Ashby** (6) is set within the grounds of the Marquess of Northampton's Elizabethan mansion house landscaped by Capability Brown. The 14th and 15th century church has an attractive tower surmounted by a pyramid roof; and within are many monuments to the Crompton family – owners of the manor. Of particular interest is a brass in the chancel floor of the rector William Ermyn (6), dated 1401. His cope is elaborately decorated with ten saints all standing under traceried canopies on the orphreys. There are coats-of-arms on the morse.

SHORWELL

The 15th century church at **Shorwell** (1,2,4,6 and 9) on the Isle of Wight is of mellow texture, set in a lovely village of thatched cottages in multi-coloured local stone. The exterior is weathered and unrestored, the interior is dark and crowded with medieval poppy-headed pews. The church has an unusual plan, with the two side aisles running the entire length of both nave and chancel, and separated by a fine stone arcade (4).

The roof beam of the chancel serves to denote the easterly limit of the nave (6). This particularly beautiful feature is characteristic of the carpenter's art of the late Middle Ages, yet it is not a rood beam as one might usually expect to find in a medieval church – with the figures of the Calvary, the Virgin Mary and St John. Instead, the beam at Shorwell represents 'Our Lord Reigning in Glory' with the figures of Gabriel and Michael on either side. The corbels upon which the roof beam rests represent 'Sin' and 'Death' – in

1

2

3

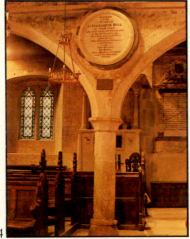

4

both cases the stonemason has displayed to advantage the full scope of his imagination and skill.

The tower was built in 1440 and the stone spire was the gift of Sir John Leigh. His splendid monument, and that of his wife (9), are in the Leigh chapel north of the high altar. In the same transept, over the northern doorway, is Shorwell's best known treasure – its medieval wall painting. Measuring 11ft wide by 6ft high, the mural depicts the figure of St Christopher at its centre, bearing the infant Christ (2), out of whose mouth issues the proclamation '*ego sum alpha et*

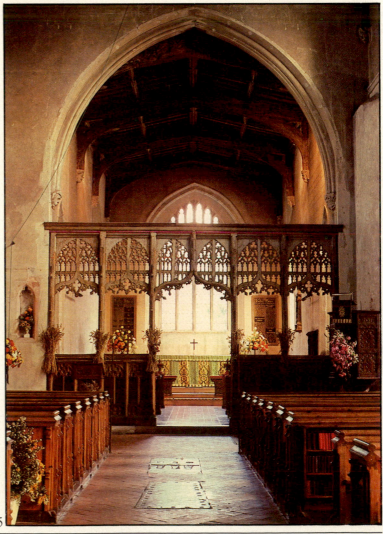

5

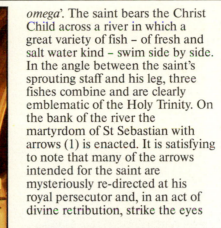

omega'. The saint bears the Christ Child across a river in which a great variety of fish – of fresh and salt water kind – swim side by side. In the angle between the saint's sprouting staff and his leg, three fishes combine and are clearly emblematic of the Holy Trinity. On the bank of the river the martyrdom of St Sebastian with arrows (1) is enacted. It is satisfying to note that many of the arrows intended for the saint are mysteriously re-directed at his royal persecutor and, in an act of divine retribution, strike the eyes that witness Sebastian's torment.

■ The parish church at **Clavering** (3,5,7 and 8) is delightfully positioned within an Essex countryside of willowy meadows and unfenced bean and corn fields. Picturesque cob-cottages (3) line the pathway to the church whose flint walls were raised during the Perpendicular period, and whose window tracery and clerestory are characteristic of this last great phase of the Gothic (7). The western tower is also of the early 15th century (8).

Its dedication to St Mary and St

Clement is probably from the 12th century when the church (later to be reconstructed) was presented by the Lord of Clavering to the Priory of St Mary at Prittlewell, whose parent monastery at Cluny in France possessed a relic of St Clement – one of the early bishops of Rome. The present church is very large for a rural parish and it is likely that the funds necessary to raise so grand a building were met by farming tithes. Indeed, the lovely and ancient custom of tying corn sheaves to the medieval rood screen at harvest time (5) may well have a deeper significance – for Clavering is an extensive parish in fertile corn growing country, and most of the money that built the church came from corn. The screen itself is a fine example of the East Anglian genre, handsomely carved, with traces of its original bright colouring. The panels reveal the faint outline of the figures of saints, including one of St Anthony with a pig – his sole companion during his meditations in the desert.

CROMPTON BEAUCHAMP/FAIRFORD

Light – the intangible phenomenon by which the world is made visible – has, since time immemorial, been symbolically equated with goodness and revelation, and has therefore been a focal point of the religions of mankind. The flowering of the art of stained glass in the Middle Ages was inspired to '*illumine mens' minds so they may travel through it (light) to an apprehension of God's light*'. At the end of the Saxon era and in Norman times, when the boom in ecclesiastical building was beginning, windows were small, and characterised by large splays which encouraged as much light as

All is of the late-15th and early-16th century (as is the building of this 'wool-church' – the gift of the wool stapler and cloth merchant, John Tame) and is thought to be of the school of Barnard Flower, Master Glass Painter to King Henry VII.

The 'Passion' occupies the east window, but otherwise Fairford begins with Old Testament scenes and continues with the early life of the Virgin, the 'Annunciation', the life of the infant Jesus, and the whole of the Gospel story up to Pentecost. In the clerestory, saints and martyrs occupy the south windows, and face the 'evil'

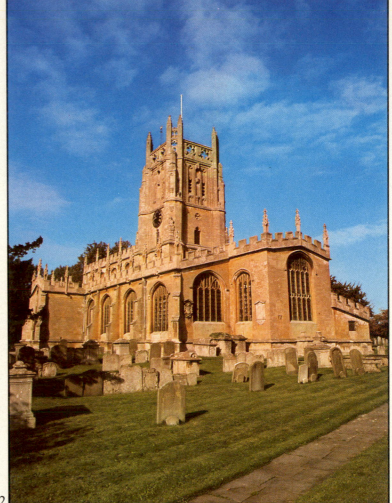

possible to seep into the church – such windows are exemplified by the 13th century chancel-light (3) at **Crompton Beauchamp** (1).

As the art of medieval bar tracery developed, cathedrals and churches became ablaze with the colour of stained glass. Windows gradually increased in size, until some 15th-century churches had the appearance of huge expanses of glass held together by narrow strips of stone. The opportunity offered by these vast areas of glazing was eagerly seized upon by artists, and their jewel-like creations are among the finest possessions of our medieval heritage. Of all England's parish churches, St Mary's at **Fairford** (2,4,5,6 and 7) contains the greatest display of medieval stained glass. As a complete series, the glass in this Gloucestershire church is unique. Its twenty-eight Perpendicular windows cover an area of two thousand square feet. Fairford is, in fact, the Bible in glass: and the whole faith of the Church is presented in vivid colour.

and the artist clearly took enormous delight in the dramatic use of reds and blues. In the fourth light (7) stands St Michael in golden armour. He suspends a pair of scales – in one pan a little soul is being weighed, whilst into the opposite pan a devil has climbed in in an attempt to pervert the balance – the innocent soul is still worthy and will proceed to the left hand side of the window tracery where the blessed, in white robes, file past St Peter up a golden stairway that leads to the heavenly bliss of the upper half of the Great West Window (5). Here, the innocent form the outer bands of worshippers who encircle Christ enthroned upon His tricolour rainbow (a symbol of the Trinity). At Christ's feet kneel His mother and St John the Baptist, while the angelic host surround their heavenly Lord to whom full jurisdiction is given. However, it is the imagery to the right of the arch-angel, in the lower tracery, which attracts most attention, for here the full rein of the artist's imagination has been allowed to run riot. He fills the panels with grotesque and fascinating detail of a hellish nightmare, wherein a blue

5

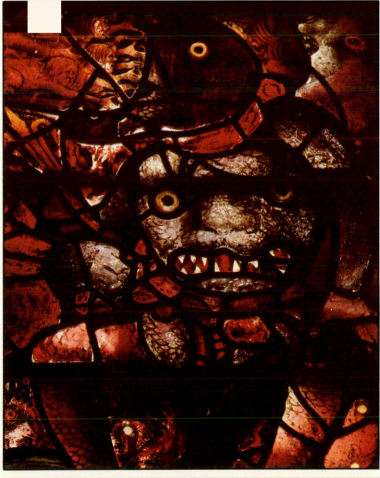

6

7

northern side, filled to overflowing with those who have persecuted the Church – with a wealth of demons in the traceries. The most spectacular of Fairford's windows – the Great West Window (5,6 and 7) – is given over to the theme of the apocalyptic end of the world, and the judgement of souls. It is the finest example of a 'doom-window'

devil (4) carts off an old man to destruction, and Satan (5) is seen with a fish's head devouring a stream of damned sinners, while his bloated stomach forms a second head with leering yellow eyes and a row of hideously sharp teeth – all bathed in the blood-red glow of hell-fire.

BRIXWORTH

All Saints' Church, **Brixworth** (1,3,6 and 7), built some two or three hundred years after the Romans left Britain, is without question the most impressive and outstanding early-Saxon building in the country. Not only is it one of the few constructions to have survived from the 7th century almost complete (6); but it has been in continuous use as a centre of Christian worship from its inception to the present day – a

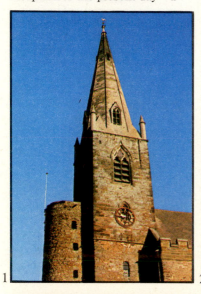

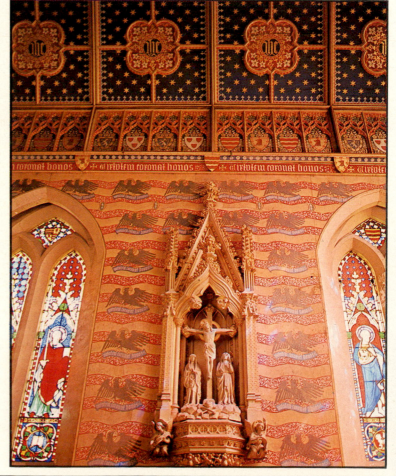

span of thirteen hundred years. Indeed, its present impressive size is now actually smaller than when the original minster was constructed.

Brixworth is built of stone rubble with a substantial amount of Roman tiles utilised in the abaci, the arches (7) and in portions of the tower. When the minster church was founded it must have proved a suitable centre from which to spread the Gospel to the heathen tribes of Mercia; and the narthex at the west end (part of which survives in the tower) was used for the instruction of *catechumens* – converts under instruction in the Faith.

The reddened stones at the west end of the church are an indication of severe heat, and such burning would agree with the theory that Brixworth was sacked by Danes in the early years of its history. During subsequent rebuilding work in the

late-9th and early-10th centuries, part of the existing sanctuary and the vaulted stair turret were built against the tower (1). The latter houses a good example of a helical staircase centered on a newel post, which permits access to the tower's upper chamber. This room has a window looking into the nave and was used – as at its fellow Northamptonshire church, Earls Barton – by persons of distinction. From this window, with its lovely baluster shafts, one can inspect the intricacies of the nave's roof construction (3) and the interplay of king-posts and tie-beams.

Various alterations were made in the Middle Ages: the Lady chapel was built in the 13th century, and the belfry and spire raised in 1350. There is also an ancient, sunken ring-crypt beneath the apse, where stood the sacred relic of the throat bone of the great preacher St Boniface. To prevent it being

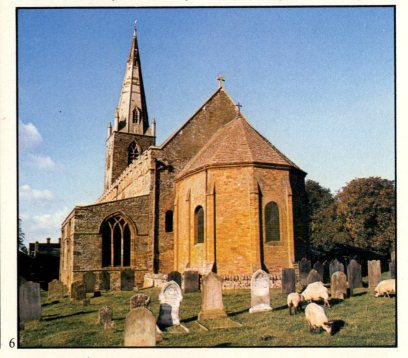

desecrated during the Reformation the last chantry priest of Brixworth, Thomas Bassenden, bricked up the treasure in the Lady chapel wall where it was uncovered three hundred years later. This priceless relic is now displayed within a heavy iron cage in the reliquary.

■ The Doomsday Book church of St Peter and St Paul **Albury** (2,4,5 and 8) in Surrey, is beautifully situated in a well timbered park, but has been disused since 1842. It has traces of Saxon stone-work, and the tower – whose interior (8) is lit by pre-Conquest windows – is part Saxon, part Norman, and is surmounted by a 17th century cupola (2). The chancel is a ruin, but the south transept was lavishly remodelled by Augustus Pugin in the early 1840s as a mortality chapel of the Drummond Family. The feel of this chapel is vividly Victorian, with stained glass by William Wailes (5) and walls and ceiling elaborately decorated in heraldry (4), coloured and gilded by Thomas Earle.

DURHAM CATHEDRAL

Considered to be the world's supreme masterpiece of Romanesque architecture, the Anglo-Norman cathedral at **Durham** (1-12) could want for no finer setting. It dominates the lofty sandstone peninsula on which it rests (2), encircled by a great loop of the River Wear on all three sides, and guarded on its landward approach by a mighty Norman fortress. The strength of its position made Durham the '*Citadel of the Holy Church of the North*', shielding the sacred relics of St Cuthbert against the ravages of Scottish incursions and Viking raids. The saint's relics proved the inspiration for the founding of the cathedral 1540, but when the tomb was opened the Reformers found that his body – despite the passing of eight centuries – had remained in perfect condition, with no visible sign of decay. To the monks, however, it had been common knowledge that the saint's hair and nails continued to grow and, from time to time, it was necessary for the guardian of the shrine to open the tomb and trim the growth. At the discretion of the King's commissioners Durham's chief treasure was allowed to rest beneath the site of his once sumptuous shrine, under a slab of stone simply inscribed '*Cuthbertus*' (1,3 and 4).

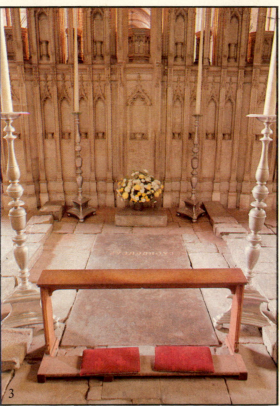

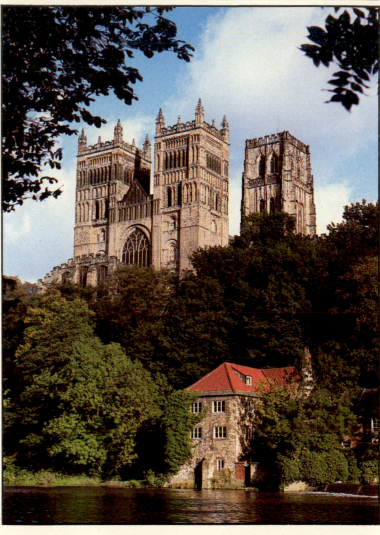

and his shrine became the 'brightest jewel of the north' – '*exalted with the most curious workmanship, of fine and costly green marble, all limned (painted) with gilt and gold; having four seats underneath the shrine for lame men to offer their devout and fervent prayer to God and Holy St Cuthbert, for his miraculous relief and succour which, being never wanting, made the shrine to be so richly invested with silver, gold, elephant tooth and suchlike things, that it was esteemed one of the most fabled monuments in all England*'. Of the many gifts that crowded the shrine, among the most unusual were part of Moses' rod, a fragment of Jesus' manger, a unicorn horn and the claw of a griffin with several of her eggs. Only men were admitted to the presence of the tomb as St Cuthbert appears to have developed an aversion to women which in medieval times resulted in the defining of a black marble boundary line in the nave, over which no female dared to tread. Cuthbert's shrine was despoiled in

DURHAM CATHEDRAL

The cathedral itself was raised during the period 1093 to 1133, and its abiding spirit is one of massive strength and overwhelming grandeur; yet despite its force, Durham is so well proportioned that nothing about it seems ponderous. The 201ft long nave (5) was considered the miracle of its day, and its lofty arcading is borne on alternating clustered piers (6 and 8) and massive circular columns – each boldly incised with swirling, almost barbaric, patterns of chevron (11), vertical flute and chequer pattern (9). Above the aisles, shadowed galleries (10) harbour England's

first flying buttresses. The cathedral is also the earliest building in Europe to have ribbed vaults throughout (7), and pioneered the use of the pointed arch to divide the nave into bays – a feature that was to be the secret of the world's greatest architecture – Durham is thus not merely the triumphant climax of Romanesque art, but also the first hint of the Gothic.

Few examples of Norman sculpture have survived which can compare with the savage splendour of Durham's bronze sanctuary knocker (12). The grotesque 'griffin head' mask (whose face once

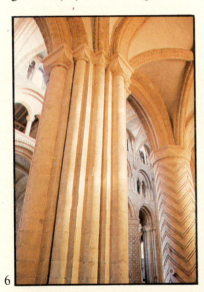

6

7

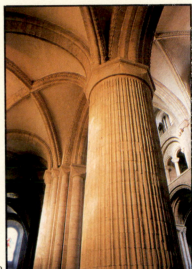

8

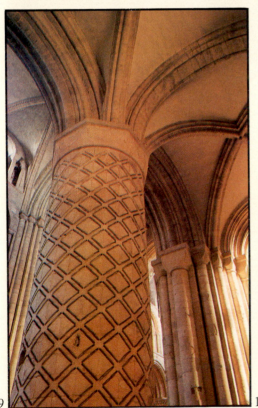

9

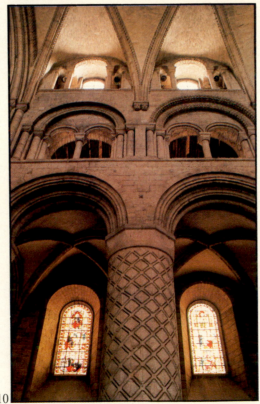

10

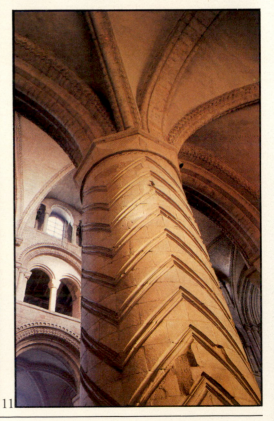

11

cathedral: he had to toll a special bell formally to signal his claim of sanctuary, confess his crime to a priest, surrender his arms and pay a nominal fee. Common law then allowed the fugitive the right to take an oath of 'abjuration of the realm', whereby (dressed in a long white robe and armed only with a crucifix) he had but nine days to quit the Kingdom.

■ The little Norman church near the abbey ruins at **Hailes** (15) in Gloucestershire is one of the most unspoilt in the country. Cement rendered on the outside, it perhaps does not look very interesting, but within everything is old. There is

Norman window. Beneath the foot of St Catherine lies the crowned head of the Emperor Maxentius whom she humiliated; and St Margaret is seen thrusting the shaft of a long-stemmed cross down the throat of Satan (in the guise of a dragon). Many of Hailes' tiles were brought to the church from the abandoned Cistercian abbey; and the oak canopied pulpit dates from the 17th century, as does much of the panelling and choir stalls. In the same county, St Mary's, **Upleadon** (13) is a 12th century church containing a fine Norman doorway which includes a sculptured tympanum. The superb

12

13

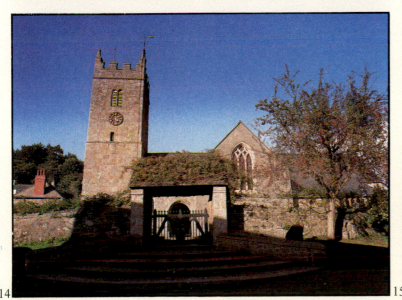

14

15

flashed with the fire of red enamel eyes) leers menacingly from the cathedral's great north door, yet would seem better suited to the prow of a Viking longship. Its frightening countenance was, however, a welcome sight to the eyes of debtors and fugitives

fleeing the terrifying excesses of medieval civil law. By clinging to the metal ring a criminal could claim the Right of Sanctuary (which dates back to the Old Testament). If he conformed to a strict code of conduct, the felon was permitted to shelter within the

medieval stained glass and a series of well preserved wall paintings of c1300 – including a representation of St Catherine of Alexandria and St Margaret of Antioch. The two saints often appear in each other's company and are painted together in the splays of a half-blocked

tower, with its pyramid cap, is of half-timbered construction and was raised in c1500.

■ The Perpendicular church of **Lustleigh** (14) has a granite tower contemporary to Upleadon and a lavishly carved mid-15th century screen.

BARFRESTON/BECKFORD

The best Norman church in Kent, St Nicholas at **Barfreston** (2,5,6 and 8) has remained substantially unaltered since the day of its completion in c1080. It is built of flint and Caen stone, and comprises a nave and chancel, joined by a finely decorated chancel arch (8) beyond which lies the glory of its altar and famous wheel-window. Barfreston's chief

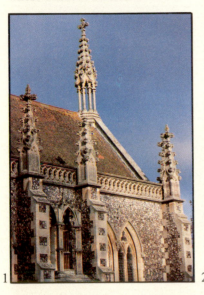

distinction is the surprising elaboration and richness of its carved decoration both within and without. The quality is similar to that of Canterbury Cathedral, but why so much skilled work should have been lavished on so small a church, set in such a remote area, has never been satisfactorily explained.

The magnificence of the south doorway (2) is world renowned and in the centre panel is a portrayal of Our Lord with His hand raised in blessing. Around him are carvings of beasts and acanthus leaves surrounded by three recessed arches: the outside moulding has figures set in ovals which include a foot-soldier drawing his sword, a sower of seed, a forester who has loosed his bow, a falconer and lure, a woman drawing from a cask, and Samson opening the jaws of a lion. There are also other interesting carvings, such as a monkey with a rabbit over its shoulder riding a goat, and a bear playing a harp. On

the door jamb can be seen the scratch-dials that indicated the times of Mass: attendance was obligatory, if the worshipper arrived after a certain stage of the service he was deemed not to have been present.

The east front of the church (5) contains an abundance of carvings and the wheel-window, corbel table and wall niches hold a fascinating array of mythological creatures – dragons, wyverns and sphinxes. The corbel table encircles the church (6), and on the northern side there is an old 'Devil's door' once kept open during Baptism to allow the Devil to escape.

■ The cruciform church at **Beckford**, (3 and 7) in Worcestershire, is another fine example of Romanesque work, with carved, 12th century tympanum over the south door showing an allegorical design – the animal creation according to the Holy Trinity. The all-seeing eye of God represents the Father, a cross the Son, and a dove the Holy Ghost: on either side are beasts possessing five horns and five ears. The Norman nave is separated from the central tower (3) – occupying the site of the original chancel before it was extended eastwards in 1310 – by a superb

Romanesque arch (7). On the northern column are two demon heads and a centaur – believed to be part of the badge of King Stephen, in whose reign the arch was raised.

■ The high standard of craftsmanship expended by the Normans on external decoration was repeated in later ages. The ball flower type of ornamentation (which resembled a small globular flower with three incurved petals) was a particular feature of the Decorated period – seen here at **Booton** (1) – whilst the Perpendicular style of architecture is characterised by the intricacy of parapets and the richness of sculptured string courses. This latter feature is seen to perfection at **Blythburgh's** 15th century church where the parapet of the south aisle (4) has perforated cinquefoils, cusped and pointed; and on the narrow string course below, roses and lions' heads are set at intervals. Over the apex of each window is a small, carved angel holding a shield.

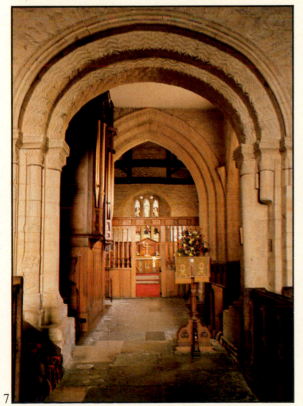

NEWTON ST MARGARET

Standing at nearly 800ft above sea level, with magnificent views over the Hereford plain to the hills of Dinedor, Garway and the Black Mountains, the church of **Newton St Margaret** (1,2,3 and 4) is superbly sited on its lonely hilltop, and although rather isolated, it possesses an abiding atmosphere of peace and tranquillity. At the time of its foundation, however, life would have been far from tranquil, for St Margaret's lies in the southern border country of the Welsh Marches - which later contained Norman castles a few miles to the south, west and north of the church. Indeed, the slight 'batter', or inward sloping, of its walls is a typical Norman feature (reminiscent of their fortified buildings) and indicates the strength of the original 12th century construction.

This simple, two-cell Herefordshire church (4) is built of shaly rubble with local sandstone dressing, and owes more to the traditions of Wales than to any English influence. St Margaret's low nave and even lower chancel are typical of many Welsh churches, yet what distinguishes this parish church from so many others is the beauty of its rood screen (1) - described as '*one of the wonders of Herefordshire*'. When the screen was built in c1540 it contained a large crucifix and supporting figures. At festivals they

the coving is a cornice with running oak foliage and brattishing in the form of scores of tiny fleurs-de-lis.

The chancel arch is obscured by the screen. This rather crude 12th century arch is the oldest surviving part of the church, and proves that the Norman building occupied the same position as the present chancel and 15th century nave. The former was partly reconstructed in the early 14th century and incorporates a typical trussed rafter collar-beam roof, with short, straight braces from the

Go and Sin no more

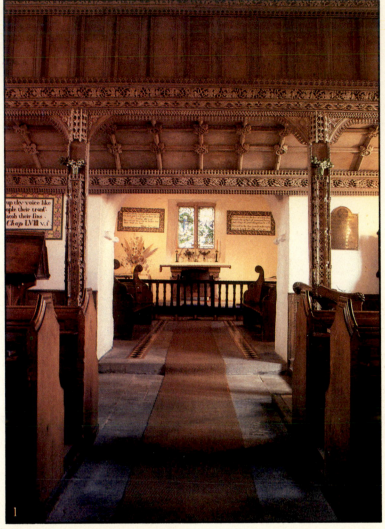

were dressed with nosegays and garlands, but during Lent were cowled in veils. After the Reformation an order of 1547 was made to destroy all such imagery, and the vast majority of roods vanished. Fortunately the destruction of the loft was left to

the discretion of each parish, and St Margaret's survived thanks to unknown lovers of beauty (in those days of violent passion) who must have considered it sacrilege to destroy such a fine piece of craftsmanship. The front of the loft is divided into twenty simple

panels by moulded muntins, and the upper and lower rails of the loft are enriched with running vine foliage (3), friezes and brattishing. The bosses of the soffit are carved with human heads (one man pokes his tongue out), lions, interlaced knots and foliage. At the base of

rafters to the collars. It is a type common to medieval England and Wales, but is not basically a 'Marcher roof' - as is the nave's Tudor vault of arch-braced collar-beam, and side and ridged purlins. A carved strip of timber dismantled during the restoration

of the nave roof bears the Welsh inscription '*Karka Dy Ddtwedd 1574*' - 'Prepare for thy end'. In a similar vein the chancel contains Commandment texts written on either side of the east window – being good examples of typically 18th century work – and, above the south door as one leaves the church, is the exhortation to '*Go and sin no more*' (2).

■ The church at **Hardres Court** (5, 6, 8 and 9) in Kent is raised in local stone faced with knapped flints, with a large brick-built porch (6). Its roof is barrel-staved and the

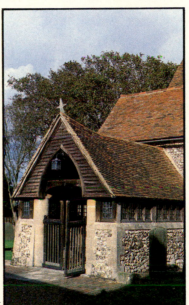

Romanesque archway gives access to the Perpendicular nave and glorious Early English chancel. The latter (5) houses a rare bracket-brass set into the chancel floor-slabs, which depicts a former rector, John Strete, who died in 1404. It is the best example of its kind in England, and shows the rector at the foot of a tall cross with the church's patrons at the top. Another of Hardres Court's important possessions is its 15th century glass in the eastern lancets (9) displaying the Hardres family arms, surmounted by figures of the

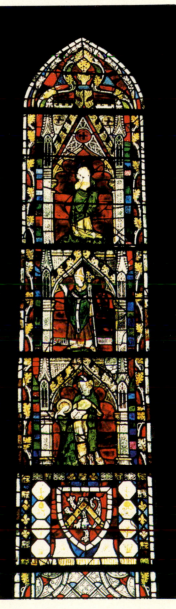

Blessed Virgin, St Edmund Rich the Archbishop of Canterbury, and the 'Salvation of Mary and Elizabeth'.

■ 7: Snowdrops adorn the graves beside the tiny priest's door of St Peter's church at **Benington**.

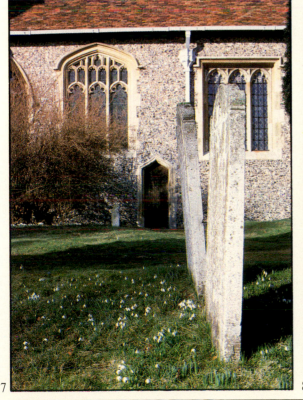

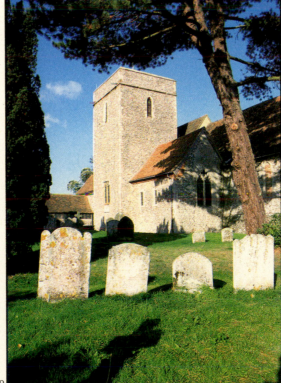

BRAMLEY

The engaging church of St James at **Bramley** (2,3,5,7 and 8) in Hampshire, belongs to the Norman transitional style, and dates from 1160. The walls of the original church are very thick - built with flint and tiles from the old Roman city of Silchester - an indication of their width can be gauged by the great splay of the Norman window (5) in the chancel, which contains medieval glass depicting St Eustace's vision of Christ crucified, held between the antlers of a stag. Later building work at Bramley utilised brick (3) and both the west tower of 1636 and the south transept were raised in a matching face. The latter, built in 1802 by Soane, is known as the Brocas aisle. The heraldic weather-vane above the family chapel represents a Moor's crowned head - a crest granted to the Crusader ancestor who smote off the head of the King of Morocco. The centrepiece of the aisle is the 18th century monument to Sir Bernard Brocas by Thomas Banks (2), beyond which rises the south window - full

2

3

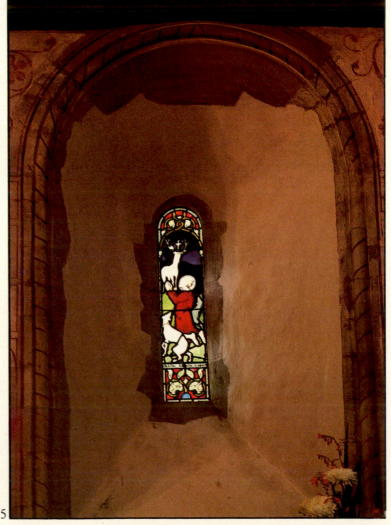

of valuable glass belonging to the period 1480-1520 - the work of Flemish glaziers of the Liege School. Stained glass of the 15th century also embellishes the Decorated windows of the north side of the nave where the heraldic Sun of York and Brocas Arms (7) are boldly exposed.

Bramley's wealth of medieval wall painting was brought to light by the Reverend Charles Eddy in late-Victorian times after many years of concealment. The oldest is a 12th century consecration cross marking the exact spot where the Bishop thrust his crozier. The chancel (8) was revealed to be

4

5

woven in the reddish-brown trails of flower and foliage, whilst the nave boasted a fine depiction of St Christopher. The most interesting painting, however, is of St Thomas à Becket's martyrdom. It was painted within fifty years of his murder (1170), and Becket is for once correctly dressed in his outdoor habit – and not, as he is usually shown, in his eucharistic vestments – for his martyrdom occurred in the evening whilst he was saying vespers.

■ The 14th and 15th century church of St Mary at **Yatton** (1,4,6 and 9) is one of the most impressive in Avon. It displays a

7

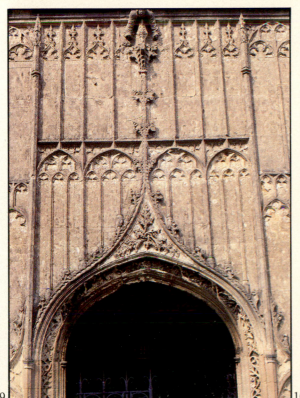

6

8

notable west front and has a central tower crowned with a truncated stone spire (6). Entry to the church is gained via a superbly carved and highly decorated south porch (9) and once within, one is immediately aware of its sense of calm majesty. There are some notable late-medieval tombs and a curious pall made from a 15th century dalmatic. Among the finest of Yatton's monuments is the alabaster table-tomb of Richard Newton and his wife (1 and 4) set before the altar.

■ **Ardeley Church** (10) in Herefordshire is mostly of the Perpendicular period, with an early-Gothic chancel and piscina. In the Middle Ages the main occupation of the village was malt production, and because of its exceptional quality Ardeley was called upon to supply the Dean and Chapter of St Paul's Cathedral in London. In return the clerics provided funds for the erection of the church of St Lawrence in the 1240s.

9

10

Lying close to the Roman wall, **Hexham Abbey** (1 and 2) was founded by St Wilfred in 674. Here he built the predecessor of the present abbey church - bringing stone from the Roman camp at Corstopitum. The crypt, built during his episcopate, is probably the finest early crypt extant in northern Europe. According to tradition it housed the sacred relics of St Andrew, brought from Rome by St Acca, Wilfred's successor. In the church above, much architecture is of the high-vaulted Early English style, and the area around the choir and high altar (1) is particularly slender and aspiring. Here, in the chancel, is 'Wilfred's chair', or the 'Frith stool'. It is scooped from a single stone and has stood at Hexham for more than twelve centuries. Tradition asserts that it was the coronation throne of Northumbrian Kings, and it has long been associated with the privilege of sanctuary (*frith* in Old English means 'peace'). In Prior Leschman's 15th century

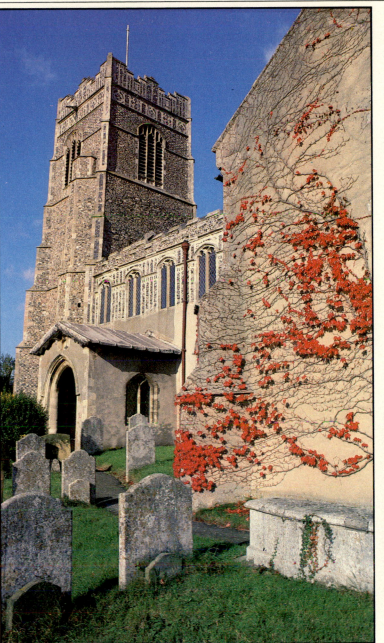

chapel there are intriguing stone characters of St George and the dragon (2), a fox preaching to geese, and representations of piety together with vanity, gluttony and other human failings.

■ **Earl Stonham Church** (3 and 6) is built upon ground that was holy long before the Christian Era. What was once sacred tended to remain hallowed ground for succeeding generations; thus the present 14th century cruciform church (3) is raised over a Roman tumulus. On entering this Suffolk church one is immediately captivated by its most noteworthy feature - the single hammer-beam roof (6) over the nave, which dates from 1460. Its timbers are chestnut and prone angels alternate with pendant, heavily carved bosses (the latter being 'false' hammer-beams). The original medieval intention of such a roof - with its profusion of angels, apostles, saints and ranks of cherubim - was to act as a forceful reminder of the praise that is ceaselessly offered to God by the

whole Host of Heaven, joined for a moment by mortal man in his offering of the *Te Deum* and *Sanctus.*

■ St Wulfram's church at **Grantham** (4 and 5) in Lincolnshire is cathedral-like in proportion. There are six pillars left of the Norman church, but its greatest beauties are its 14th century additions - the Lady chapel, the double-vaulted crypt with its fine altar (5) and the splendid 272ft steeple. Above the south porch is a parvise in which Grantham's chained library (4) is housed. The oldest book was printed in Venice in 1472.

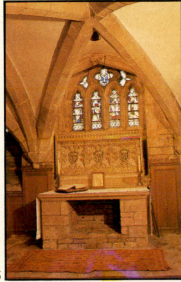

The original church of St Nicholas at **Arundel** (1,3,4 and 10) became derelict and was pulled down after the privation of the Black Death, which stalked England in 1349 and claimed over a third of her population. It was rebuilt in 1380 by Richard, the 4th Earl of Arundel, as a collegiate chapel, and is a fairly complete example of Early English architecture. On the walls are traces of medieval murals, and there is a most unusual and lovingly-carved stone pulpit (1) designed by the King's Master Mason, Henry Yevele. An unusual - if not unique - feature of the church is that, although it is an Anglican parish church, one end of it is the Fitzalan Chapel, where Roman Catholic services are held. The chapel is a fine example of Perpendicular Gothic and has been attributed to William Wynford, whilst the magnificent timber roof (10) with its stone bosses, may originally have been the work of Hugh Herland, who was also responsible for the contemporary hammer-

1

2

3

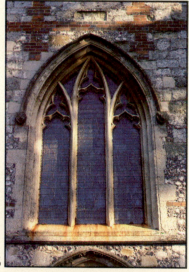

4

5

6

beam roof at Westminster Hall. The chapel fell into disrepair after the Dissolution of the Monasteries and was further desecrated by Parliamentary troops who used it as a stable. Because of its vantage-point St Nicholas' also suffered the indignity of having a cannon hoisted to the top of its tower (3) to bombard nearby Arundel Castle. The chapel was restored to its original beauty and purpose in 1886 by the Catholic 15th Duke of Norfolk, who now rests beneath his bronze monument amid the many tombs of his distant predecessors. One particularly interesting alabaster monument is to John,

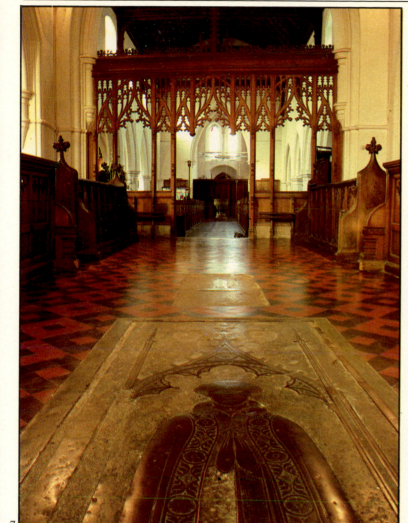

the 7th Earl and the Duke of Touraine, who died in 1435. An open tomb carries the effigy of the Earl resplendent in armour and surcoat, whilst beneath, by way of contrast, is an emaciated cadaver (4) - a gruesome reminder of the mortality of Man.

■ The flint and rubble church of St Peter and St Paul, **Hambledon** (2,5,6 and 9) in Hampshire, is a mixture of many architectural styles. The nave still retains signs of Saxon work. The church was enlarged in Norman times, added-to greatly in the 13th century –

when the chancel (9) and tower were raised – and finally restored in the last century. A huge yew stands in the churchyard (5) and, nearby, the graves of famous cricketers (2) recall the halcyon days of the 1770s and 1780s when the village of Hambledon won for itself the title 'The Cradle of Cricket'. The ancient yew is one of the thousands that exist in parish churchyards throughout the country. They are in some cases older than the church itself, and it is quite possible that the yews are vestiges of groves once used for

pagan worship. King Edward I further enlarged the stock of yews growing in parish graveyards by ordering that they be planted by reason of their close growth, which afforded protection for the church against the high winds and storms raised by witches. Twigs and boughs of the tree were used to decorate the church at Easter and, because the yew lives for over a thousand years, the tree was regarded as a symbol of everlasting life, and as such its branches were used to line newly dug graves.

■ The Cambridgeshire church of **Fulbourn** (7) possesses one of the finest priest brasses in the country. It is set in the chancel floor and dates from 1391. The brass shows William de Fulbourne dressed in his cape, with his initials WF on the orphreys and his Coat of Arms on the morse. At **Snarfield** (8) the February snow and unseasonable sun intensify the rich texture of the church masonry. Its simple stone pyramid cap is surmounted by a gilt cockerel weather-vane.

HOLME LACY/APPLETON

As rich in beauty as it is in history, the Herefordshire church of St Cuthbert at **Holme Lacy** (2,3,4 and 5) is set in the verdant meadowland of the Wye Valley. It is of Norman origin with a low roof and six-bayed, 14th century arcade dividing the nave and the south aisle – which are almost of the

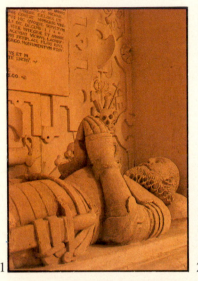

1

2

3

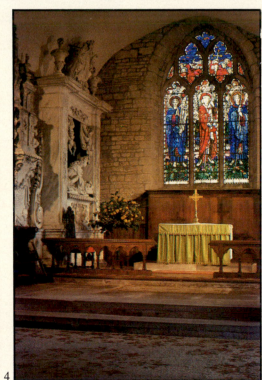

4

5

same width. The late-17th century font is carved, and the church's notable medieval choir stalls have misereres. In the chancel (4) are early murals executed in a pleasing red-ochre pigment (3 and 5), and there are many fine monuments dedicated to members of the Norfolk and Scudamore families. Perhaps the most splendid is to be found mid-way between the

chancel and the south aisle, raised in 1571 to Sir John Scudamore (2), whose alabaster effigy – in full panoply of the tournament – is in striking contrast to the Classical elegance of carved figures (on the opposite side of the altar) representing his 17th century descendants.

■ Devonshire churches have as rich an inheritance of bench-ends

and rood screens as those of any county in England; and the Perpendicular church of St John the Baptist at **Plymtree** (8 and 9) contains magnificent examples of both. Its gilded screen (8) displays all the exuberance of the wood-carver's art in its massive fan vault (9), and all the intricacy of his craft in the cornice's bands of elaborately wrought vine trails –

which stretch from one side of the church to the other in one glorious, unbroken line. The painted panels of the screen's base are especially clear and well-preserved, and represent one of the country's most complete series. Its theme depicts the 'Annunciation'; the 'Salutation'; the 'Journey of the Magi', and some unusual saints – including St Anthony, St Sitha, St

and a simple basket of wayside primroses (10) placed upon the altar makes a touching tribute to Easter's message of peace.

■ 1: The Elizabethan effigy of Sir John Fettiplace, in **Appleton Church**, who died in the year 1593.

■ 7: The tower of **Puttenham Church** in Surrey.

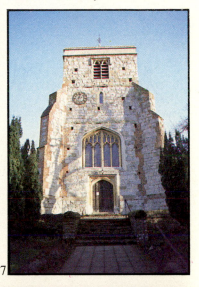

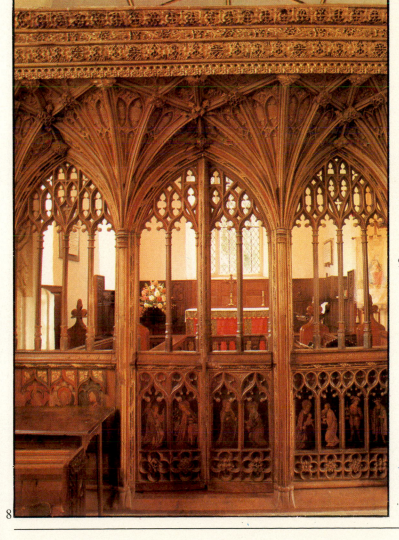

Sidwell, St Agnes and St Edward the Confessor.

Plymtree's wagon-roof, the arcades' carved-foliage capitals (confined solely to this area in the 15th century) and its old square-headed benches, will all be noted as West Country features - as characteristic in their own way of Devon as the fields of red-earth and steeply banked lanes teeming with fern, foxglove and honeysuckle, that form the surrounding countryside. In neighbouring Somerset nature forms a spring-tide carpet of wild flowers (6) in the churchyard of St Peter and St Paul's, **North Curry**,

STOKE-BY-NAYLAND

St Mary the Virgin, **Stoke-by-Nayland** (1,2,3,5,8 and 10) is one of the largest and most stately churches in Suffolk – a county so noted for its sacred buildings that it won the title '*selig*' meaning 'holy' (which in recent times has been corrupted to 'silly' Suffolk). The church stands at the very heart of Constable country, and its tower (8) became one of the artist's favourite subjects. It stands 120ft high, built largely of brick with stone dressing, with four pinnacles that dominate the surrounding countryside. From its stepped battlements the picturesque village with its group of half-timbered

cottages may be seen in the arch of its shadow (3). The nave soars up with splendidly proportioned arcades and there are many interesting memorials and brasses – the earliest and finest of which is to Sir William de Tendring (1) who fought alongside King Henry V at Agincourt, and who is here depicted '*upon the Pavement before the high Aultar*' (2) in full armour, resting his head upon his helm which bears a crest of feathers.

The 15th century font (5 and 10) is octagonal, its panelled sides being carved with the emblems of the Evangelists over a course of cherubs and a shaft of ogee-canopied niches. The base is formed of three raised steps to give the font greater dignity. Indeed, it is from this century and in East Anglia in particular, that the font reaches its highest development – as exemplified at **Surlingham** (4) in Norfolk, whose font is surrounded by lions at the stem, and whose bowl depicts lions alternating with angels holding shields bearing symbols of Christ's

Passion (6) – the spear, the scourge and the goblet of vinegar raised on high.

From the Stoke-by-Nayland font, looking eastwards down the nave, one can see that in this church, as in many others, the alignment of the chancel with the nave inclines towards the north. Guide books like to suggest that such inclined or 'weeping' chancels represent the angle of Our Lord's head upon the cross, but this is pure fantasy. Owing to the skill of medieval builders, it is quite unlikely that the 'fault' was accidental, and it is probable that the church faced the risen sun on

the dedication or patronal festival when it was built, but over the centuries that position would change slightly, and a new or rebuilt chancel would be set out to face the new sunrise position – thus being slightly out of alignment with an earlier nave.

■ As with many East Anglian churches, that of **Old Weston** (9 and 11) in Cambridgeshire exudes an air of calm and serenity, where simplicity is itself a vehicle to beauty. The altars of the chancel (9) and of the south aisle (11) display neither reredos, nor elaboration, but rely merely upon the effects of an eastern light

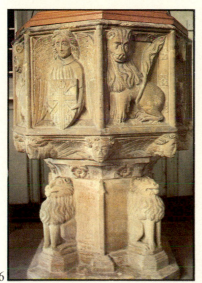

6

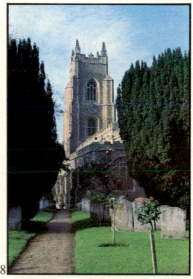

8

9

10

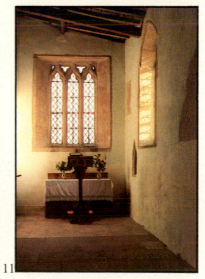

11

flooding through plain, leaded windows.

■ At **Chiddingstone** (7) in Kent, the parish church has a Perpendicular tower and faces a single street lined with a group of peerless Tudor half-timbered houses built when the Wealden iron industry was at its height.

The parish church of **St Mary Redcliffe** in Bristol (1,2,3,4 and 6) is accredited universally as one of the finest examples of Gothic architecture in Europe. The opinion most commonly quoted is that of Queen Elizabeth I who, on her visit to the church in 1574, described it as '*the fairest, goodliest and most famous parish church in England*'. It is distinguished first and foremost by its size and plan, which are almost those of an abbey. St Mary's contains distinguished work from the early-13th to 15th century, the best being that of the late-14th century.

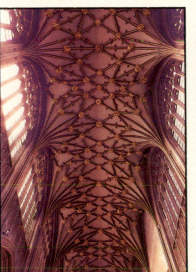

2

3

The munificence of local merchants whose fortunes were amassed by trading fleets based at the nearby harbour (John and Sebastian Cabot, the discoverers of Newfoundland, being notable patrons) contributed to the architectural embellishment of the medieval church. It was during this period that St Mary's achieved its greatest glory, and it is hard to conceive of anything more gracious than the piers of the nave (1) and clerestory – where the absence of capitals gives added delicacy to the pillars by allowing the line from the floor to vault to remain unbroken –

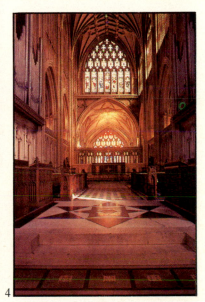

4

or anything more beautiful than the roof, with its lierne vaulting of tufa rubble (2), with which almost the entire church is covered. The bosses of the vault are especially fine – there are more than one thousand two hundred of them, all different, and each one covered in pure gold. In the south transept (3) – which is architecturally interesting for the rare distinction of possessing double aisles – are some of the loveliest roof bosses, whose gilding was added in 1740 when the women of the city donated their gold jewellery to be melted down.

In marked contrast to the tower of St Mary Redcliffe (6) – richly decorated and soaring for 285ft - is the three-storey, pagoda-type tower of the Priory Church of St Laurence, **Blackmore** (5) built of local oak in the 15th century. Only by careful study of these timbers can one fully appreciate the strength and beauty of the tower's construction, and the skill with which medieval craftsmen selected and handled their materials.

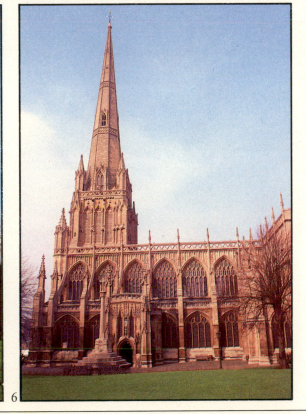

5

6

FOTHERINGHAY

The magnificent tower of **Fotheringhay Church** (1,3 and 4) is an outstanding Northamptonshire landmark, and was a beacon for travellers through the Forest of Rockingham. It rises in stages and the whole building has a profusion of windows. On the corners of the first stage are four small turrets, and crowning them in place of a spire, is an elegant octagonal lantern with two sets of lancet windows in each face, adorned with tracery. Above are eight pinnacles, surmounted by the gilt badge of the House of York – the Falcon enclosed by a Fetterlock.

Of the collegiate church endowed by Edmund Plantagenet, fifth son of King Edward III and founder of the Royal line of York, nothing now remains. What we see today is a truncated church of great beauty erected by his son Edmund, Duke of York, who was slain at Agincourt in 1415 and whose monument now resides in the sanctuary. The lofty nave has flying buttresses (3), and the large interior has numerous windows

1

2

3

which allow light to flood in. Fotheringhay's austerity is relieved by the fan vault under the tower; by a fine pulpit (a gift of the Yorkist sovereign, Edward IV); and by an 18th century reredos (4).

■ Like Fotheringhay, St Mary Magdalene's at **Cobham** (5,6,7 and 8) was also a collegiate church in the Middle Ages. Early in the 13th century the de Cobhams moved to Kent and the family began to provide money for the rebuilding of the old village church. Of their work the splendid chancel of 1220 survives. They seem to have regarded it as their own chapel and mausoleum, and made it

4

exceptionally large for a parish church. The years 1360-70 were a time of intense building – at the expense of Sir John de Cobham whose fine brass memorial records: '*From earth was made and formed and in earth and to earth is returned the former John of Cobham Founder of this place*'. The 'Founder' rebuilt the present nave – which is even now smaller than the chancel – and raised a college to house priests to say daily masses for his forbears. His last great work was to add the tower (6) and lengthen the two aisles he had earlier built, to clasp it.

In the mid-16th century the

COBHAM

5

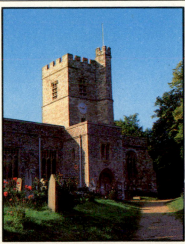

6

7

chancel was dominated – to the detriment of its liturgical function – by a large and extremely elaborate altar-tomb (8) which effectively blocks the view of the high altar from the nave. This is the tomb of George Brooke, Lord Cobham, who died in 1558, and his wife Anne Bray. Their figures are life-size, and the tomb's highly tinctured heraldry enriches the pale honey-coloured surface of the alabaster. Lord Cobham's head rests on his tilting-helm, with its Saracen's head crest (the original of which hangs on the wall above him) and his feet on a heraldic goat. The work is executed with

great exuberance and illustrates both the virtuosity of the sculptor and the arrogance of the family that commissioned such a colossus.

On the wide chancel floor below the altar-tomb is a double rank of brasses – nineteen in all – which stretches from wall to wall. Their stylised forms depict members of the Cobham and Brooke families (5 and 7) and span the years from 1320 until 1529. They represent the finest collection of brasses to be found anywhere in the world. It is estimated that as many as 150,000 brasses were laid in English medieval churches, but of these only 4,000 still survive. However, the number is still greater than that which remains in the whole of the rest of Europe. The effigies were cut out of a sheet of latten and inlaid into tombslabs. The method of treating figures as silhouettes is peculiarly English. Continental brasses, and those executed in this country by foreign artists, are engraved on a rectangular plate.

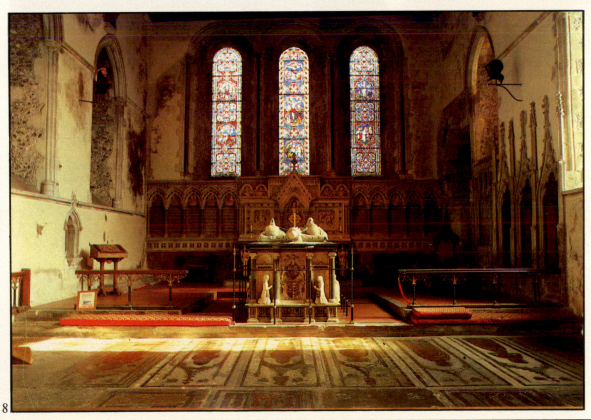

8

SELWORTHY/ASHTON

The Church of All Saints, **Selworthy** (6 and 9) is superbly sited on a densely wooded hillside where its churchyard (9) affords a famous view over the thatched roofs of the village, and across the Vale of Porlock to the distant heather peaks of the Dunkery Beacon – the highest point on Exmoor. The 14th century interior (with Tudor additions) of Selworthy church possesses, in its south aisle, what Dr Eeles of the Central Council for the Care of Churches has described as '*one of the greatest treasures of English architecture*'. Its windows and arcade, its roof and proportions, are all of inimitable grace and beauty. The delicacy of the carving and the refinement of the window tracery surpass everything else in West Somerset. Indeed, the design and execution of the south arcade – all carried out in Dundry stone – are unequalled for delicacy even in the Perpendicular stonework of East Anglia. The roof of the aisle is

representing prophets and saints. Each has his or her own emblem – St Appollonia, whose help was invoked for toothache, holds a pair of pincers – the costumes are of the 15th century and the style suggests a Flemish influence (7).

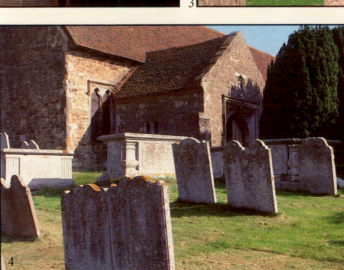

among the finest roofs in England and has an angel holding a shield at every brace (6).

■ Another singularly attractive church is that of St John the Baptist, at **Ashton** (7 and 10) which lies on the western slopes of Haldon, where they cascade down to the Teign valley. Entirely rebuilt and refurnished between 1400 and 1485, Ashton is a typical Devonshire church at its best. White Beer stone arcades and plastered walls set off the colouring of the lavishly carved parclose screen (11) and rood screen – with its cornice of birds pecking at bunches of grapes. Within their panels are a host of painted figures

■ St Peter and St Paul's, **Seal** (2,3,4,5 and 8) possesses what has come to be regarded as a traditional 'Kentish Tower' (3). These are either Perpendicular or early Tudor, and are invariably constructed of Kentish ragstone with a prominent octagonal stair turret at one corner projecting above the tower. There are no pinnacles and the belfry windows are usually square-headed. Seal Church crowns a slight knoll (8) and possesses an interior that is far more spacious than the outside of the building would indicate. This is effected by the addition of aisles positioned on either side of the

nave (2) – the south aisle is of the 13th century, whilst that of the north was raised in Victoria's reign. In the Lady chapel there is fine heraldic glass of 1858 displaying the arms and devices of the Marquis of Camden (5), and by the south porch are impressive examples of table-tombs (4) – built to mimic an altar – raised above the ground so as not to become overgrown with nettles.

■ The finest work of the sculptor Nollekins is to be found on a tomb in the sanctuary of St Mary's, **Tittleshall** (1) in Norfolk. The tomb depicts the deceased with an angel hovering attentively over her. Below, a cherub holds up a bleeding heart – an allusion to the sentiments of the bereaved. The white marble monument was erected in 1805 in memory of Jane, the first wife of Thomas William Coke – the famous 'Coke of Holkham' whose farming innovations brought about England's agrarian revolution.

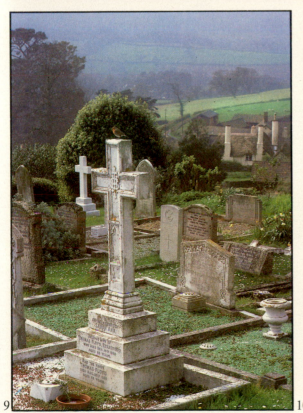

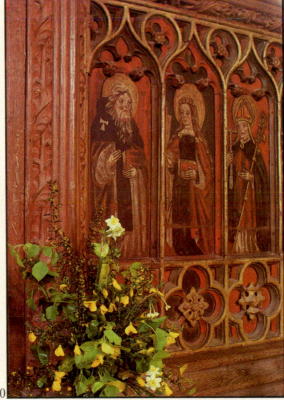

BRADFORD-ON-AVON/HALES

The tiny church of St Laurence, **Bradford-on-Avon** (1,3,5 and 6) is one of the very few Anglo-Saxon churches to survive intact – a unique and superb example from pre-Conquest England. It is thought that the church was built by St Aldhelm – the first Bishop of Sherbourne, and a close relative of King Ine of Wessex – who lived in the late 7th century. The plan and 9ft 8ins high by 3ft 6ins wide; the tapering of doorways and arches (a Saxon feature); the three original windows which are splayed on both sides, and the figures of ministering angels hovering with outstretched hands veiled by napkins – no doubt originally on either side of a figure of Our Lord upon the Cross.

Above the tiny altar stand the

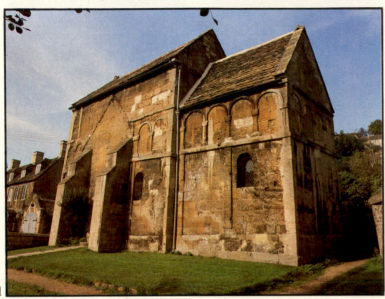

1

much of the fabric of St Laurence's dates from this early period, but the external decoration is of the late 10th century when the blind arcading of the outside walls (1) was formed by cutting into the stonework of the existing church. This embellishment was probably carried out at the behest of King Ethelred, who chose to hide the relics of his half-brother, St Edward the Martyr (the King murdered at his stepmother's instigation at Corfe Castle in 978) within the church '*that therein might be found a safe refuge – impenetrable confugium* (referring to the dense woods then surrounding Bradford) – '*against the insults of the Danes*'.

After the coming of the Normans, the Saxon church was put to secular use and its true purpose was forgotten. Old deeds reveal the name '*Skull House*' and it is likely that it was used as a charnel house during the Middle Ages, and to this fact St Laurence's owes its preservation in its original state. Rediscovered by chance a century ago, it now stands revealed as one of the oldest and smallest – the height of the nave (6) is greater than its length – churches in the land.

Internally the chief features are the dimensions of the chancel arch,

2

3

vertically. The dendrological method of determining age has traced the construction of these wooden walls to the year 845. At this time the whole building – both chancel and nave – was of timber, and its affirmed antiquity makes St Andrew's the oldest surviving wooden church in the world. The dormer windows, the porch and the brick-built chancel were all added during the reign of the Tudors, as was the wooden tower with its small, shingled spire.

remains of a Saxon cross (5) – one of seven set up by order of Ecquin, Bishop of Worcester, to denote the resting place of St Aldhelm's bier when it was carried from Doulting, where he had died, to his shrine at Malmesbury.

■ Another of England's architectural treasures, the Church of St Andrew at **Greensted-juxta-Ongar** (7) in Essex, also dates from the Saxon era; where the walls of the nave consist of massive oak trunks cleft in half and set

■ The rounded 'apse' – or chancel based on the old basilica plan – is a rare feature which gives a firm indication that a church is of early Norman foundation. One such example is St Margaret's, **Hales** (4) whose stone-built tower and thatched roof are charmingly set among the verdant water-meads of Norfolk.

■ 2. The parish church of **Moonstoke** in Hampshire.

WALSOKEN/BADINGHAM

The large and beautiful parish church of All Saints, **Walsoken** (2,3,4,5) is one of the 'Marshland group', situated on the edge of the Cambridgeshire fen. Of late Norman and Early English design, it has much ancient decoration – foremost among which is its Romanesque nave arcade (5) with alternate round and octagonal columns with scalloped capitals and chevron mouldings on the round arches. The chancel arch is Transitional Norman (the arch has become pointed) and there is some interesting blind arcading on the tower (4).

As so often in East Anglia, the clerestory was added in the 15th century to throw additional light into the main body of the church and to illuminate the great rood. The elaborate roof is of this period as are the carved 'poppy-heads' of the stalls – a fine example depicts a falconer and his hawk (3). The font is elevated and dominates the western nave – being a well known example of the 'Seven Sacrament' type – gracefully incised with

1

2

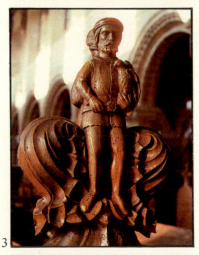

3

panels representing Baptism, Confirmation, the Eucharist, Penance, Ordination, Matrimony and Extreme Unction.

■ A font with the same Seven Sacrament theme is the prime treasure of the church of St John the Baptist at **Badingham** (1) in Suffolk, where a horned and winged fiend expelled by confession awaits the penitent in the north-west panel of the font. Badingham's flint tower with stone quoins is very old and the lower stages probably date from Norman times – as witness the narrow lancets with the voussoir at the top carved out of a single stone.

4

WORTH/FLAMBOROUGH

Perhaps the most interesting cruciform church to survive from Saxon England, St Nicholas at **Worth** (2,4,5 and 7) in West Sussex, dates from the late 10th century. It has retained its main features, notably the magnificent chancel arch (5) and two transeptal arches. The former, at 22ft high by 14ft wide, is the largest Saxon arch in the country. Its head is a semi-circle of plain stones with an archivolt built of smaller stones

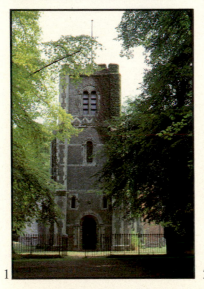

1

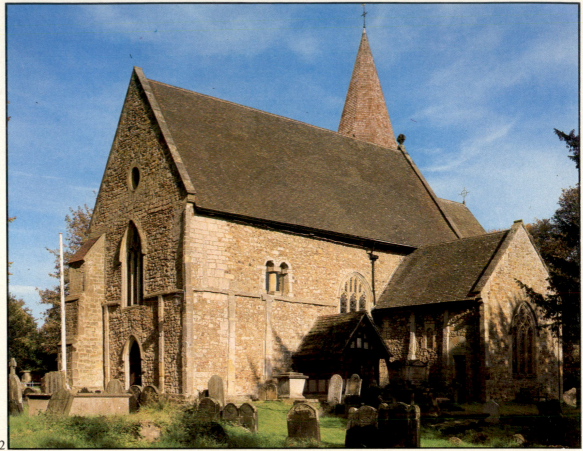

2

3

projecting from the arch below. These rest on large capitals each with a square, grooved abacus and a rounded lower member over a flat cushion. The 15ft high arches of the transepts are equally massive and retain a similar rugged dignity. The church's ground-plan remains unaltered (save for the addition of the tower in 1871) and the nave contains three remarkable examples of Saxon window-lights, separated by a stone baluster. They

are relatively small and are set high up in the wall above the external stone string-course that surrounds the building: two are in the north wall and one in the south (2). Below the string-course on the outside walls can be seen a series of vertical pilaster-strips which are particularly noticeable on the apse (7) – they are a feature of late-Saxon architecture and divide the walls into distinct bays of masonry. Of a later age, Worth's elaborately

4

carved pulpit (4) bears a Low German inscription and the date Anno 1577. It has projecting columns with composite capitals, carved pedestals below and entablature above: between the columns are arched panels with figures of Christ and the Evangelists.

■ Where the chalk cliffs of Yorkshire's wold plunge into the sea, stands the sentinel-like village church of St Oswald's **Flamborough** (3). The rich interior is noted for its early-16th century rood screen and rare rood loft (3) which retains

traces of its original colouring. The rood loft is among the finest in the country, and has a double cornice with canopies of exceptionally elaborate tabernacle work, grape-vine trails above, and an ornamental rose branch weaves between rows of brattishing. Indeed, if one imagines the effect that the enrichment of gold and colour must have had upon the work, one can visualise a little of the magnificence of the pre-Reformation church.

St Oswald's also contains some curious 'finds' – notably a pair of

white paper gloves which custom decreed were worn at maidens' funerals and then hung within the church; a cartouche to 'Wild' Walter Strickland whose pardon, granted by King Charles II, is framed in the nave; and a monument to Sir Marmaduke Constable, who died in 1520, which shows him with a bared heart – a reference to the gruesome story that his heart was eaten by a toad that he had swallowed.

■ The leaf-embowered church of St Peter, at **Hurstbourne Tarrant** (1 and 6) in Hampshire lies in the valley of the Bourne Stream. It has two faded murals – the larger one showing three kings hunting in a forest where they encounter three skeletons.

■ The brass lectern is used to hold the Bible from which the lessons are read. That of Christ Church, **Guildford** (8) is fashioned in the popular form of an eagle – symbolising the Gospel carried on wings to the four corners of the earth.

ALTARNUN

After the bare greyness of Bodmin Moor, the appearance of **Altarnun Church** (1,2,3,4,5,6 and 8), sheltered by hills and tall trees, presents a wonderfully soft and refreshing sight. It stands amid the simple, yet well-cared-for cottages of the village (2), by an old pack-horse bridge spanning a fast-flowing river. This is the supposed *Penpota* of the Doomsday Survey – granted to Robert, Earl of Mortain and Cornwall, by his uterine brother King William the Conqueror – but the church's ancient title, meaning the '*altar of St Nonna*', survives. In this respect it follows the traditional Cornish

1

2

also many miles of rolling hills, green valleys and scattered tors. The masonry is granite moorstone and the capitals and bosses are each carved from one large slab. The pinnacled tower – which is one of the loftiest in the county – took over a generation to raise, and in the second half of the century the nave and side-aisles were built and crowned by their admirably carved wagon-roofs (5).

The church's greatest treasures, however, are the seventy-nine carved bench-ends which date from the period 1510-30. They follow the West Country's traditional style of square heads,

3

practice of naming a parish after the old Celtic saints who brought Christianity to the West Country fourteen hundred years ago. Altarnun is thus the church where St Nonna's altar was preserved. She was the mother of St David, and came here from Wales in the 6th century.

The Cornish cross at the entrance to the churchyard may date from the days of St Nonna, but of the original building nothing now remains. Nearly six hundred years after the foundation the Normans built a church here – of which only the piscina bowl and the font survive. The latter, however, is one of the glories of Altarnun (6) – possessing a Romanesque capital, roundels on the bowl and large, bearded, staring faces at each corner of the font.

In the 15th century the building of the present church commenced, and was carried out upon a suitably grand scale – as befits England's largest parish (15,018 acres). The district embraces Dozmary Pool – the resting place of Excalibur, and

4

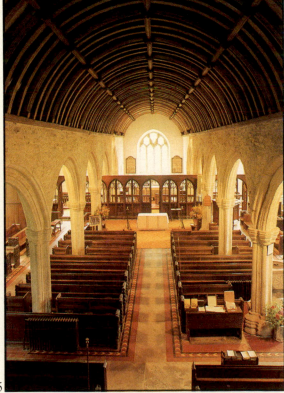

5

6

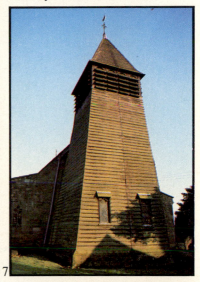

7

back to the Tudors, and was probably old even then – for which Altarnun is famous. The priest always celebrates the Holy Eucharist from the east side of the high altar, thus facing the people. This practice was universal in the early days of Christianity, but only the Pope and the Vicar of Altarnun have carried on this unbroken tradition to the present day.

■ Noted primarily for its 15th century wooden tower and

8

9

and are all the work of one man. He was Robert Daye, as will be noted from the inscription on the bench-end next to the font (4), and they reflect his interpretation of religious subjects – the symbols of the Passion (8) – parish worthies; Renaissance design; common sights, including a piper, a sword dancer, a jester and a fiddler, and strange mermen (1 and 3).

There is a curious custom within the parish – that certainly dates

pyramid cap (7), the church of St Mary **Raskelf** in North Yorkshire is largely a 19th century rebuilding around the original tower.

■ **Lillingstone Lovell** (9) in Buckinghamshire is one of the least altered small churches in the country. The Norman tower with its saddle-back roof dates from 1210, whilst the remainder of the building was raised during the Decorated period at the behest of the le Barbur family.

HEREFORD CATHEDRAL/BATH

Hereford Cathedral (2,3,4 and 5) owes its foundation to King Offa of Mercia who, in AD 792, was responsible for the murder of St Ethelbert. In expiation he built a costly shrine to receive the body of the martyred East Anglian King. The present cathedral is substantially of Norman date, and to this style belong the columns, arches and triforium of the choir, the great arches under the tower, the columns and arches of the nave, and the font (2) of about 1140 – sculpted from a single block of sandstone with figures of the Apostles occupying each of its twelve niches. Throughout the Middle Ages extensions and partial reconstructions were carried out in the styles fashionable at the time: thus, simply by looking up (5) it is possible to see three great innovations of medieval architecture uniquely positioned one above another: the rounded Norman arch, the Early English pointed arch, and finally, the glorious triumph of the Perpendicular fan vaulting.

The Lady chapel (4), built between 1217 and 1225, has a series of five narrow lancets (unusually elaborate for the period, with thick clustered shafts in the window embrasures) which lend

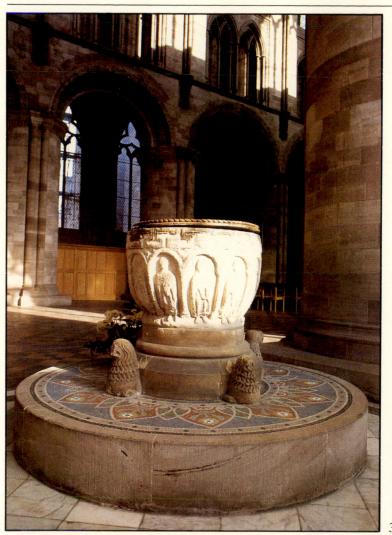

2

3

special dignity to the chapel. Among their glass is a depiction of Christ carrying a crucifix of 'green' wood to Calvary – a touching use of medieval symbolism to illustrate the everlasting power of the cross. In the mid-13th century Hereford was brought to the forefront of fashion by the Savoyard Bishop, Peter Acquablanca who, by building a northern transept, completed the cruciform shape of the present cathedral. His architectural style is perhaps the most lavish – being the most extreme example of that phase of the Decorated style known as 'Geometric'.

■ Raised in 1499, and a masterpiece of Perpendicular architecture, **Bath Abbey** (1) occupies the site of the Saxon abbey in which Edgar was crowned King of the English in 937. Transformed into a vast minster by the Normans, it is now renowned for its huge and elaborate windows and its superlative 16th century fan vaulting (1) designed by William Vertue.

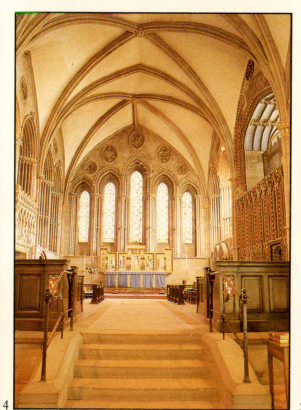

4

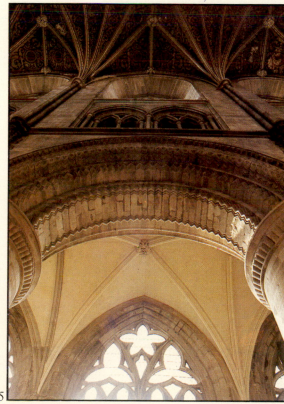

5

IVYCHURCH/CAVENDISH

The large, late-Decorated church of St George at **Ivychurch** (1 and 3) is one of seven Kentish churches dedicated to England's patron saint. Such dedications became popular after the founding of the Order of the Garter by King Edward III – Ivychurch was rebuilt during his reign, in the 1360s. Its plan is unusual, with three parallel aisles of equal length running uniformly from the east wall to the west wall (1) without structural division – the immediate impression is of spaciousness, enhanced by an absence of pews. Indeed, the church follows the ancient precedent whereby the

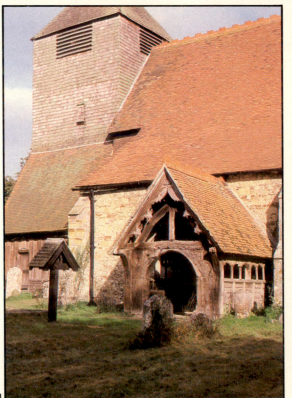

only seating was a line of stone slabs on the south wall, set aside for the aged and infirm – the weakest, quite literally, going to the wall. At the east end of the south aisle is the medieval altar platform (3) of St Katherine, below which is a large vault used in the 18th century for stowing contraband.

■ Also in Kent, **High Halden** church possesses a fine medieval oak porch (4). Benches on the east and west walls recall a time when it served as the village's first school. Here also the wedding service commenced; and penance too was served, with the sinner forced to stand in a white sheet in full view of his neighbours. Such was the importance of church porches that legal documents were drawn up, and Coroner's inquests held, beneath their roofs.

■ The 14th century tower of St Mary's, **Cavendish** (2 and 5) in Suffolk rises above a traditional English scene of thatched cottages encircling a village green. The church itself – with its lofty clerestory panelled in flint

TEWKESBURY ABBEY/ABBOTS ANN

6

Beauchamps. Its greatest glory, however, is its Romanesque nave, tower and Great West Window arch – all Norman work of the highest calibre and comparable to the best found anywhere in Southern England. The latter, the arch of the West Front (7), is a recessed sixfold arch, 65ft in height and the largest of its kind in the Kingdom. The tower (6) is equally impressive, being 132ft tall and 46ft square: the pinnacles were added later and are regrettable, yet even these cannot detract from its majesty. The view from the tower battlements is wide and far-reaching, stretching away to the Severn Valley, the Malvern Hills and the distant vision of the misty-blue mountains of Wales.

■ **Abbots Ann** (8) in Hampshire is the only church to continue the medieval custom of awarding Maiden's Garlands. The ceremony connected with the custom takes place at the funeral of an unmarried person of good character who was born, baptised and died within the parish. The 'crown' is made of hazelwood and is ornamented with roses. It resembles a bishop's mitre, and attached are five parchment

7

8

flushwork – contains an extremely elaborate Renaissance altar-piece (5) which probably originated in 16th century Flanders. There is a fine medieval brass eagle lectern, and a Tudor wooden one.

■ Among the largest abbey churches to have survived the Dissolution, **Tewkesbury Abbey** (6 and 7) has been used as a parish church ever since. It possesses some of the finest medieval tombs in England – notably those of the De Clares, the Despencers and the

gauntlets which represent a challenge to anyone who may wish to dispute the worthiness of the deceased person. At the funeral the crown is suspended from a rod and carried in procession by two young girls dressed in white. After burial, the garland is hung from a bracket (8) together with a small scutcheon bearing details of name and date. Here it remains until it decays and falls with age; the earliest remaining crown is dated 1740, and the latest, 1959.

BOSBURY/SELSEY/BROOK

Sited in one of the country's most important hop-growing regions, the grand, late-Norman red stone church at **Bosbury** (2 and 4) contains two splendid Elizabethan tombs. Both are dedicated to members of the Harford family – that on the south wall of the chancel is to John Harford (and is signed by the sculptor: '*John Guldo made this tomb with his own hands 1573*') and that on the facing wall is dedicated to Richard Harford, who died in 1578. The latter is flamboyant and over-decorated, but interestingly displays the carving of a demonic composite of man and tree; the

Bosbury was erected between the years 1186 and 1200, during the bishopric of William de Vere, who also rebuilt the Bishop's Palace at Hereford. The church is comprised of nave and chancel, and is in the transitional style of architecture between Norman and Early English. The north and south aisles were added the following century. There is a massive, unbuttressed, separate tower (2) – one of seven in the marcher county of Hereford – divided into three stages and built forty or fifty years after the main body of the church. Now used to house bells, the rugged tower was originally a

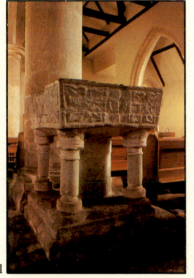

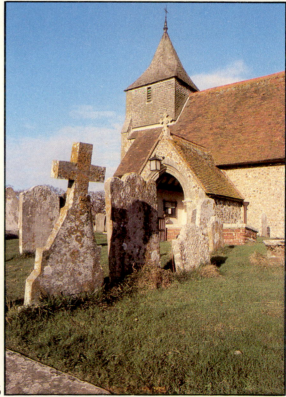

pagan 'Green Man' (4), or 'Jack-in-the-Green'. His presence in the chancel indicates that even after a thousand years of Christianity the old Celtic gods of fertility – who rekindled life in the earth each spring – had not altogether been banished from the minds of country folk.

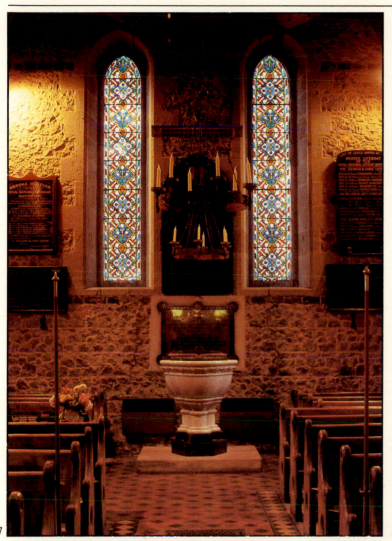

7

8

9

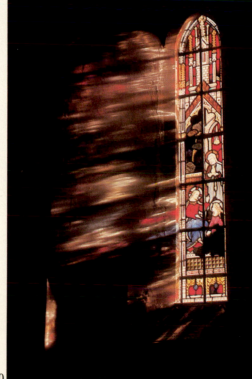

10

refuge and fortification against the incursions of marauding Welsh in their constant forays across the border.

■ An unusual feature in the history of St Peter's **Selsey** (6) is that the original 12th century parish church, built at Pagham Harbour, was dismantled in 1864 and the stones transported on farm trucks to the present site. St Peter's was re-erected within eighteen months and re-consecrated on April 12th, 1866. Two years before the transportation of Selsey Church, a disastrous fire had gutted St Mary the Virgin, **Brook** (7) on the Isle of Wight, and only

by public subscription was the architect, Mr W. Mullins, able to re-glorify the interior in its present mid-Victorian style. The stone rubble from which the walls are built is left unplastered and is brought roughly into course at intervals by lines of local ironstone. The western end of the nave (7), with its trefoil font of white Sicilian marble and twin lancet windows admirably demonstrates the harmony of the refashioned masonry.

■ Grace and composure are also apparent in the 18th century tower of St Nicholas' Church, **Moreton** (3) in Dorset. It stands beside the

River Frome, to the south of the conifer forests and Thomas Hardy's Egdon Heath. Built in 1778, Moreton is an unusual and cheerful little church, full of light and air, with pale-blue and white apsidal chancel, and an aisle and porch added in the 'revival' style of the mid 19th century. From the churchyard (wherein lies the grave of Lawrence of Arabia) there is a fine view across parkland to the Georgian mansion of the Framptons, who built St Nicholas'.

■ The parish church of St Mary, **Sidlesham** (1,5,9 and 10) possesses a fine font (1) typical of those of early Sussex design. Its weather-beaten appearance suggests that it was removed from the church and buried in the graveyard during the Commonwealth. At the Restoration of the Monarchy it was replaced in its rightful position within the nave. The imposing west tower (5) has a battlemented parapet – as has **Timworth Church** (8) in Suffolk – and an octagonal stair turret at the south eastern angle of the tower.

WINCHELSEA

Dedicated to the memory of St Thomas the Martyr, **Winchelsea Church** (1,2,4,5,6,7 and 8) in East Sussex has been hallowed by the prayers and worship of untold thousands since 1288 when its conception and building was inspired by King Edward I. The port of Old Winchelsea – situated on a low-lying island about three miles south-east of the present church – was destroyed by a phenomenal high tide which *'flooded twice without ebbing with a horrible roaring and a glint as of fire on the waves'*. The inhabitants were forced to raise a new town upon the plateau known as Iham, above

the River Brede marshes. Each received from the king a plot of land similar to that lost to the sea; but the 2 acres that crowned Iham Hill were reserved for the building of a great church planned to surpass in magnificence and beauty every other place of worship in the neighbourhood – in fact, a foundation worthy of Winchelsea's importance as an eminent member of the Cinque Ports.

The building consisted of a Chancel and choir with two side chapels, a central tower, transepts and a great nave. However, Edward's grandiose plan was blighted when the new walled

1

3

4

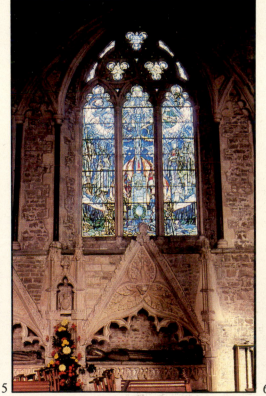

5

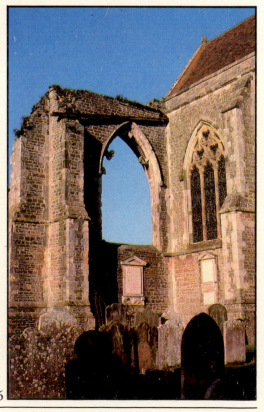

6

Although much was destroyed, very great beauty still remains. Foremost are the many examples of rare and beautiful stonework, executed during the Decorated period under royal patronage. There is a richly canopied sedilia and piscina with crocketted gables, and nearby, in the south aisle, two canopied, early 14th century tombs with recumbent effigies of Gervase Alard (7) – England's first admiral – and Stephen Alard (4), Admiral of the Western Fleet. The hands are raised and enclose a heart, whilst the main gables of the recessed canopies spring from the sculptured heads of their patrons – King Edward I and his son, Edward II (2). In the north aisle (5) – which has highly coloured and heavily leaded glass by Strachen – are three more effigies carved from solid blocks of black marble. The figures (8) lie beneath three sepulchred canopies with fine S-shaped, feathered tracery heads. So beautifully are these effigies sculpted that one can not only feel the chain links of the Knights

town of Winchelsea was mercilessly attacked and taken by the French in 1337 – the first of four such assaults upon the town and church. Women and children were at mass, and others had fled to the church for shelter, yet the soldiers 'killed all that withstood them without regard to age, sex, degree or order'. By the time of the last raid (that of 1380 by the Castilian fleet) all that remained were the chancel and the side aisle. These form the present church; and the ruins of the transepts (6) may still be seen on either side of the north porch.

Templars' armour but realise that it is shaped to the muscles beneath in both leg and arm. A more light-hearted carving in St Nicholas' chapel depicts a hunchback (1) believed originally to have upheld a statue of the saint.

■ Dating from the 12th century, the church of St Giles at **Bredon** (9) in Worcestershire has a central tower with a 160ft spire immortalised in the verse of Housman and Masefield. Inside there is a curious dragon's head (3) of Norman design on the nave arcade.

WELLS CATHEDRAL

The earliest completely Gothic cathedral in Europe is also one of England's most beautiful. The graceful West Country cathedral of **Wells** (1-13) was begun in 1176, a few years after William of Sens had introduced the new style of architecture at Canterbury. Bishop Reginald de Bohun was greatly influenced by the design and caused the present building at Wells to be raised on a similarly grand scale. His idea that '*the honour due to God should not be tarnished by the squalor of His house*' could well be taken as the

sense of harmony (8) is dashed, however, the moment one passes into the nave, by the sudden and unexpected drama of the great inverted 'strainer arch' (3) standing directly ahead and dominating all. It has been likened to a gaping 'hell-mouth' with ascending horns and huge roundels on either side of the intersection looking like glowering eyes. The monumental 'sinew in stone' is thrice repeated – at the nave and at the entry to each of the transepts. It was not planned, but improvised to solve the crisis of the dangerous westerly

1

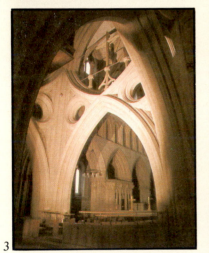

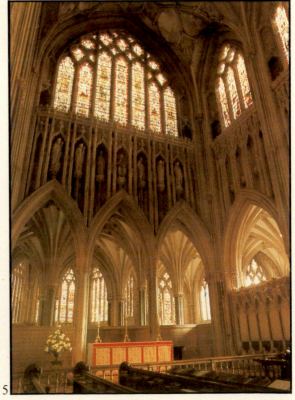

dictum of medieval architecture, and here resulted in the construction of a cathedral filled with air, light and space, possessing the typical ribbed vaults and pointed arches that represent the emergence of a purely English style of Gothic Art. Wells Cathedral seems to hold the spirit of the Middle Ages forever in its mellow stonework. The outward

3

4

5

WELLS CATHEDRAL

tilting and cracking of the central tower in 1340.

By the year 1239 the choir and transepts were finished and the nave was suitably advanced for the cathedral to be consecrated. Much of the work was undertaken by Adam Lock, whose influence is everywhere apparent. His piers are at once massive yet delicate – consisting of twenty-four shafts that conceal rather than display the line of upward thrust – and gently lead the eye along the vertical of the nave (6) towards the upper church. The progression is

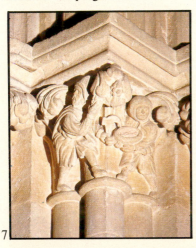

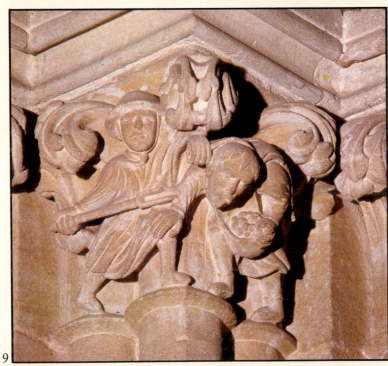

accompanied at every level by a host of carved detail which fills both capital and corbel with some of England's finest sculpture. They not only exemplify marvellous skill, but capture for eternity the humour of the age. Much of the carving depicts scenes from everyday life – two beggars steal apples from an orchard (7) and are apprehended by an angry farmer (9); men are shown toiling in vineyards; a fox makes off with a goose, and a cobbler perpetually mends shoes whilst a poor woman who cannot afford shoes carefully pulls a thorn from her bare foot.

The chapter house was raised during the episcopacy of William de Marchia in 1300, and completed six years later. It is uniquely elevated upon an undercroft (which served as a treasury) and is approached by a marvellous stairway of broad flags which curve up towards a double-arched doorway of miraculous delicacy. The flight (4) – which has been compared to a flowing river – has been worn down through the ages by the tread of countless generations of the faithful. Once inside the Chapter House, a superb marble central pier (10) fans out

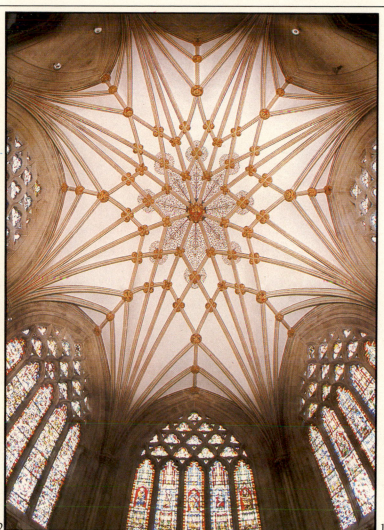

11

13

through the choir towards the Great East Window – the 'Golden Window', ablaze with the translucent colouring of greens, yellows, and ochre – the comparative simplicity of the Early English nave gives way to the lightness and richness of the high altar which is extremely florid and beautiful, having stone tracery which climbs over every available inch of wall to tangle its tendrils in the fantasy of the roof's net vaulting.

■ At **Broad Hinton** (15) in Wiltshire there is a fine example of a late-Elizabethan tomb showing Sir Thomas Wroughton – at one

14

15

into thirty-two ribs. It is the apotheosis of the tierceron vault, which never fails to stir a sense of the marvellous: indeed, it is perhaps the most beautiful of all those polygonal chapter house interiors which are unique to English cathedral architecture.

The Lady chapel (2) – with its incomparable vault (12) and 14th century stained glass (11 and 13) – and the central tower (1: seen to best advantage from the gardens of the Bishop's Palace) were both designed by Thomas Witney during the period 1310-22. The

former is joined to the choir by a rectochoir built by local mason William Joyce; his main work however, was the reconstruction of the cathedral's eastern end, providing the beautiful vista through the open arches to the high altar (5). As one passes

time Sheriff of the County – and his wife Anne. Their heavily stylised effigies kneel in the attitude of prayer, whilst below their feet the diminutive figures of their four sons and four daughters likewise kneel – in humble submission to their parents (14).

SOUTH HARDING/SHERBORNE ST JOHNS

The church of St Mary and St Gabriel, at **South Harting** (1,2 and 5) lies at the foot of the South Downs in West Sussex – the green of its broached copper spire and the red flash of its roof tiles making a colourful splash against the distant swell of turquoise hills. This impressive cruciform church was rebuilt and enlarged at the end of the 13th century, and the plain arcading, sans capitals, of the Early English nave (2) and the font of Purbeck marble, originate from this time. The Chancel (5) is lit by a triplet of lancet windows, and the elaborate Elizabethan tie-roof (raised after a fire in 1576) is an unusual feature for Sussex.

■ In the neighbouring county of Hampshire the church of St Andrew, **Sherborne St John** (3,4 and 6 – 10) was built mainly during the Perpendicular period, yet it reveals shades of an earlier history in the west and south walls of the nave, in the Norman font and in the south door – all of which date from 1150. The tower (6) was built to the level of the nave roof a

1

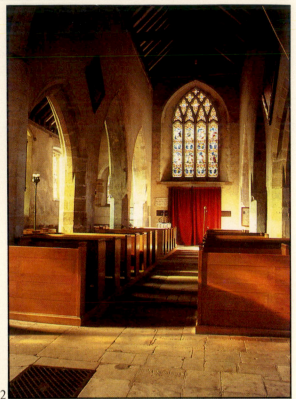

2

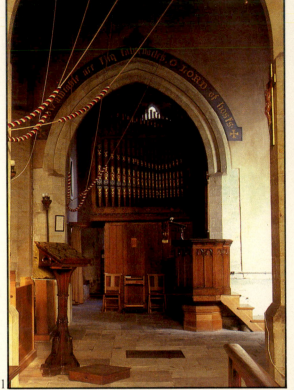

3

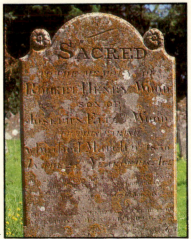

4

century later, and raised to its present height in 1834 to accomodate bells.

There are some interesting brasses in the Brocas chapel – the family mausoleum of the influential owners of Beaurepaire Park. The earliest brass, of about 1360, depicts Raulin Brocas and Margaret his sister. Other such engravings commemorate John Brocas and his two wives, and William Brocas (7) who died in 1506. Perhaps the most interesting of all the family brasses is of Bernard Brocas depicted as a skeleton wrapped in a shroud – a popular subject between the years

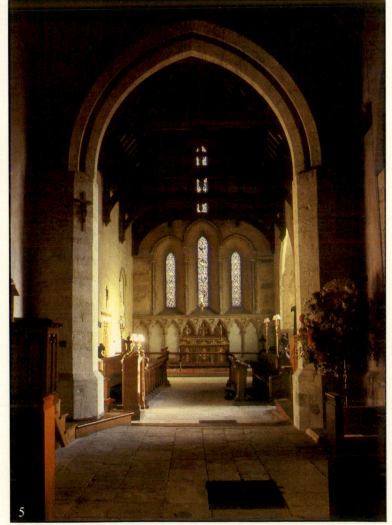

5

SHERBORNE ST JOHN

1480 and 1510 as a reminder of the mortality of earthly vanities. However, the most impressive memorial is undoubtedly the Renaissance altar-tomb (9) positioned between the chapel and the chancel (8). The subject is Ralph Pexall and his wife Edith Brocas from whom he inherited the Beaurepaire estate.

The south porch (10) is a fine example of Tudor brickwork – and is a contemporary of the Pexall tomb, c1535 – and the small relief sculpture above the door is of the donor and his wife: the inscription reads, '*of your cherete pray for the soal of James Spyre departed in the*

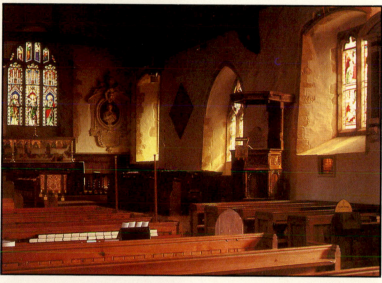

yere of our lord A. MDXXXI, on his soal Jesu have mursi.

The churchyard at Sherborne St John is full of delights, and displays all the characteristics that one would expect from an ancient foundation. The oldest graves are to be found south of the church – people avoided the shadow of the church falling across their graves, and a similar fear of darkness led to the association between the north side of the graveyard and the Devil. Thus it is that the sheer volume of internment has raised the ground level above that of the nearby path and porch door sill. Here also are found the oldest gravestones – assailed by weather and encrusted with lichen and moss (3 and 4) – they date, for the most part, from the 18th century and are charmingly carved with the emblems of mortality: the skull, the hour glass, the scythe and the closed-book; or with symbols of eternity: the yew branch, the torch and the clarion of salvation.

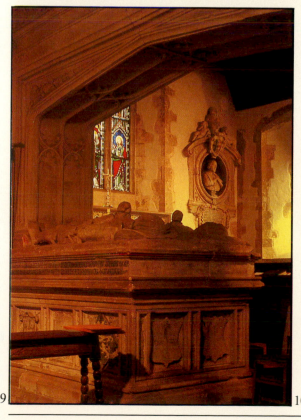

DEANE/KERSEY

Overlooking one of the most picturesque of all Suffolk villages, the Church of St Mary at **Kersey** (2,3,6 and 8) dominates a scene of rare medieval charm and beauty. The village street, which runs up opposing slopes of a valley and crosses a water-splash of the River Brett at the bottom, is crowned on the south by its imposing church, and on the north by the ruins of Kersey Priory. St Mary's suffered terribly after the Reformation at the hands of iconoclasts who smashed and mutilated, with an insane fury, all that the world deemed beautiful. In spite of this wanton destruction and sacrilege the church still retains, in a unique way, an atmosphere of peace – as if the fury which had been hurled upon it could not destroy its ancient calm. There are still treasures to be found – in the medieval screen of the north aisle, in the south porch roof and in the lectern with its carved eagle – all of which are over five hundred years old. Greater even than these is the unforgettable loveliness of the vista

which the 14th century church, with its flint tower of 1481 (6), presents to the eye – whether it be viewed from the churchyard (8), or from the surrounding countryside in the mellow half-light of a Suffolk evening (2).

■ Unlike the church at Kersey, which had known and benefited from the medieval prosperity that cloth-weaving could bring, the hamlet of Deane was never large, and its church seldom boasted more than eighty members in its congregation. However, the magnificence of their church belies the size and wealth of the village it served. All Saints, **Deane** (1,4,5

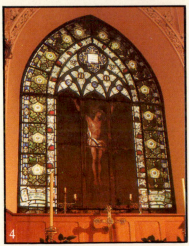

and 7) is described as being the best example of 19th century Gothic Revival in the county of Hampshire. Its most notable features are the coade stone chancel arch (5) and screen (1), and the painted crucifix (4) mounted in the east window, surrounded by stained glass. All Saints' was rebuilt on the site of a medieval church in 1818, and a window in the south porch retains a reminder of that earlier church in a panel of 16th century stained glass depicting a saint holding a *monstrance* (7) – a vessel of silver or gold in which the consecrated host was exposed to the congregation. The church itself

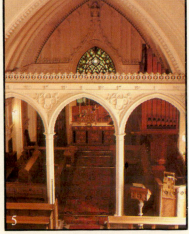

6

possesses a silver Elizabethan *tazza* or shallow chalice, of which there are only two in the world – Deane's is placed for safe-keeping at Basingstoke museum, and the other is in the Kremlin.

■ After the richness of Deane, the stark formality of **Whitcombe Church** (9 and 10) in neighbouring Dorset comes as something of a shock, yet here can be found a residual beauty born of simple and unpretentious aspiration. The nave is largely of 12th century construction, although it incorporates pre-Conquest masonry at the west end (10); and the chancel (9) – lit by a triple

7

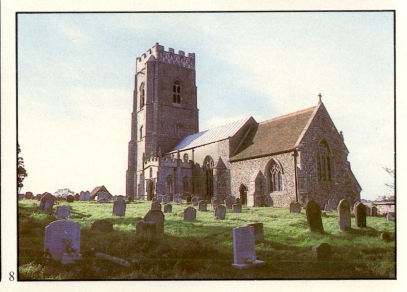

8

9

10

lancet – possesses great dignity. On the rough-hewn flags before the altar is the tender rustic memorial to a baby aged '*6 months one week and 5 days*', the inscription on which reads; '*Grive not for me my Mother dear, But be content think unto you I was but lent, Short were my Days long is my Rest, God call'd me whenever he thought Best.*'

To the east of Whitcombe's blocked Norman door is a large medieval painting of St Christopher. The saint wades across a river with the Christ Child on his shoulders, who blesses the saint with his right hand and in his left upholds an orb. St Christopher (the name means '*Christ-bearer*') has a bandeau round his temples which falls in folds around his shoulders. Two figures look on: that of the donor of the painting, and below him a mermaid who is combing her hair and holding a mirror.

WORCESTER CATHEDRAL

When viewed from the River Severn or the distant Malvern Hills, the serene prospect of **Worcester Cathedral** (1 – 8) seems to typify all that is England. It is dominated by a magnificent 14th century tower which rises from the *green heart of Albion* – a land from which Elgar drew his music and, centuries beforehand, Langland his vision of 'Piers Plowman'. The tower (1), built by John Clyre to beckon pilgrims to the shrines of St Oswald and St Wulfstan, is an architectural jewel which

and ring, but having received his bishopric at the bidding of Edward the Confessor he would resign the office to none but the dead king. Wulfstan fixed his crozier into the Confessor's tomb saying '*take this and give it whom it pleaseth thee*'. None could withdraw the staff save the Saxon bishop, '*whereat the stone resolved to let the staff go out, as if it had been soft earth or clay*'.

In Wulfstan's new cathedral the relics of St Oswald were housed in the Romanesque crypt (4) – one of the largest of its kind and

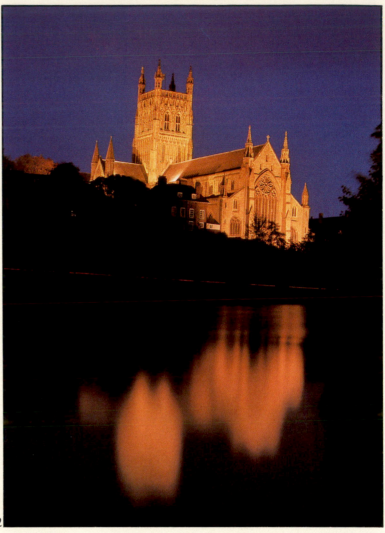

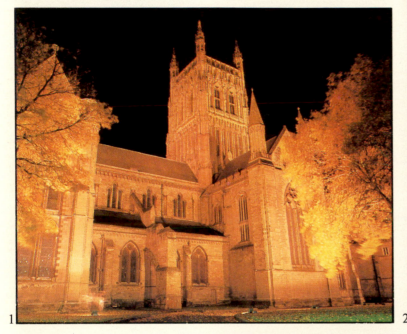

complements light as well as any gem – especially (in the words of Langland's verse) '*in somer season, when soft is the sonne*'. The tower houses Worcester's famous set of fifteen bells (8).

In the late 10th century a Benedictine monastery under the dedication of the Virgin was founded here by Bishop Oswald. Within ten years of his death he was revered as a saint, but his shrine and church were razed to the ground in 1014 under the raven-banner of the Norse. The fabric was allowed to moulder away until the appointment of Wulfstan who, as bishop, began the construction of the present church, and later, as saint, enriched its coffers. He stands alone among his contemporaries as the only Saxon bishop to continue in office after the Norman Conquest. Legend decrees that Wulfstan was summoned to Westminster Abbey to show good cause before William the Conqueror why he should not be dispossessed of his See. He was asked to give up his pastoral staff

WORCESTER CATHEDRAL

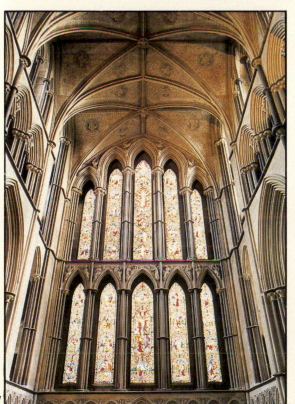

Worcester's most remarkable architectural feature. It was built in 1084 and embodies the mastery of elegant simplicity – its function dictating its design. Much of the cathedral dates from the early years of the 13th century – the consequence of Bishop Wulfstan's canonisation in 1203 which attracted many pilgrims from an England dominated by foreign rule, to the grave of their Saxon kinsman. Their wealth kept Worcester's masons constantly in work. Immediately behind the high altar (where stands the elaborate, carved marble reredos of Christ in Majesty seated between the four Evangelists) (6), Bishop William de Blois began the construction of the Lady chapel (7) in 1224. This impressive building – with its superb east window of ten lancets – makes great use of marble shafts to give the impression of richness and variety. The Early English style of architecture established in the Lady chapel set the yardstick by which the rest of the cathedral was to be measured. Its delicacy

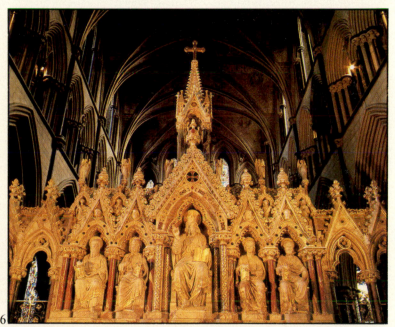

dictated the standard of the choir, transepts and nave – where Norman work was reconstructed to forge a vista of exceptional unity (3).

The cathedral houses the marble tomb of King John, the oldest royal effigy in the realm. Some months before he died, the sovereign instructed that his body should rest between St Oswald and St Wulfstan – thus fulfilling the prophecy that he, of all his line, should rest *inter sancto* – 'between the saints'. In 1526 King Henry VIII had the sacrist construct a more elaborate base for John's tomb in an attempt to enhance the reputation of his able, but erratic, ancestor. He wished to portray John as a monarch willing to stand before the Pope in defiance – a path he himself was soon to tread. Henry's own brother, Prince Arthur (from whom he inherited both his title – Prince of Wales – and his wife, Katherine of Aragon) rests within the last great medieval addition to the cathedral – the chantry chapel (5).

WALPOLE ST PETER

The great church of **Walpole St Peter** (1-10) is one of the finest in the country and, as a member of the Marshland group of churches, is known as the 'Queen of the Marshes'. In this respect it is the worthy equal of Ely and Blythburgh. Its quality is at once apparent in the lovely south porch (6), whose entrance displays at its apex the arms of the See of Ely (the Abbey owned the advowson since 1021), and whose interior contains fine bosses – the subjects of which include the 'Last Judgement', the 'Assumption of

The present church stands on the site of an earlier foundation which was destroyed (all except the Barnack-stone tower of 1300) by a sea flood in 1337. The nave we see today (5) served as both chancel and nave when built in 1360. In style it is a very early example of Perpendicular Gothic, which might more correctly be termed 'transitional Perpendicular'. The arcades have not yet lost the beauty of the pointed, Early English arch; and there is a very unusual feature – a west screen (7) of 1610 which runs the entire

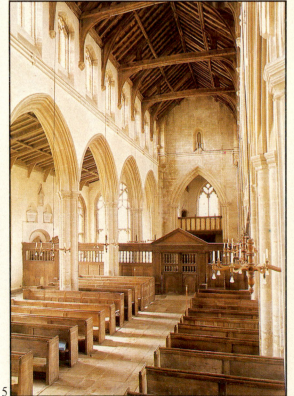

Our Lady' with God the Father's head and hand in blessing, the Dove of the Holy Spirit, and the Pelican – the symbol of the Holy Communion. The carving in the north-west corner is a Pieta, a very rare subject in England.

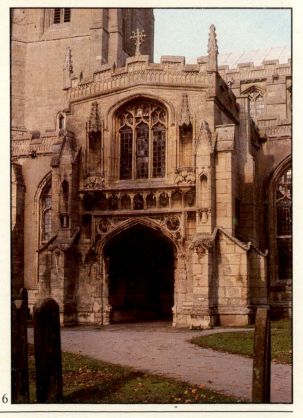

WALPOLE ST PETER

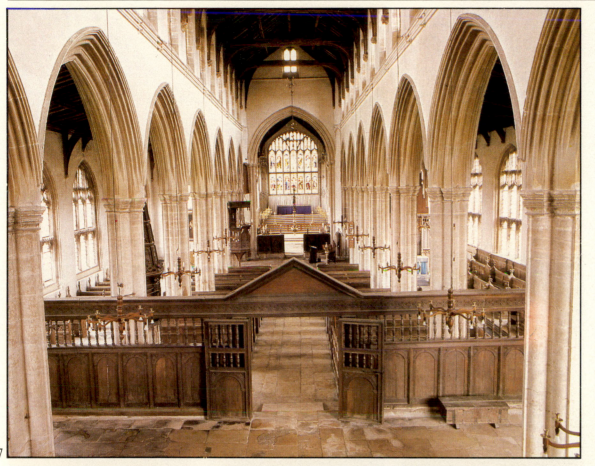

7

high altar was raised to its present height to allow a processional right of way to be built underneath it. If the nave can be said to be transitional, then the chancel is pure Perpendicular, and was probably added in 1425 at the expense of the Rochford family – the Constables of neighbouring Wisbech Castle – many of whom are buried in the Lady chapel. The chancel stalls have been restored, but still possess much 15th century craft, especially in their carvings. Of particular merit are an antelope (whose horns were supposed to become entangled in sin); a carving of a griffin (1) – a beast to be feared, which drew the chariot of the vengeful Nemesis – and the head of St Edmund guarded by a wolf.

Everywhere there is a profusion of sensitive detail, even in the pinnacles of the eastern nave. The church is battlemented (added in 1634) and the carvings of gargoyles and corbel heads leer down from the parapets of walls and towers. Those of the chancel have bodies attached, which is unusual. The very fine bell-cote still contains the sacring bell used to tell the time of the Elevation of the Host. Looking

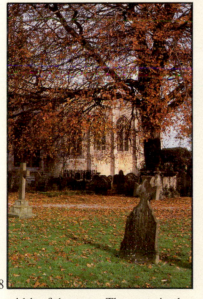

8

9

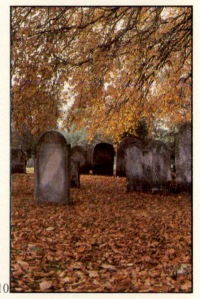

10

width of the nave. The seats in the south aisle (3), which face inwards beneath huge windows, are interesting because they have 15th century carved ends, with Jacobean seats and rails.

It is evident that the chancel (4) was added to make the church – at over 160ft in length – even grander in design. Such is its great size (9) that the building reaches the eastern extremity of the church boundary, and in consequence the

up at the detail of St Peter's from the churchyard, one is made aware of the apparent similarity between the aspiration of the church's Perpendicular tracery – of intricacy striving towards heaven – and the delicacy and form of nearby beech trees. This is particularly noticeable in late-autumn (8 and 10) when the golden leaves are shed and the tree's massive, yet graceful, boughs are revealed in all their glory.

STOW/MUCH MARCLE

St Mary's, Stow (1,3,4 and 6) in Lincolnshire is one of the most monumental and impressive Saxon churches, and one of the most important in that it retains its true cruciform plan – with low central tower (1) and crossing arches of equal proportions. The earliest church is said to have been raised by King Ecgfrith of Northumbria in AD 678 in respectful recognition of a miracle. Whilst his wife, St Ethelreda (the foundress of Ely Cathedral) was in flight from him following a quarrel, she stopped at Stow and drove her staff into the ground, whereupon it took root and became an ash tree. Ecgfrith's

(6) – with its incomparable stone ribbed-vault (3) of such richness that it seems an extraordinarily magnificent piece of architecture for a parish church.

■ Set among Herefordshire's cider orchards, the 13th century church at **Much Marcle** (2 and 5) holds an exquisite 14th century effigy of Blanch, Lady Grandison (5), her splendidly fitted gown flowing away gracefully and her beautiful hands seeming barely to touch her rosary. The painted wooden effigy of a man (2) carved in oak with slender folds is one of the rarest of its kind found in England.

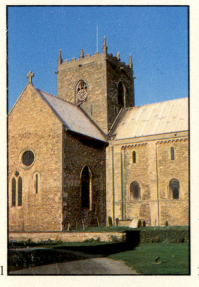

1

2

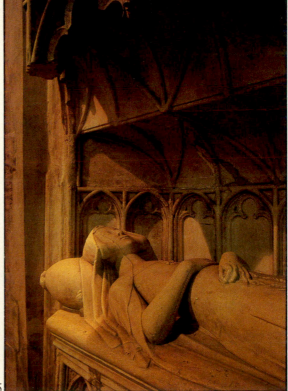

3

church was pillaged by Danes in 870, and again by Canute in 1016, but forty years later the ruin was reconstructed by Leofric, Earl of Mercia, and his wife – known to history as Godiva. By the time of the Norman Conquest the transepts and crossing had been built. Remigius was appointed the first Norman bishop, and before he moved his See to Lincoln in 1073 he inaugurated the magnificent nave (4) of this, his '*Head Minster at Stow*'.

The richness of the church may surprise many people – one is apt to think of Saxon work as being heavily built with great rugged stones, yet the ideal church for the Anglo-Saxons was one whose exterior shone like polished stone, and whose interior was a worthy home for God and all his saints who flocked into the great spaces high in the church to hear the prayers of the faithful. In accord with this view, and in keeping with his own epithet, Alexander the Magnificent, Bishop of Lincoln from 1123 to 1147, raised a chancel

4

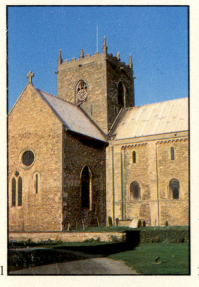

5

LONDON CHURCHES

Medieval London possessed over one hundred churches all crowded within the square-mile of the City. In 1666 the Great Fire swept through the capital and destroyed many of them. Very few churches were spared the flames – save for rare exceptions such as the Guild Church of **St Ethelburga, Bishopsgate** (6) which is the third oldest in the City.

The Fire's destruction heralded the advent of Classicism, and the awesome task of rebuilding ecclesiastical London befell the King's Surveyor General, Sir Christopher Wren. Of his fifty-one

wealth of architecture – it must not be supposed that all Classical towers and spires of the late-17th and early-18th centuries are of his design. Like most great men he had his disciples – Hawksmoor and Gibbs, Flitcroft and James of Greenwich – who have also bequeathed to us individual examples of excellence. Of them all, the Scottish architect James Gibb was the most illustrious, and it is he who has left us with what is, in many respects, the finest and most influential church of Georgian England – namely the Royal Parish Church of **St**

City churches only fifteen now survive, but fortunately that number includes **St Margaret Pattens, Eastcheap** (2) where Wren built a splendid tower of Portland stone, surmounted by a gracious, lead-covered wooden spire. The church itself is a clerestoried oblong with a west gallery and a northern aisle: the walls are white plaster, columns and pilasters are grey and capitals gilded – the effect contrasts with the dark woodwork of the pulpit, swordrest and choir stalls. However, it is Wren's spires that are the true testament to his genius. Unfettered by any constraints upon upward growth (the body of the church was always restricted by the size of the site it occupied) he topped his churches with that forest of elegant masonry – Wren's spires and steeples – which arose over a city crowned by the dominating dome of his cathedral-church of St Paul's.

Although Wren did so much – and looking at what he left behind it is hard to believe that any single man could have produced such a

LONDON CHURCHES

5

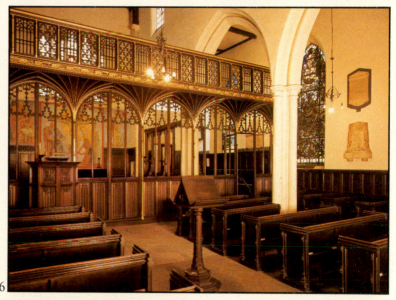

6

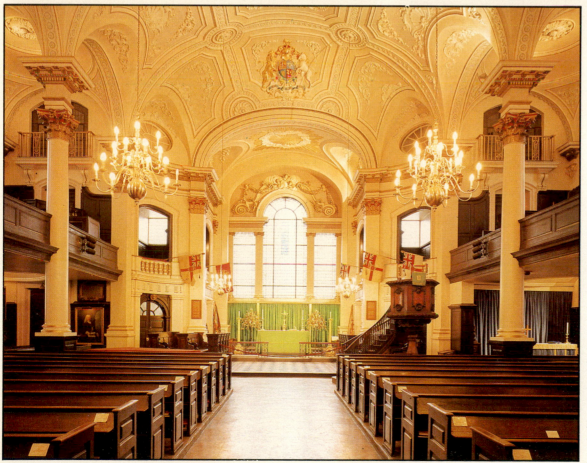

7

Martin's-in-the-Field (4,5 and 7). It was built between the years 1722 and 1726, and influenced ecclesiastical architecture not only in Britain, but also in America, where many churches were erected in accordance with Gibb's arrangement for St Martin's. The rectangular church is approached by a broad flight of steps and has a great Corinthian portico, above which rises the Ionic pilastered steeple (4) and spire. The interior is equally lavish. To the left of the altar (7) is the Royal Box, and to the right, the Admiralty Box (5). The flags on the left are the personal ensigns of King George V and of the Queen as Lord High Admiral, whilst those opposite are the flags of the South Atlantic, East Indies and Far-East Fleets.

The largest parish church in the City of London, St Sepulchre-without-Newgate (1) has associations with the old prison opposite. Here a handbell rang in the condemned prisoners ears the night before execution, and the tenor bell in the tower sounded their death-knell at 8 in the morning. From Newgate gaol, in a tumbril, to Tyburn, the condemned passed St Sepulchre's and there traditionally received a nosegay, and at St Giles a cup of beer.

St James' Church, Piccadilly (3) contains some of the most memorable craftsmanship in London, notably by Grinling Gibbons whose font and altar are masterpieces of Anglo-Classicism. The wood he used for carving the altar and reredos (3) is lime, which Gibbons was the first to use in preference to oak. Of his work the diarist Evelyn wrote: 'Dec 16th – I went to see the new Church of St James', elegantly built. The altar was specially adorned, the white marble enclosure curiously and richly carved, the flowers and garland about the walls by Mr Gibbons, in wood: a pelican, with her young at her breast, just over the altar in the carved compartment... There was no altar anywhere in England, nor has there been any abroad, more handsomely adorned'.

KINGSTON/BRIDEKIRK

Since the 12th century, Kingston in Dorset has been a chapelry of Corfe Castle, and was served by the Castle Rector or his assistant. During the years 1874-80 the 3rd Earl of Eldon raised the present church of St James, **Kingston** (4,8 and 10) at an expense to himself of £60,000, intending it originally to be a private family chapel; but in 1921 Lord Eldon consigned the church to the Church Commissioners. The eminent architect of this notable building was G.E. Street, whose enthusiasm for the Gothic is exemplified by his design for the Law Courts in the Strand. The Dictionary of National

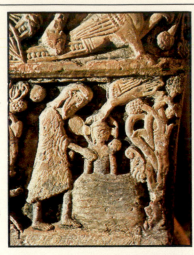

2

3

Biography says of him: '...one of Street's favourite designs was that of Kingston Church; it is a cruciform building, with an apse, central tower and narthex, built throughout of Purbeck stone, with shafts of Purbeck marble...the mouldings are rich, and owing to the character of the materials, the building has a model-like perfection'. Indeed, so ornate is his design – in the stone-vaulted chancel (8), in the arcading and rose-window of the nave (4), and in the beautiful wrought-iron screen – that it is more suggestive of the Ile de France than the Isle of Purbeck. The massive appearance and evident use of the finest materials, are complemented by St James' lofty central tower which, together with the rest of the church, is regarded as one of the most successful of the Victorian era.

■ The church of **Bridekirk** (1,6,7 and 9) in Cumberland was also raised on a cruciform plan with an apsidal chancel (9), but at a very much earlier date. The features indicate a Norman foundation, and

4

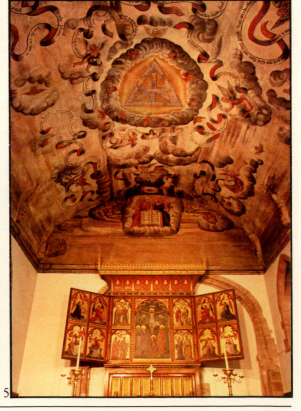

5

the church is known to have flourished in 1291 when it was referred to as *Bricekirk* – 'the church of St Bride' – in the *Taxatio ecclesiastica*. Its greatest treasure is undoubtedly the magnificent Norman font, ornamented with mystical monsters and remarkable inscriptions. The relief, although roughly executed, never fails to stir the senses with the naturalism and originality of its composition. On one side the Baptism of Christ is depicted (1), showing John the Baptist in his hair-robe and Christ encircled by a nimbus with a dove of the Holy Spirit in attendance. A vine runs its entangled course around the font recalling Christ's words '*I am the Vine, ye are the branches*'. However, the basic Christian theme of the Bridekirk font is enlivened by allusions to the paganism of the area's Viking past – represented by such fabulous creatures as a Hydrahead, which bites its own tail, and carved wyverns (6) which strongly resemble those of the Bayeux Tapestry.

■ The church of St Mary the Virgin, **Bromfield** (2 and 5) in

6

7

8

9

10

Shropshire is mentioned in the Doomsday Book, but only the north-east wall of the chancel remains from this period. The early-Gothic tower (2) houses a peal of six bells, and the nave has a fine oak roof dating from 1577. However, it is the painted chancel which draws greatest praise. This work is of 1672 and originally covered the whole chancel with depictions of angels and symbols of the Trinity – the roof alone now remains (5): and has been described as the best specimen of the worst period of ecclesiastical art.

KINNERSLEY

1

windmill, a pelican in her piety (7), a man holding the roots of a tree (5) and the marks of Christ's Passion. Of similar merit is the richly gilded 'tester' or canopy, over the high altar (9). The church's greatest glory is, however, its noble rood screen of the fan vaulted type, with local variations – probably made at Taunton in the early 16th century. One member of the sumptuously carved cornice contains the Apostles' Creed in Latin running the whole width of the screen. The lower panels contain elaborate tracery carvings in place of the more usual painted figures, and there are leaden stars

2

3

A solemn Worcestershire church of quiet dignity – St James' at **Kinnersley** (2,3,4 and 6) is best viewed in winter when the reddish hue of its stonework seems to shine out against the greyness of the day. It lies close to a Jacobean Castle (2) and possesses an imposing, saddle-back tower of the 14th century (3) – a style of gable that invariably indicates that the tower remains unfinished. Within, the arcade draws the eye along the length of the nave and into the beautiful chancel (6) where stands Kinnersley's magnificently carved reredos (4) whose gilding serves to highlight the subtlety of its creation.

■ Another church renowned for its finely carved and painted woodwork is **Bishops Lydeard** (5,7,8,9 and 10), which lies at the foot of the Quantocks in West Somerset. The church was rebuilt in the 15th century, and its fine array of carved bench-ends date from early-Tudor times. They display, amongst other things, a three masted ship, a miller and his

4

in the 'webs' of the fan vaulting (8 and 10).

The splendid tower of Bishops Lydeard was raised in 1470 and is of the 'Somerset' type – but unlike most others in the county it is built of the local red stone with yellow stone dressing from Ham Hill. There are additional pinnacles on the buttresses and the second tracery filling of the belfry windows gives a lace-like apearance to the grace and massiveness of the whole structure. In the base of the stair turret is a small room in which the Royalist troops, under the command of Sir John Stawell, stored their weapons while

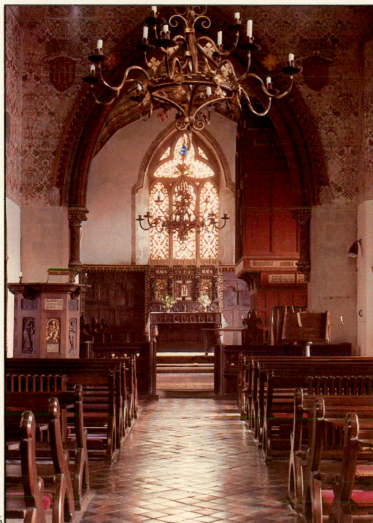

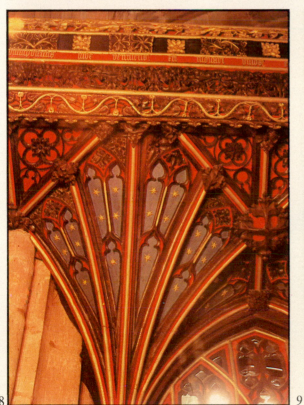

5

6

Cromwellian forces occupied the neighbourhood. Close by the village his enterprise was crushed by Robert Blake, the Parliamentarian general.

Near the tower is a medieval churchyard cross upon which is carved 'Our Lord in Majesty', with a lion and a scroll representing the world; and Christ rising from the tomb, attended by angels. In one of the steps is a hollowed-out niche provided as a kneeling-place for penitents. Within the church porch is a small panel engraved to the memory of John Geale, vicar from 1714 until 1733. He asked to be buried under the first flagstone of

7

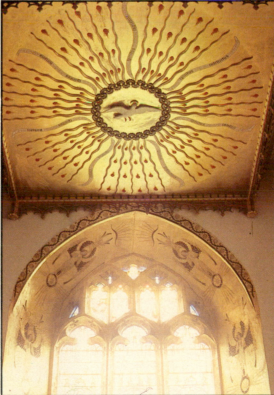

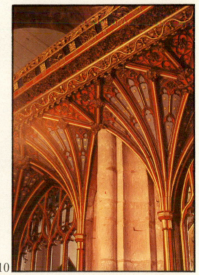

10

the porch, saying: *'my parishioners were ever wont to walk over me whilst I am alive; they shall not be denied this pleasure when I am dead'.*

■ 1: The flint-faced church of **Broxted** whose timber belfry and red tiled spire are typical of the Essex countryside.

8

9

LONG MELFORD/LAVENHAM

Two of the finest Perpendicular churches in the country, **Long Melford** (1) and **Lavenham** (4), owe their size and splendour to the prosperity of the 15th century, when Suffolk cloth was highly prized, and Suffolk wool was practically as valuable as gold (today the Lord Chancellor still sits on the Woolsack). Their well-proportioned towers emphasise the vertical lines of Perpendicular architecture and set the style for the rest of the church. Within, nave and chancel almost disappear in perspective, and an air of spaciousness pervades all. In characteristic fashion the walls are virtually 'sides of glass' and through their window tracery, and through that of the clerestory, light floods in, illuminating the church's many treasures – at Lavenham, the lovely Spring chantry chapel with its parclose screen around the tomb of its founder – a wealthy clothier who paid for the steeple – and at Long Melford the brasses of the Clopton family and, directly behind the high altar, the vestry

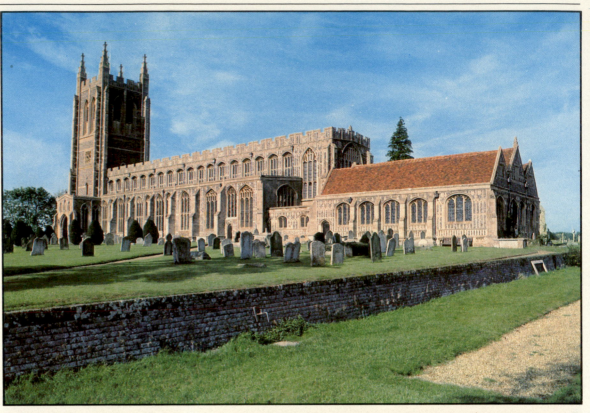

1

2

and marvellous Lady chapel, surrounded by an ambulatory.

■ The church of **St Clement Danes** (2 and 3) has stood on its site in the Strand since the 9th century; and it is said that when King Alfred expelled the Danes from London those who had English wives were permitted to remain in the area – hence St Clement (of the) Danes. The original church was rebuilt in Norman times, and again in the Middle Ages. It escaped the flames of the Great Fire, but became unsafe in 1680 and was demolished and rebuilt again by

Sir Christopher Wren. He recased the medieval tower with new stone and surmounted it with obelisks. The spire – which houses the famous peal of eleven bells that ring out the well known tune '*oranges and lemons*' – was added in the 18th century by Gibbs. The interior (2) is striking – black oak predominates up to the height of the gallery, whilst above, all is brightness and light, in white, grey and gold. The panelled ceiling is supported by elegant columns which lead the eye down the body of the church to the richly gilded focal point of the high altar (3).

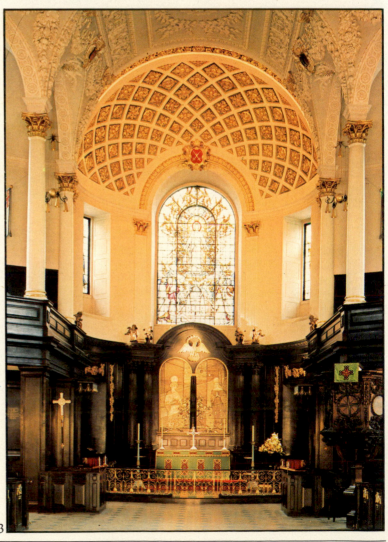

3

WHALEBY/FRISTON/AMBERLEY

Set in a Lincolnshire landscape that is three-quarters sky, the lonely church at **Whaleby** (1,2 and 5) lies on the Viking Way. Samphire moss grows among its ancient graves, and the tower (1) has stood for centuries against the piercing squalls driven off the cold North Sea. No longer used as a parish church, its appearance and features are simple and unpretentious, imparting upon the church an overriding sense of brooding dignity, which is further enhanced by the quiet majesty of the carved rood (2) and the sombre march of its sturdy, rounded arcade (5) which serves to separate the nave from the transepts.

■ If Whaleby appears to be a 'foothold' gained by man in spite of the harshness of the terrrain, then the tiny Norman church of St Mary the Virgin at **Friston** (3) is the exact opposite, for it seems to have taken its birth from the countryside around it. Indeed, so natural is this fusion of church and nature that it seems as much a part of the gently rolling Sussex downland as the tall

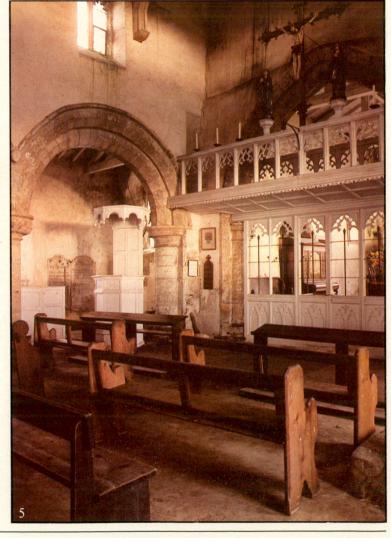

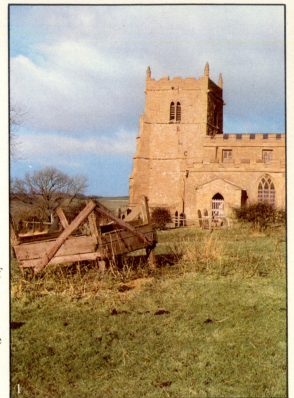

beech trees which crown the chalk scarp, or the lily-covered hammer-ponds which bejewel the area. Both Friston's 11th century nave and 13th century chancel were raised in local flint, and even the font, which is of Puritan parentage, is of Sussex 'marble' quarried locally and sometimes termed 'winkle' stone because fossil deposits can be seen in it. The church's shallow western tower is surmounted by a Sussex-cap – a humble version of a full spire and a characteristic feature of South Downland churches.

■ In the same county, St Michael's at **Amberley** (6 and 7) forms a

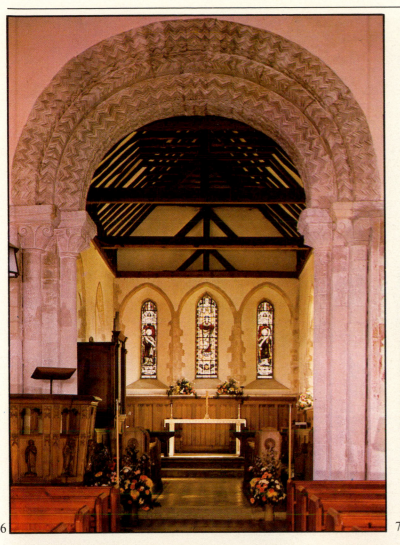

medieval group with the castle – a former palace of the Bishops of Chichester. Indeed, it was the munificence of Ralph Luffa, the first Bishop to the new See (transferred from Selsey in 1075), that caused the Romanesque nave and chancel arch to be raised. It is likely that a team of masons brought over from France worked both on Chichester Cathedral and on Amberley Church. Their skill is best exemplified by the magnificence of the chancel arch (6) which has three orders, richly ornamented with chevron moulding. Their capitals are of the volute type, with spiralled foliage.

A second period of enlargement of St Michael's was instigated by Bishop Ralph Nevill who, in 1230, provided funds for the extension of the chancel and sanctuary, and for the addition of a large buttressed tower and south aisle. Their architectural style is pure Early English, and lancets (a particular feature of Sussex) adorn all sides of the church (7) with the usual arrangement of three such windows at the east end. Another local characteristic is the way in which the roof of the nave (of red tiles – as so often in South East England) also covers the south aisle in one large sweep.

6

7

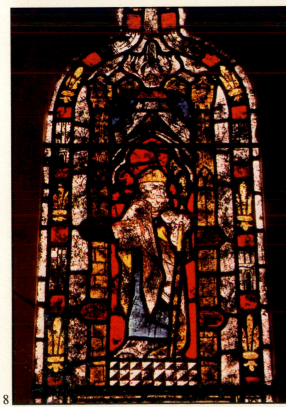

8

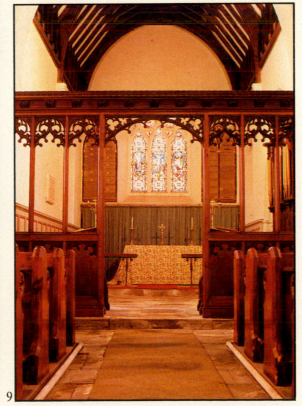

9

■ The wool-church of St Peter's **Winchcombe** (4) in Gloucestershire was begun in about 1460, and is famous for its forty grotesque gargoyles (although they do not function as water-spouts as true gargoyles should). The medieval sense of fun depicted fantastic monsters and figures caricaturing local dignitaries in every possible attitude – they are noted for their ugliness, and seldom display any drawing-room manners: one devil (4) for instance, is shown with his legs bent upwards behind his head, displaying the area where it was popularly supposed the satanic kiss should correctly be planted.

■ **Linwood Church** (8 and 9) in Lincolnshire, is one of only two foundations dedicated to St Cornelius. Little is known of this early martyr, but a panel of medieval stained glass (8) in the south wall of the chancel (9) depicts St Cornelius in his vestments as Bishop of Rome.

WESTON ZOYLAND

At the heart of Sedgemoor the 15th century tower of St Mary's, **Weston Zoyland** (1,2,3,4 and 11) looms over the marshes – its yellow-grey stone a familiar landmark within the flat, fen landscape. The building is one of the great Perpendicular churches of Somerset, satisfying both within and without. The interior is mainly of the 14th and 15th centuries, being high, light and uncluttered, with a tremendous tie-beam roof (4), carved with angels holding shields (3). In addition, there is a vast expanse of flagstone flooring, an intricately carved rood screen (2) and a nail-studded north door (11) where the carved ornamentation at the head mirrors the window tracery of the period.

In 1685 the church achieved notoriety when the Battle of Sedgemoor took place about a mile away. The forces of King James II routed the untrained and poorly armed rebels of Charles II's

1

illegitimate son, the Duke of Monmouth. A number of prisoners were shot or hanged on the spot, and some five hundred were locked up in Weston Zoyland church overnight. Many of those interned were wounded, and five died in the church. The following day the survivors were herded to Bridgewater, some being hanged *en route*.

■ The church of St Michael and All Angels at **Eaton Bishop** (5,7,9 and 10) stands at the highest point of the Herefordshire village. The oldest part of the church is the tower (5) which dates from the decade immediately following the Conquest, and its staunch walls – 4ft thick in places – were originally intended to guard parishioners

2

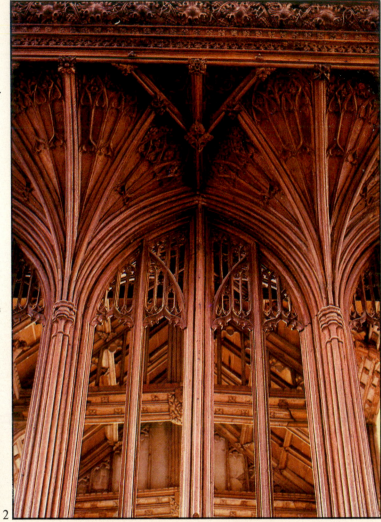

4

3

5

against raiders from the west. The present nave, aisles and chancel arch were raised c1200 – the rounded pier and Early English capitals and bases of the arcade being typical of the period. There is a clerestory of lancet windows and, like several Cotswold churches, a window over the chancel arch (7). The chancel itself was built between the years 1320 and 1330 – the large Decorated windows serving the double purpose of providing more light, and as a framework for the wonderful stained glass which is the chief treasure of the church, and also dates from the 14th century.

Eaton Bishop has some of the finest glass in Europe, of the unmistakable Decorated colour harmony of brown, green and yellow, with a little red and still less blue; and of the sophisticated, highly emotional draughtsmanship more familiar to illuminated manuscripts, which belongs to the same style. Of all the panels in the eastern window, that illustrating the Madonna and Child (9) is the most exquisite – the graceful, humanised figure of the Virgin holding Jesus is English stained glass at its most original and beautiful. Mary's figure no longer seems stiff and awkward as in

earlier glass, yet it is still boldly simplified and stylised. The appearance of suppleness is created by the relaxed S-shaped pose. Natural details and lively, realistic facial expression add charm and individuality to the scene. The window (10) also depicts St Michael weighing souls, and around the panel a trellis background of ruby glass links it with that of the Archangel Gabriel (hand raised in benediction) and the Crucifixion panel at the centre. The inquisitive are well rewarded, for every inch of glass seems to contain intimate detail – be it the singing birds which perch

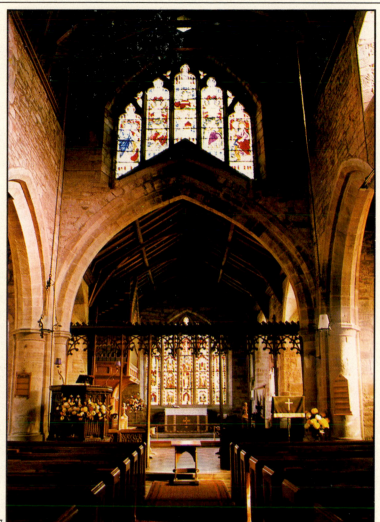

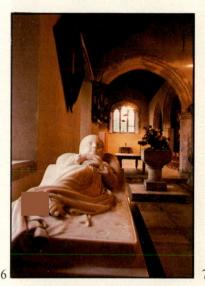

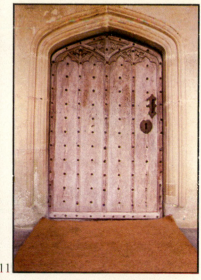

on the topmost pinnacles of the canopy, or the acorn motif; the vine trail, or the leopard faces.
■ St Mary's at **Brading** (6) is the largest medieval church on the Isle of Wight, and contains a tenderly sculpted monument to Elizabeth Rollo, who died aged fourteen months.

HILLESDEN

The lovely church of All Saints, **Hillesden** (2,3,5,6 and 10) is set in a quiet corner of Buckinghamshire – seemingly lost to the outside world. Here, amid green fields bordered by hedgerows, ash, oak and elm, is an example of Perpendicular architecture that is rarely surpassed. The walls of All Saints are impressively crenellated and there is a two-storey north vestry and sacristy with a delicate canopy to the tower (3). Below the chancel roof is a *Te Deum* stone frieze of alternate scroll-bearing and instrument-playing angels. The church possesses an imposing late-Gothic nave (6) and some fine monuments – foremost among which is the marble memorial to Sir Alexander Denton and his wife (5), by Sir Henry Cheere. The rood and parclose screens have linenfold panelling, and the 16th century stained glass is among the finest in the country. The influence of Flemish glaziers is apparent in the richly coloured and lively windows depicting eight stories from the miracles of St Nicholas. One panel

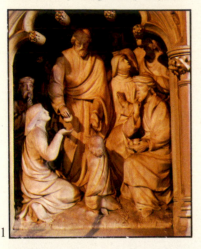

1

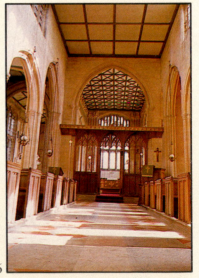

2

3

4

5

6

illustrates the tale of the 'Boy and the Gold Cup'. A rich nobleman promised that if he had a son he would present a gold cup to the altar of St Nicholas. A son was born and the cup duly made, but at the last moment a worthless duplicate was offered to the Saint instead. On the voyage home the boy is seen falling into the sea with the original gold cup spinning from his grasp (10).

■ **Margaretting Church** (1,4,7 and 9) in Essex contains stained glass from the 15th century – earlier than that of Hillesden, yet comparable in quality and verve to that of the St Nicholas miracles.

The glass is also Flemish in style, and is housed in the Perpendicular tracery of the Great East Window (7) – behind the high altar with its intricate reredos of 1678 (1) – and can boast a complete 'Jesse Tree window'. The 'Stem of Jesse' was one of the most popular subjects of the medieval glazier's art and derives from Isaiah's prophecy of the coming of the Messiah from the Royal Line of David, '*and there shall come forth a rod out of the stem of Jesse, and a Branch shall grow out of his roots*'. The artistic interpretation of the prophecy made Jesse the stem, or root; Mary the rod, or shoot; and Christ the

fruit, or flower. The theme is in fact genealogical, and the Margaretting 'tree' traces back Jesus' ancestory through round medallions of glass (4) around which the tree's stem twines, showing the Madonna and Child, King Solomon (holding the tabernacle), King David (playing the harp), Joseph, Jacob, Abraham and another sixteen figures until it reaches Jesse.

Once outside the church (9) the tower is seen to be built on ten wooden posts of immense dignity and strength. It supports four pre-Reformation bells, one of which is ascribed to Robert Borford, c1400, and is the oldest bell in Essex. One account of Henry VIII's reign states that they were rung '*for all the weddings of our Royal bluebeard*'.

■ The thatched Norfolk church of **Thurton** (11) displays the figure of the two-headed god Janus (8) at the terminus of the hood-mould on one of the lancet windows of the south nave.

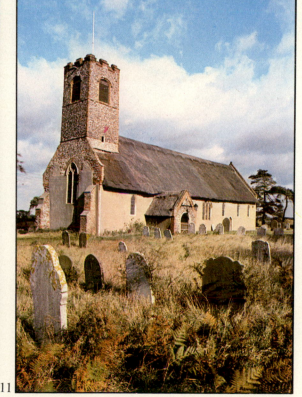

Situated on the east slopes of Dartmoor, the charming granite church at **Manaton** (2,3,8 and 9) has remained a place of peace, security and beauty for over six hundred years. It is perhaps at Eastertide that the church is raised to its greatest glory – decked throughout in spring flowers (8 and 9) whose vernal 'birth' after winter's 'death' proves faithful tribute to Christ's own Resurrection. The church we see today dates from the early 15th century when both nave and chancel were built. To these were added side-aisles later in the century, and the tower (4) was

corpse three times round the old cross before burial. This practice so annoyed one rector that in the last century he arranged for the cross's 'disappearance', and it was not found again until the early 1900s when it served as the base to a stile. From this degradation it was saved and re-erected in its present position.

The church of Manaton is justifiably famous for its rood-screen (2) which boasts unrestored, painted panels from c1500. They depict the twelve Apostles, four Latin doctors and other saints (3), but sadly suffered damage at the hands of Cromwell's troops. In an

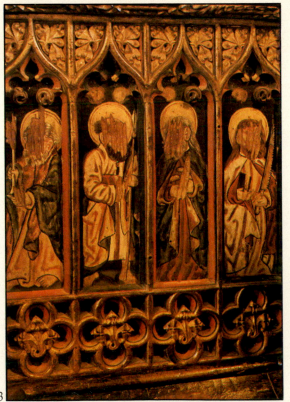

raised not long after. The latter houses three bells at least as old, if not older, than itself: the tenor was cast at the Exeter foundry of Robert Norton in about 1499, and the others cast locally by Johanna Hill, widow of a London bell-founder, whose marks date the two bells to 1440 and 1443. One is dedicated to St Catherine (a fairly usual practice), but the other is to St George, a rarer dedication which must have some connection with the village Guild of St George: a group whose interests lay in tin production.

As with many of the 'Dartmoor Crosses', that of Manaton – between the lych-gate and the porch – is very ancient and certainly pre-dates the Perpendicular church. It marks the place where itinerant friars would gather their congregation to hold a service in the days before the area boasted any church at all. Tradition states that in medieval times the cross was held in such veneration that it became the practice for bearers at funerals to carry the

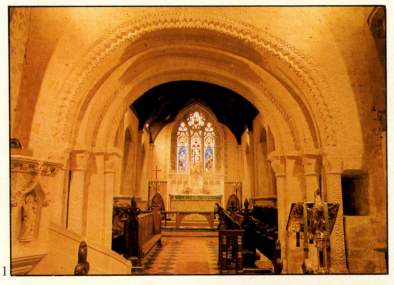

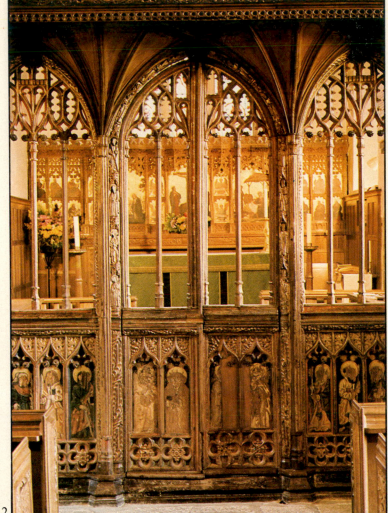

5

6

7

8

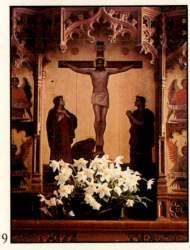

9

elaborate Renaissance tomb beside the high altar.

■ At **Kemsing** (7) in Kent, the church – of Norman origin but with later additions – is full of beautiful craftsmanship. It contains a stained glass medallion of the Virgin Mary (to whom the church is dedicated) made in 1220: she wears a green skirt and a yellow underskirt. In the churchyard there once stood a shrine and miracle-working statue of St Edith – the illegitimate daughter of King Edgar – who was born in the village in 961. Local farmers and yeomen brought grain to the shrine to be blessed by the parish priest before mixing it with their seed corn.

■ The precious, 11th century crypt beneath St Mary's **Lastingham** (6) in the North Riding of Yorkshire is one of the four apsidal crypts in England, and the only complete specimen with chancel, nave and side aisles. It was built between 1078 and 1088 as a shrine for St Cedd, who died here in 664. His relics were placed in the crypt's altar in accordance with the words

effort to purge 'popish imagery' they knocked the heads of the carved saints from the uprights of the screen doorway – as was their almost traditional practice – but the obliteration of the saints' faces within the panelling looks more like gouging with a sharp chisel than the slashing of a blunted sword.

■ Also in the county of Devon are the churches of **Powerstock** (1) and **St Werburghs** (5). The former has an impressive 12th century chancel arch with four rows of ornaments remaining from the original Norman church, whilst the latter possesses an interesting and

of the Book of Revelations '*I saw under the altar the souls of them that were slain for the word of God, and for the testimony which they held*'. The massive pillars of the vault show a gradual growth of ornamentation, but most have a simple ram's horn capital. Here, amid ancient stones, graced by the tread of saints, and hallowed by centuries of pilgrimage, it is wonderful to think that, except for the floor, which used to be of rough cobblestones, not a stone has been touched since 1088.

ST PAULS/ST MARY-AT-HILL

Britain's only Classical Cathedral, St Paul's (1,3 and 4) in London, is also the only one conceived and completed by one man in the course of his own lifetime. Sir Christopher Wren's mission to rebuild St Paul's took thirty-six years, and its grandeur and sheer architectural brilliance are a towering monument to his genius.

The catastrophe of the Great Fire in 1666 put an end to one of the proudest medieval cathedrals of its age – whose nave and chancel were longer than any other in England, and whose spire (an almost unbelievable 489ft in height) was the tallest in Europe. The architectural scope for the rebuilding of St Paul's offered a unique opportunity to create an entirely new cathedral upon a virgin site – the first since Salisbury was founded four hundred and forty years beforehand. The classical idiom – the nearest that Protestant England ever came to the Baroque, with ornate gilded mosaics and saucer domes (4) –

1

2

used with such assured confidence suggests a break with the past, but St Paul's is, in fact, the traditional cathedral plan with twin-towered West Front and the central dominating feature over the crossing. Even though this latter feature is the magnificent imperial dome (and not a tower) the method used by the architect to poise the 68,000 ton downward thrust over the huge central space – eight enormous pillars (3) – was inspired by the Gothic precedent set by the octagon at Ely.

Within the burnt husk of the medieval ruin, Wren found a piece of shattered grave-slab upon which the solitary legend '*Resurgam*', '*I shall rise again*', was inscribed. In gratitude for the fulfilment of this prophecy, the finished building has a phoenix rising from the ashes of a funeral pyre carved above the entrance to the south transept.

■ Another Wren masterpiece, the church of **St Mary-at-Hill** (2), has a similar plan to that of his great cathedral – cruciform with a dome over the crossing. The plaster-work is in the Adam style, delicate and airy, which contrasts with the massive and splendid woodwork of the nave, pulpit and altar (2)– it being one of the loveliest and least spoilt interiors in the City.

3

CIRENCESTER/CHIPPING CAMPDEN

The magnificent Perpendicular Gothic churches of the Cotswolds owe their extreme beauty to the surrounding sheep pastures and meadows of the gently rolling Gloucestershire uplands. These churches were raised through the munificence of 15th century wool merchants. Two excellent examples of these 'wool-churches' are at **Cirencester** (1) and at **Chipping Campden** (2) – both were built at the height of England's medieval prosperity. The former

columns, foliage on the capitals (6) and endless carvings of men, women and wild and imaginary beasts. There is a unique apsidal Lady chapel in the south transept, and an Easter Sepulchre – one of the three finest in England – in the chancel.

■ The Essex church of **Little Easton** (3,4,8 and 9) contains spectacular treasures of its own. There is an outstanding 12th century painting of a seated prophet in the nave and, opposite,

1

has a particularly lofty nave (1) supported by six soaring arches on either side, and above these a tall clerestory with fine glass which reaches to the richly bossed and panelled roof. Both the east and west windows, as well as that above the chancel arch, have rich medieval glass that reflects glowing colours onto the stone and woodwork below. St James' at Chipping Campden is equally spacious, and possesses in its chancel an excellent brass of William Grevel and his wife (2).

■ Just as wool provided funds for the Cotswold churches, so it was that a thriving local market enabled the church of **Patrington** (5 and 6) in the East Riding of Yorkshire to be built in the sumptuous style of Decorated Gothic. The building is known as "*The Queen of Holderness*" and is a cathedral in miniature. The glory of the exterior is Patrington's noble 189ft spire which is set in a corona that rests upon the central tower (5). Within the church there are thirty arches with clustered

3

4

5

6

7

8

wall-standing monument which blocks the eastern window is dedicated to William, 2nd Baron Maynard (4) who reclines in a Roman toga against marble reliefs entitled 'Justice, Fortitude and Charity': in one corner sits a weeping cherub (3).

■ The church of St John the Baptist at **Penshurst** (7) stands beside the great mass of Penshurst Place at the centre of a handsome red-brick and sandstone village of the Kentish Weald. It is reached through an ancient lych-gate around which a two-storeyed Tudor house was raised. The church originally dates from the 12th

9

a series of eight frescoes from the early 15th century depicting scenes from Our Lord's Passion. On the south side of the chancel is a chapel originally built by the Bourchier family, but rebuilt and enlarged two hundred years later, in the 17th century, for the Maynards. By the chapel gate is the famous brass of Henry, Viscount Bourchier, who dutifully wears a Yorkist collar around his neck, and traces of the original coloured enamelling can still be seen on his garments.

At the centre of the Bourchier chapel's south wall is the magnificent alabaster tomb of Henry Maynard (9) whose eight sons and daughters kneel in the front panel at the base of the tomb-chest. Five of the boys hold skulls to indicate that they pre-deceased their father. The large, century, but there is much work remaining from the 13th, 14th and 15th centuries. The tower (7), with its four prominent pinnacles, has windows that were formerly in Penshurst Place but were set in the tower in 1627.

CULBONE/HAPPISBURGH

There is a tradition which refers to the site of **Culbone Church** (1 and 4) as being an ancient spiritual centre long before the time of Christ. There is also a local Somerset legend which claims Culbone to be one of the places made sacred by the visit of Jesus as a young man. Indeed if Christ did – as Blake suggests – '*walk upon England's mountains green*', there could be few lovelier places than this remote combe-glade beside a stream on a steep wooded cliff 400ft above the sea. The church itself (1) is dedicated to St Beuno, and lays claim to being the smallest complete medieval church

completely demolished when Happisborough was rebuilt in the 14th century. This in turn was virtually swept away in a rebuilding programme of the following century: only the chancel was allowed to remain unaltered. The nave (5) was raised in the Perpendicular style, rising to a lofty clerestory and a square-headed window above the chancel arch. However, the most splendid feature of the 15th century rebuilding is the magnificent west tower (2) with its battlemented parapet and elaborate base-course, both panelled in flint flush-work. The tower, which rises to 110ft, is a

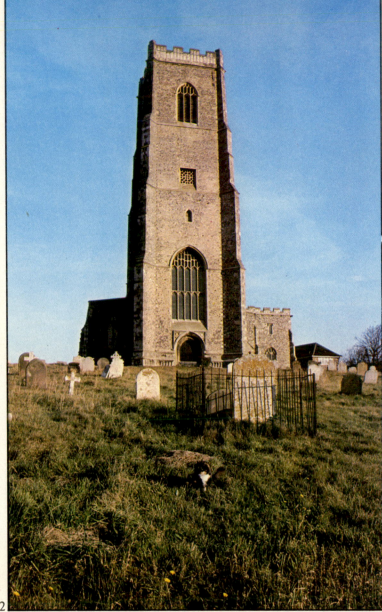

in England – with a mention not only in the Doomsday Book, but also in the *Guinness Book of Records*. Within (4) it measures 33ft 10in long by 12ft 4in wide. Basically Norman, it probably replaced an Anglo-Saxon chapel as one of its windows dates from pre-Conquest times, being a remarkable two light window carved from a single slab of sandstone.

■ In contrast to the size of Culbone, St Mary's, at **Happisburgh** (2,5,6 and 9) is one of the largest and most successful of East Anglia's Perpendicular churches. The name is pronounced 'Haisbro' – being one of the many Norfolk place-names which appear to have slipped the anchorage of their spelling. There was a Norman church upon the site, but this was

landmark for shipping; and the graveyard is a sad resting place for the many sailors driven ashore on this, the most treacherous part of the Norfolk coast. The large green mound on the north side of the churchyard marks one of many tragedies – the grave of one hundred and nineteen crew from *HMS Invincible*, which was wrecked on Haisbro Sands in 1801 when on its way to join Nelson's fleet at Copenhagen.

Happisburgh's delicate square-headed rood screen and magnificent font also belong to the 15th century rebuilding programme. The latter (9) is typical

of the period, and the font panels represent figures of angels holding musical instruments, interspersed with Evangelistic Symbols – the Four Living Creatures having the faces of a man (for St Matthew), a lion (for St Mark), an ox (for St Luke) and an eagle (for St John) which were seen by St John the Divine in his heavenly vision.

Happisburgh also has a wealth of carved creatures leering from its shadowed recesses (6). This follows a tradition of ornamentation which reached its peak in late-Norman times. The most decorated and highly carved are the doorway arches of churches such as **Windrush** (7 and 8) in Gloucestershire and Adel in West Yorkshire – both of which possess rounded Norman arches (8) incised with the heads of birds and animals all with long beaks (they are known as 'beak-heads') which extend over a convex moulding. At **Adel** (3) the imagery of fabulous beasts even encompasses the closing-ring of a door which depicts a monster swallowing a man.

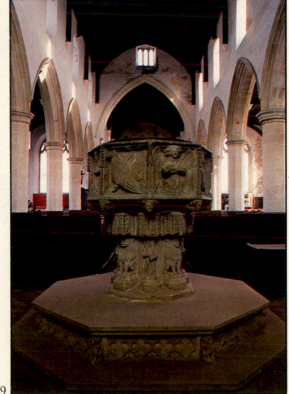

Index

Harting's 16th-century chancel roof.

The chancel at Harting.

Cowper family monument.